Actionable
Web Analytics

Actionable Web Analytics

Using Data To Make Smart Business Decisions

Jason Burby

Shane Atchison

Wiley Publishing, Inc.

Acquisitions Editor: WILLEM KNIBBE
Development Editor: PETE GAUGHAN
Production Editor: DEBRA BANNINGER
Copy Editor: TIFFANY TAYLOR
Production Manager: TIM TATE
Vice President and Executive Group Publisher: RICHARD SWADLEY
Vice President and Executive Publisher: JOSEPH B. WIKERT
Vice President and Publisher: NEIL EDDE
Book Designer: FRANZ BAUMHACKL
Compositor: KATE KAMINSKI, HAPPENSTANCE TYPE-O-RAMA
Proofreader: IAN GOLDER
Indexer: TED LAUX
Anniversary Logo Design: RICHARD PACIFICO
Cover Designer: RYAN SNEED
Cover Image: ALICIA MCVEY

Dear Reader

Thank you for choosing *Actionable Web Analytics: Using Data To Make Smart Business Decisions*. This book is part of a family of premium quality Sybex books, all written by outstanding authors who combine practical experience with a gift for teaching.

Sybex was founded in 1976. More than thirty years later, we're still committed to producing consistently exceptional books. With each of our titles we're working hard to set a new standard for the industry. From the paper we print on, to the writers and artists we work with, our goal is to bring you the best books available.

I hope you see all that reflected in these pages. I'd be very interested to hear your comments and get your feedback on how we're doing. Feel free to let me know what you think about this or any other Sybex book by sending me an email at nedde@wiley.com, or if you think you've found an error in this book, please visit http://wiley.custhelp.com. Customer feedback is critical to our efforts at Sybex.

Best regards,

NEIL EDDE
Vice President and Publisher
Sybex, an Imprint of Wiley

Dedicated to Bill Burby

Acknowledgments

First and foremost, we must thank our clients for allowing us to work with some of the best brands in the world in an ever-changing and fast-paced environment. Thank you for keeping us challenged and letting us try new things. Our ability to continue to learn and grow is based on the companies and people we work with.

Thank you to all our great co-workers at ZAAZ for supporting us while we were writing the book, giving us great inspiration, and allowing us to share some of our stories. Special thanks to Chris Kerns, Pam Shales, Ryan Turner, Ryan Clukey, Elena Moon, Erin Abbey, Nigel Morgan, Dmitria Lukoskie, Sinjin Maloney, Anil Batra, Brad Gagne, Iris Lamband, Kanishka Surana, Julie Rosefsky, Marietta Szubski, and Peng. Our sincerest thanks to Dave Brede, Julius Brown, Joel Calvo, and John Farris for enabling us to chase new opportunities and ideas.

Special thanks and prayers go out to Brother Scott Greene, the country of Brazil, Hong Kong, Griffey & Luna, and the Tiges. Nothing in life is possible without you.

This book would not have been possible without the hard work of Joe Shepter, Sarah Asher, John Simpson, and Norman Guadagno. Thank you to Willem Knibbe from Wiley for approaching us with the idea to write this book and all the kind encouragement (and teaching) throughout the writing process.

Thank you to Jim Sterne, Eric Peterson, and Avinash Kaushik for providing input and contributing ideas for the book.

Finally, a special thanks to our families and friends (Frank, Jan, Nancy, Mel, Carol, John, Georg, Beau, Keegan, Frances, Tasha, Cade, Blake, DM, Destia, Rod and Aaron) for supporting us during the process of writing this book, especially during long nights and weekends when we were locked in an office in front of a computer.

About the Authors

Jason Burby

Jason Burby is the Chief Analytics and Optimization Officer at ZAAZ, Inc., a web business consultancy implementing data-driven business initiatives for long-term clients across the U.S. Using performance score-cards, A/B and multivariate testing, tool reconfiguration, and other techniques, Jason helps companies better use web-analytics data to improve site business results.

Jason has worked with eTrade, Ford, Sony, PayPal/eBay, Blockbuster, Washington Mutual, Reuters, T-Mobile, Converse, Alaska Airlines, Microsoft, Sprint, Levi Strauss, Qwest, Hallmark, Nintendo, and A&E Television Networks. Jason speaks frequently at confer-ences and seminars around the world, helping spread the word about the effective use of web analytics.

Jason has contributed to several web-analytics books in the past few years. In addi-tion, he has written a web-analytics column on ClickZ.com for the past four years and is the co-chair of the Standards committee of the Web Analytics Association.

Shane Atchison

In 1998, Shane Atchison co-founded ZAAZ to advocate a different approach to web services—one that respected and delivered on the power of the individual and the promise of web technologies. As CEO, Shane leads the company's long-term strategic vision of working with leading financial service organizations, consumer brands, start-ups, nonprofits, and community-based organiza-tions, helping each realize the potential of the Internet and its meaningful impact on their business.

Shane has more than eight years of strategic con-sulting, business development, and advisory experience in web marketing, design, and customer-relationship man-agement. He has led efforts to develop compelling online experiences for clients such as Disney, Fox Television

Network, Microsoft Corporation, *National Geographic*, PBS, Warner Brothers, Boeing, and Washington Mutual.

At ZAAZ, Shane's responsibilities range from setting the company's overall strategy and communicating the ZAAZ brand and service offerings to working with clients, leading partnerships, and fostering the internal culture of the company. Outside of ZAAZ, his advocacy for creating meaningful, effective visitor-centric digital strategies continues through media and speaking engagements. Shane has been a keynote speaker for major conferences and business associations, including CREDO and AIGA.

ZAAZ

ZAAZ helps the world's most powerful brands grow and thrive online with performance-driven design, analytics, and optimization services. As a full-service interactive agency, ZAAZ provides web strategy, design, development, user experience, analytics, and optimization to Global 1000 companies including Microsoft, Sony, Ford Motor, Converse, and others. Founded in 1998, ZAAZ has offices in Seattle, Portland, and Detroit. ZAAZ is part of the WPP group of companies. For more information, visit www.zaaz.com or www.webanalytics.com.

We welcome your comments and input. You can send e-mail to Shane (shane@webanalytics.com) or Jason (jason@webanalytics.com) and let them know your thoughts about the book. We welcome any input you may have and any suggestions on future books you might like to see.

You can also visit WebAnalytics.com for an ongoing dialog about *Actionable Web Analytics,* real-world examples of the content, useful analytics tools, and information about upcoming events. We look forward to your getting engaged in the conversation.

Foreword

Half of your web marketing investment is being wasted—you just don't know which half.

Marketers will point back to the turn of the century as the before-and-after divide. Before the new millennium arrived, advertising and marketing was more art than science, more guess than test, and more imagination than information.

Then came the Age of Accountability. Sarbanes/Oxley ushered in the defense against Enron, and the CMO was put on the hot seat along with the rest to prove the value of their investment. Expectations ran high, with talk of websites being the ultimate marketing measurement machines.

Those involved with postal mail understood the direct response characteristics immediately. But the rest of the advertising and marketing departments were still debating which shade of teal would go best on the new campaign. As long as sales were up, they got to keep their budgets. And then came the day that they were made accountable for those sales.

All this at a time when customers are in control and tried-and-true marketing techniques are proving to be tired and suspect. We're recognizing that our customers think differently than we do. We can no longer judge a promotional campaign on how we feel about it, because we aren't the target audience. All we can do is run tests, measure the results, and adjust out sails.

The Web, as it turns out, is the perfect place to do that sort of testing. New tools and data-management methods make it possible to optimize not just the website, but marketing and business as well.

Website Optimization

Once we got over basing our judgment on hits, visits, and page views, we climbed out of the primordial ooze and took our first steps on dry land.

Your website isn't a bunch of pages. It's not a library of marketing literature, patiently waiting for prospects. Your website is a series of customer processes. They're trying to discover, learn, compare, configure, price, locate, purchase, join, discuss, and the list goes on.

Making web analytics actionable means optimizing those customer processes. Who comes to your website? What are they trying to accomplish? If you change this, that, or the other, will it make it easier for them to achieve their goals?

Walking around on dry land was a good move. The next step is learning how to run.

Marketing Optimization

Although web analytics has been good for the website, it turns out it's a monstrously powerful market research and perception tool. It's a window into the hearts and minds of your marketplace.

Which is better?

- Two For the Price of One
- Buy One Get One Free

You may have strong opinions about which is best. You can argue eloquently for one versus the other. You can hold meetings until all hours of the night to thrash out whose belief is stronger. (Hint: the one with the biggest paycheck.)

But you'll never know until you run controlled, statistically significant tests. Testing will reveal which headline people respond to better, faster, and more profitably. An email blast can reveal your best positioning approach within days. A side-by-side test of creative options can expose the better offer in minutes.

The Internet makes this sort of testing so quick and compelling, that the results are driving marketing message decisions on all other media. The Internet isn't a world unto itself. If people respond well to landing page A over B, then they will respond to that creative option and call to action on television, in print, and in their postal mail. Testing that takes a couple of days with minimal cost and informs the proper course for all the other forms of promotion.

Walking upright on dry land and supported by solid numbers feels good. But the next stage is learning to fly.

Business Optimization

Customers respond to more than just marketing messages on your website. Through their behavior, they show how they feel about your products and services. They click-vote their way through the hype and the fluff to find the features and benefits that mean the most to them.

Smart companies, leading/competitive advantage companies, are recognizing this online behavior as signals about how they're running their firms.

Which configuration of cars or laptops is the most prevalent? Manufacturing and distribution planning have a brand new early-warning system and no longer depend on sales forecasts.

Which is your most frequently asked question? Perhaps you can impact customer satisfaction by changing your product, your process, or your promise.

Which is your most popular article? Customer interest is constantly shifting, and you have to know which way the wind is blowing in order to create the right offerings tomorrow.

Asking the Right Questions

Helping other companies make websites has always been difficult for one simple reason: Not knowing what is possible, companies haven't known what their goals should be.

Before the turn of the century, many companies spent a good deal of time and money on finding, installing, and implementing the right web-analytics tool. Then, they threw it out because the reports weren't providing the magic answers they were looking for. Once they replaced the tool, they found they were no better off. They hadn't invested in the human side of the equation.

We've reached a point where we have too many answers. We have more data than can be consumed. It's no longer a matter of looking at the reports and following business rules based on the results. The winners will be those who ask really good questions—really good business questions.

Jason Burby and Shane Atchison have been approaching their clients with a rigorous metrics structure, which forces the discussion of goals and business questions to happen right up front, before any pages are created, which is where it belongs. Goals reveal indicators. Indicators point to metrics. Metrics identify technologies. All of it needs good people who know how to analyze a lot of data.

Jason and Shane have been using this approach for so long that they've come to recognize the best practices and the worst pitfalls that are common across companies and industries. They've shared their wisdom in articles, on their website, on the stage of the Emetrics Summit—and now in these pages.

Which metrics matter to top executives? How do you justify your budget? What does a web financial model look like? How do you jump-start the use of analytics by the business users? Jason and Shane outline organizational dynamics, requisite talents and skills, and functional operations.

Jason and Shane share examples of monetization models to help overcome the age-old analytics problem of a ton of data, but little action. This book is filled with tips and tricks to get people excited about and see the value in the recommendations you uncover on your website. They've included case studies about how companies have changed the way in which they act on data and prioritize opportunities. Their insights will make a significant difference in your investment in web analytics and your return on that investment.

This book (and the associated website) is part manifesto, part guidebook, part workshop. It's the *Hitchhiker's Guide to the Galaxy* of marketing ROI.

Don't Panic.

Jim Sterne
Santa Barbara, California

Contents

Introduction

If you're like us, one of the things you may recall from high school physics is the phrase "For every action, there is an equal and opposite reaction." You may also recall that this is Newton's third law of motion. Newton's genius was in taking the natural universe and all the behaviors and elements in it and managing their complexity through some simple laws. Today, we're all struggling with ways to explain an increasingly complex universe of our own creation: the Internet. Interestingly enough, Newton's law still has something to teach us.

We want to propose the first law of web analytics: "For every action, there is an opportunity for an intelligent reaction." In physics, we know that if we push on a door, the door must push back on us. Online, the same must be true: If we click, the site must react somehow, through some action. That action—that response to activity on the Web—is the subject of this book. It's also one of the most important issues in marketing today. In fact, it's one of the most important issues in *business* today.

Actionable Web Analytics is first a marketing book. We wrote it with the marketer in mind and with a clear focus on how that marketer can demonstrate real ROI from their web investments. But it's more than just a marketing book. It's also a practical book for everyone involved in web design, management, and analysis. This is a book for just about everyone in the organization. The key to using it successfully is to understand that it isn't a "how-to" book on web analytics, but it will help you understand the "why to." If you're unsure you're the right audience for this book, ask yourself this question: "Do your customers interact with your business online?" If the answer is "yes," then you should be reading this book. If the answer is "no," you may want to ask yourself "why" and then come back to this book later.

Our basic premise is that the vast data being generated by users of your website can explicitly and insightfully show you the actions you should take to make the site better. It's essential to remember that this data is more than just the clicks generated by visitors to your site. It's also the attitudes and perceptions of your customers (survey and usability data), data about your competitors (site traffic comparisons), data from your marketing (ad click-through and search ranking), and data from your financials (cost of sales through multiple channels). All this data is part of your marketing universe and needs to be considered holistically when you take any action.

Throughout this book, we'll come back time and again to this premise and to its corollary: Web analytics are of no real value unless someone takes action based on the data. By *action* we don't mean any random action, but action that is driven by specific business goals. This is action that is meaningful. The Web is a vast machine being engaged billions of times every hour by visitors around the globe. Those interactions generate vast amounts of data, and that data is begging for insights that will make it real and valuable. Someone must take action, or the data was collected in vain.

The topics covered here range from the types of data that need to be collected to the way in which you select agencies to help you make sense of it all. We'll discuss design and creativity as well as monetization and key performance indicators (KPIs). Marketing connects all these things together and makes them work for the business and to make the business better. Each element of your interactive strategy needs to be examined, integrated, and improved time and again. Web success comes only through endless incremental action.

What's Inside

We've structured the chapters of *Actionable Web Analytics* to flow logically from front to back but also to be able to stand alone. Part I of the book gives you a high-level view of the key issues involved in the industry today. You'll find a big picture in Chapter 1 that sets the stage for all the discussion that follows. Although much of the focus in the first chapter is on marketing and marketing themes, it's applicable to every reader who is interested in understanding how websites have become a fundamental element of modern business. Chapter 2 digs a bit deeper into the overall theme and opens up the discussion around performance marketing. Think about how you're measuring marketing performance in your organization now, and then think about it again after reading this important chapter.

Part II (Chapters 3 and 4) talks about shifting to a culture of analysis. This touches on the somewhat delicate subject of how an organization functions. A lot of this section concerns the work people do and the room for improvement that may exist. It may seem familiar to some readers as you reflect on your organization. For everyone, it will be a time to take stock of the environment around you and determine how you're going to get the most value from this book and web analytics in general.

The hard work starts in Part III. Here is where the nuts and bolts of web analytics come into play. The chapters flow logically from one to the next in much the same way you'll work through the issues in your own business. First, in Chapter 5, we provide an overview of methodology. This may be deceptively simple, but it grounds every decision you must make on a day-to-day basis. Chapter 6 discusses the concepts of measuring success through goals and KPIs. KPIs are discussed throughout this book, and soon enough you'll go into just about every meeting ready to discuss them.

All your efforts in making web analytics actionable are likely to drive more revenue and earnings for your company. In Chapter 7, we discuss monetization and provide some practical models for measuring it. We suggest that you make a copy of some of the information here for your CFO (or buy them their own copy of the book!).

Chapters 8 and 9 zero in on the types of data that are important and then the mechanics of analyzing and reporting on the data. You'll find a lot of terminology here that will be useful in working with analytics reports. Chapter 10 takes you up again to a higher-level view of prioritizing.

Another name for Chapter 11 could be "Action." Optimization is a rapidly emerging discipline, and it's all about taking ongoing action to improve your KPIs and meet your business goals. We think this is an important subject and believe you'll agree with us once you finish this chapter and start implementing some of the methods discussed.

Finally, Part IV is about taking the final steps to put everything into action and transform your business. At the heart of this is working with companies outside your own, such as interactive agencies and software vendors. They're important participants in the web-analytics ecosystem, and you should understand how to engage them successfully. Chapters 12 and 15 cover the basics of engagement. Chapter 13 dives deep into the mysteries of the creative process and will empower you to walk into a room full of potentially hostile designers and walk out with a set of new partners. You'll also find out in Chapter 14 how build a great staff (or be part of one) and make web analytics an essential part of the business.

As you read this book, we recommend that you refer back to earlier chapters as often as necessary to keep yourself grounded in basics as well as some of the overarching business issues raised by online marketing. Throughout the book, we refer to the *culture of analysis* you should be building in your organization, much as we have in our own.

During the past eight years, we've worked with dozens of businesses, from small startup companies to global companies such as Microsoft, Nike, and Ford; from not-for-profit brands like PBS to iconic brands like Converse; and with each of them, we've learned more about how to make smart decisions and take effective action. This book is an attempt to share that knowledge with you and help your company succeed.

For marketers and those who want to think like them, this book should help put the emerging discipline of web analytics into the broader context of classic marketing and branding. We hope you find something informative and are empowered to go forward and take action.

Actionable
Web Analytics

The Changing Landscape of Marketing Online

I

As we begin our discussion of web analytics, the first part of this book will cover the broad foundation issues. To start, we need to ground our overall content in the larger marketing landscape, something that Chapter 1 should accomplish. Chapter 2 will drill down deeper into the specifics of web analytics and provide domain-specific knowledge necessary for the rest of the book.

The Big Picture

1

The Web has become one of the most powerful vehicles for marketing and communication ever created. It allows fast and easy communication with millions of customers in a timely fashion. It has transformed the speed at which companies and their brands can be created and grow. The Web has also created new opportunities for marketers to become better at their discipline. This chapter provides an overview of the changes in marketing that have resulted from the Web's existence and then a discussion of the key guiding principles you should remember for the rest of this book.

Chapter Contents
New Marketing Trends
The Analysis Mandate

New Marketing Trends

"Because its purpose is to create a customer, the business has two—and only two—functions: marketing and innovation. Marketing and innovation create value; all the rest are costs."

—Peter Drucker, 1977

According to *Fortune* magazine, the five largest American corporations in 1977 were Exxon, General Motors, Ford Motor, Texaco, and Mobil; Microsoft was a two-year-old startup venture, and the Internet had not even been invented. Yet, Peter Drucker saw the future clearly. He realized then something that is even truer now: Businesses must create customers, and the best way to do that is through marketing and innovation. The nature of "marketing" and "innovation" in 1977 were markedly different than they are today (or at least than they appear to be today), and the connections between business and customer were orderly, predictable, and easily managed.

The contemporary marketing executive faces unprecedented challenges and limitless opportunities. The distance between the business and the customer, both physically and emotionally, has been shortened to the duration of a single click. Those *clicks*, perhaps the most over-examined phenomenon of the last decade, are the staccato sound of a new engine of commerce and of the near instantaneous decisions made by customers to buy or not to buy. The marketer hears the clicks as a fanfare for success or a funereal march of doom. It may sound overly dramatic, but looking at the success of companies like Amazon, eBay, and Google shows that reality may be even more dramatic still.

The challenges inherent in navigating the world of business today are daunting, but the resources available are far more sophisticated than ever. The tools and tactics available now are probably an order of magnitude more powerful and more useful than they were five years ago. In the world of online commerce, marketing has become innovation. Innovation brings with it a new level of complexity as well as confusion, and marketers have to work harder and harder to stay ahead of their competitors and their customers.

Tools and tactics are essential, but strategy wins the war. Marketing leaders know that perspective and vision help create and drive a strategy. In the online world, it's often easy to become consumed with minutiae and forget the overarching business goals. Being able to show improvement in how many new clicks your site gets isn't useful if you can't show how much you invested to get those additional clicks and you have no baseline data for comparisons. Strategy dictates that metrics are grounded in historical context, and return on investment (ROI) is predicted before and reviewed after any program is implemented. Strategy must also lead to action, and action is the governing principle behind this book.

Marketing in the twenty-first century is about change and innovation. Change is no longer driven solely by the ideas of big companies ("let's introduce a diet version of that drink and see what happens") and their competitors. Now it's also driven by customer demands (and customer revolt). Information on good and bad products used to take months or years to become general knowledge. Today, new products are often discussed and dissected before they're even released. Change has come, and customers are doing innovation as fast as companies.

All of this change and innovation generates data—lots and lots of data. Data is the click made *real*. Data is the transformation of customer needs and buying decisions into marketing and innovation. Data is also the endless wave that threatens to overrun every marketing department in the world. Data is in danger of becoming the enemy of progress instead of the foundation of success. Throughout this book, we'll return to data and the specific actions you need to take to make that data valuable.

Before becoming completely consumed with data (and this book will show you exactly how not to be consumed *by* data), it's important to examine some of the larger trends that are driving the data onslaught. These trends are as follows:

- The consumer revolution
- The shift from offline to online marketing
- Instant brand building (and destruction)
- Rich media and infinite variety

We'll look at each one briefly and weave together the larger pattern of what marketing and innovation will look like in the near future. From that pattern, we'll set the stage for the "Analysis Mandate" and a plan for using the rest of *Actionable Web Analytics*. First, we go into the hearts and minds of the consumers.

The Consumer Revolution

Among the more than 100 million websites online (according to netcraft.com) and the billions of pages that form those sites is just the page you want. If you can find it, you'll click it. If you click it, you'll receive the satisfaction you so richly deserve. Welcome to infinite choice, Mr. and Ms. Consumer.

Most of us are familiar with the Industrial Revolution as part of a broad historical tableau that saw manual labor slowly replaced by automated labor and the manufacture of machines to power that automation. It was a significant revolution for businesses because productivity soared and costs dropped. For the worker, it was a time when their livelihood was often threatened by machinery; but they benefited from the cheaper and more readily available goods created by those machines. The revolution continued for many decades as each change produced a series of other changes, such as railways producing an infrastructure for wider distribution of manufactured goods and then allowing goods to be centrally manufactured as raw materials were transported. In many ways, the Industrial Revolution solidified the role of the *consumer* in the economy. Someone had to buy all the output from efficient and automated production, and thus the consumer class was born.

From the time of the Industrial Revolution in the late eighteenth and early nineteenth centuries until the beginning of the twenty-first century, the role of the consumer was pretty fixed. Consumers *consumed* the goods and services produced and distributed by industry. This was a sweeping and broad statement of how markets worked, and everyone accepted it as true. Consumers were, at least for the most part, passive participants in the ecosystem.

The Internet changed all that completely. The full extent of this change is still being observed and documented.

Consumer-Driven Choice

One of the authors recalls purchasing new stereo equipment in the late 1980s. Once the right receiver was chosen based on a review in a magazine, finding it involved a lot of driving around and making phone calls to stereo shops. The magazines gave something called a "suggested retail price" for an item; the actual price was something secretly determined by stereo salespeople (or so it was rumored among aficionados). Having finally purchased the equipment, the author then wanted to show it off. He even recalls making a photocopy of the instruction manual cover page to display to friends.

Consumers had the choices presented to them back then. If you walked into a store and there were only red shirts, you couldn't get black. If you bought something and found it defective, you could bring it back for a refund, but that didn't help the next guy who bought the same thing. If you loved a book or movie, you would go out of your way to tell some friends about it, and they would tell some friends, and you hoped all your friends would know about it before it left the theater (and remember when the only place to see movie trailers was in the theater?).

As a marketing manager in 1985, you would have had a fairly straightforward job (not an easy job, but still straightforward): Identify a market segment for your product, and then place some ads, do some promotions, and ensure that the target audience knew about the existence of the product. Then, wait for the sales data to come trickling in. Review all the data, and determine if something needed to change about the product or campaign. Make the changes, and start waiting all over again.

You can quickly see how different the situation is today. In 10 minutes, you can sit at your computer and find information about the latest receivers, compare prices, read reviews by hundreds of other buyers, check out the technology blogs to determine if a new model is coming out soon, and purchase your equipment for delivery the next day if you want. Not only that, but you may find that if you ask a question about the product on a discussion site, the marketing manager located across the globe responds to you in real time (and it's definitely way after working hours for them). They may send you a discount code so you can get the receiver at 10% off at a preferred online retailer.

The Internet shifted the power of choice from manufacturers, suppliers, advertising agencies, and stores to the single most important element of the system: the consumer. The flow of data has changed from trickle-down to a wide-open river, with the consumer being able to drink when and where they choose. The tools of communication make everyone equal (recall the classic *New Yorker* cartoon with the caption "On the Internet nobody knows you're a dog").

Marketing managers everywhere have had to make a radical shift in how they view their markets and their customers. There is little value in trying to hide information about your product or spread misinformation about your competitors—the Internet is a self-correcting ecosystem that almost always lets the truth shine through. The power of millions of consumers is always stronger than the power of a single company. Transparency is the only strong strategic move left when marketing.

But savvy marketers have a weapon at their disposal that consumers don't have. That weapon, as you'll see again and again in this book, is the data. The ability to engage in web analysis lets you harness the power of consumer choices and use it to predict and direct future behavior. As in any good system, there are always ways to find order amidst the chaos.

What Time Does the Store Open?

It may seem trite to write about shopping in your pajamas, but not that long ago it was a cutting-edge concept. For decades, the general rhythm of shopping was aligned with the rhythm of most jobs and most schools: Stores opened in the morning and closed in the evening. Unless you were a shift worker, your schedule was the same as everyone else's schedule. The only people shopping in their pajamas were doing so from a mail-order catalog or watching the Home Shopping Network. Impulsive desires ("I must have a pair of yellow pants now!") were rarely satisfied and usually forgotten by morning.

Professional marketers never gave much thought to the "when" of a purchase. From books to clothes to electronics, it was all about the customer being in the store to purchase the product. Making sure the channel was full of inventory was the key to success. If there was a run on a product, you usually saw it coming with plenty of time to spare. Likewise, if a product was going to be a flop, it took some time for the data to filter back to you. Price adjustments were done in a well-considered fashion.

On a typical day in the twenty-first century, the average consumer spends far more time browsing and buying online in a week than they would normally do in person in a month. The consumer chooses when to shop, where to shop, and what they buy based on their priorities, not the marketers. Living online is an empowering state for the consumer and should be equally empowering for the smart marketer.

Here are examples of some of the questions businesses now face. Did you know that more red sweaters sell between the hours of 7:00 AM and 10:00 AM with a 10% off coupon than with a $5 off coupon, but that the reverse is true between 8:00 PM and 11:00 PM? Will you run more ads at nighttime for your romance novels and more in the daytime for your business books? How are you connecting the reality of your stores closing at 10:00 PM with your online discounts decreasing at the same time?

The power of the always-on consumer is also the power of the data-smart marketer. As the shift toward more time online continues, having a strategy driven by the data of consumer behavior across time and across channels is the way in which companies will succeed. Chapter 5 of this book goes into considerable detail about making your marketing decisions using data.

The Shift from Offline to Online Marketing

Advertising used to be a simple game, or so it seemed. Print, TV, radio, outdoor, sponsorships, and direct were the channels, and it was a matter of determining how much you spent on each. The big money usually went to TV, because that was where you could get the big returns. It was all about the number of viewers—the *impressions*— you could get for your ad. Marketing strategy often meant advertising strategy, because that was the predominant way in which companies could connect with their audience.

The Interactive Advertising Bureau reported in November 2006 that Internet advertising revenue for Q3 of that year surpassed $4 billion. A decade earlier, the revenue was under $250 million. Just a few years earlier, the revenue was nothing. All that money had to come from somewhere.

The statistics across all forms of marketing spending are clear: The money is shifting from offline to online. There are two key reasons for this: The audience is spending their time online; and measuring marketing success online is orders of magnitude more accurate and informative than for any other medium. It's a data game now, and the team that knows how to analyze the data best wins.

 Note: It isn't having the *most* data that wins; it's being able to do the best analysis.

If we examine the migration from offline to online more closely, we see a natural evolution of the *relationship marketing* rigor and methodology pioneered by Lester Wunderman decades ago. Online allows marketing messages to be precisely targeted and often ensures that the audience is receptive to receiving those messages. Online also gives nearly infinite flexibility to test variations of a message or campaign in near real time. Imagine being able to run a slightly different TV commercial in 10 major cities at the same time and then knowing which was most effective at conversion before the hour was done. What is impossible offline has become routine online.

Many businesses are pursuing a marketing strategy online that means spending money on ads and buying keywords. Some companies dedicate vast resources to this effort and have detailed quantitative analyses of how each ad performs and which keywords are doing well on each of the major search engines. Marketing departments and advertising agencies have come to a point where they believe they know how to make online marketing work successfully.

Have you ever clicked a banner ad that promised something specific (such as "Click here to get 20% off our latest release") and ended up on the home page of a site with no information about that 20% discount to be seen anywhere? Perhaps you did a search and clicked one of the ads for your keyword (such as "wool socks") and found yourself on a site that sold everything from wool blankets to wool sweaters and wool socks. But you were still two or more clicks away from what your heart desired.

Unfortunately, occurrences like these are standard around the Internet in 2007. Some marketers treat banner ads and keywords as another form of mass advertising, like billboards, instead of as highly targeted doorways to specific destinations on their sites. Analytics data can quickly demonstrate how many of those people expecting wool socks decide to leave the site after landing in the wrong place and how many stick around to buy a few pairs. Likewise, analytics can help drive tactics that allow you to test pairs of ads and landing pages together to see which have the highest conversion. Chapter 11 of this book will discuss site optimization in detail and help you take action based on the insights you glean from analytics.

The Winning Site

Your website has the potential to be the most powerful marketing tool in your arsenal. If you've invested five or six figures into the site, you probably have a great deal of confidence in its ability to deliver your core messages. The website probably has a whole team dedicated to ongoing maintenance and improvement. Clearly, you've made the move to online from offline and are reaping the rewards. Right?

How many visitors did your site have yesterday? Which of those came to you immediately after visiting a competitor? How many were looking for a job, and how many were doing comparison shopping? If you can answer any of these questions, you're probably already doing some *web analytics*. By this we mean collecting web-usage data and reporting that data back to the organization.

What is your web strategy for the next two versions of your site based on your ongoing A/B site test? Which of your currently running social-networking campaigns is yielding the highest conversion rate? What is the ROI on the money you've invested in your corporate blogs? If you can answer any of these questions, then you're well on the way toward doing *web analysis* (and are, we hope, finding new and useful tips in this book to make your team even more successful). Web analysis means taking the data from web analytics and using it to make changes to your site and business decisions based on the data.

The ongoing shift in marketing focus from offline to online is only the first step. The longer-term reality will be a seamless blending of the online and offline worlds. Many businesses are already treating the two channels as points along a continuum instead of discrete entities and in doing so are elevating the stakes for everyone in their industry. The investments being made in the online channel will continue to grow. In fact, it's possible that the investments being made are increasing faster than the ability to measure their success.

Instant Brand Building (and Destruction)

Near and dear to the heart of every marketer is branding. Branding is usually the center-piece for every marketing strategy and is the thing that often generates the most discussion at the executive level. We've heard plenty of senior executives talk about "building the brand" and "extending my brand online." Everyone seems to be able to talk about branding, from the CEO to the entry-level marketing manager to the 18-year-old kid on their MySpace site. Sometimes it seems that branding has become core curriculum in elementary school, just like reading, writing, and arithmetic.

Brand building is exceptionally important, and every marketing plan must treat it as such. Measuring the success of branding, however, is a different story. Many companies build websites to promote their brand but then have no idea how effective an endeavor that was. Some companies think of all sorts of clever ways to extend their brand online, often with no thought to how doing so accrues value back to their core brand and their core business. What is the point of a tire company building a rich and interactive website so they can point to it at the next distributor meeting if that site provides no business value to its users? Is the simple presence of a decorative outpost at www.yourcompanyhere.com worth the investment made? Can it hurt your brand more than it can help it?

The concept of the brand will weave its way throughout this book, much like the thread that holds together the parts of a quilt. The agencies you may hire to perform your web analytics will want to know all about your brand. The team you hire to drive your web strategy will want to know all about your brand as well. This is because the brand is often the intangible element that can separate the great online business from the mediocre.

Once it's clear that an online opportunity exists for your business, then you have to think about how it will connect to and build your brand. Let's return to the tire company as an example. They already have a simple website in place, and its primary purpose is to let potential customers find a local dealer. Looking at the data over the past year has convinced the CMO of the company that people come to the website wanting more. Perhaps the most common search terms that bring people to the site are "tire safety comparison", "reliable tires", and "buy new tires". The dealer network is glad to be getting referrals from the site, but they would like to have more qualified leads instead of just random shoppers. Some visitors are even hunting around the site for multiple pages, apparently looking for coupons.

The tire company has a well-known brand that stands for value, reliability, and safety. Maintaining those brand characteristics is a key function of the marketing team. The CMO decides to hire an agency to help build a new site, put in place a rigorous analytics model, and drive vertical integration into the sites of the largest regional dealers. All this is also part of a plan to extend the brand to the younger generation of car buffs who like to customize all the components of their vehicles.

The RFP (see Chapter 12) process helps secure an agency that seems to be able to meet all the requirements of the project. The first thing they do is review the existing website and the current set of analytics data. From there, they propose a plan for a new site and new measurement approach. They promise to extend the brand to a new audience and ensure that the traditional audience is able to find the information they need to compare and buy tires. The CMO tells them to steam ahead.

Everything seems to be aligned for a successful extension of the brand online and increased satisfaction for customers and the dealers. The agency proposes that the new site start out with an elaborate animation of a car being customized with wheels and tires, after which a visitor can race the car around their favorite city. Once the visitor gets past the opening Flash, they're given the opportunity to compare tire models, find local dealers, and play another race game to earn a $25 coupon.

What may happen here? If you look back at the search terms that have brought people to the site in the past, they're about finding facts related to the core attributes of the brand—safety and reliability—and being able to find a dealer and buy tires. Now, when people arrive at the site, they're confronted with an attempt to extend the brand to a new audience. It's likely they will wonder if they arrived at the correct site at all.

That new target audience may find the customization and racing games interesting. But they may also consider them disingenuous and false, given the historical brand attributes of the company. Trying to be cool online is often the worst way to reach an audience. Consumers know cool when they see it, and it isn't easy to pass off a fake as the real thing.

Brands are precious assets, and the online world presents many new challenges in maintaining and growing those assets. Emerging phenomena such as user-generated content and social networking provide opportunities for brand building to be put into the hands of consumers. As we are writing this chapter, the Super Bowl is on TV, and several companies are showing commercials created by their customers, not by ad agencies or marketing departments. Consumers are in control, and brands can be created, enhanced, or destroyed overnight in the online world.

The strength of your brand can be measured in many different ways. Being able to track carefully what happens on your site as well as the conversations that take place across the Internet (have you checked today to see how many blog entries discuss your latest marketing campaign?) is key to business growth and demonstrating ROI. You must be able to create and track brand metrics online in order to succeed. If you don't control the fate of your brand, then someone else will.

Much of the actionable strategy found in this book ties tightly to the value of your brand. Websites don't function in a vacuum, and analytics must be driving important business metrics. Brand building helps define the types of goals and key performance indicators (KPIs) discussed in Chapter 6. Likewise, Chapter 13 discusses how to write creative briefs. These briefs are all about defining the brand and ensuring that your agency (or internal creative team) understands how to translate that brand into online experiences.

Rich Media and Infinite Variety

In January 2006, JupiterResearch published a report stating that the average online consumer spends as much time online each week—14 hours—as they do watching TV. This fact is stunning in many ways, but most interesting of all is the question of what they're doing during those 14 hours. Are they shopping? Reading the news? Chatting with friends and building websites? The infinite variety of things to do online provides choices for everyone, but the killer applications online in the future are going to be rich media.

Broadband connectivity has become so pervasive that many consumers have as much bandwidth at their house as they do at their office desk. They're just as likely to have more data storage at home as at work (it's a lot easier for you to go buy a 300GB disk drive for a couple of hundred dollars than it is for your IT department to requisition you a new one). In industry vernacular, "fat pipes" are here and ready to be filled up. The rich filling inside those pipes includes video and audio. Movies and TV. New albums and classic songs. Radio shows, podcasts, and video chat. Rich media is driving consumer engagement and providing new opportunities for your marketing machine. Are you ready?

A decade or so ago, in the early days of web analytics, there wasn't much debate about what had to be tracked and reported. The Web consisted of mostly static pages of text, and user behavior consisted of clicks—one click followed by another and followed by another (what is referred to affectionately as the *clickstream*). Any motion or sound on a page was all but ignored by web analysts and web-analytics software. Banner ads were the standard for advertising; even if they had fancy animation, the things that mattered were impressions and clicks.

For many sites today, the page and the text on it is the least important element of the consumer experience. From the Flash animation that drives navigation to the consumer-generated videos playing in the background, the contemporary web experience is rich and vibrant. Consumers watch the latest episodes of their favorite TV shows and catch the limitless number of videos available at sites like YouTube. Some of those videos are about your product and your brand.

The flip side of consumers spending 14 hours per week online is that they're generating 14 hours per week of data! That data can be used to fuel your marketing strategy and help you make informed decisions. If rich media is the honey enticing your audience online, then you need to be able to measure just how sweet that honey tastes. You must be able to track how your media is shared (your audience will do a lot of your marketing for you by sending those great videos to their friends and coworkers) and how often it's watched. You must be able to discriminate between rich media that drives ROI-enhancing events like purchases and rich media that distracts people from purchases. Sites that become so full of entertainment that people forget to buy a product are delivering negative ROI (trust us, it happens far more often than you might think).

Rich media can enhance your dialog with your consumers and do so in a profitable way. From creating an immersive experience to providing incentive for viewing advertisements, new media types bring the Internet closer to the world of TV without having to sacrifice the measurement advantages of being online.

You may recall how TV ratings were conducted many years ago: Families received a diary in the mail in which they were to record the shows they watched each evening (the *Nielsen family*); they mailed the diary back every few weeks. From that highly scientific and precise survey, the TV networks determined the ad rates for their shows. No one questioned the model because it was the best the medium offered. Today we have digital cable and Internet Protocol TV (IPTV) bringing all the media channels closer together in both spirit and technology. The lessons learned in measuring the Internet over the past decade will provide the framework for eventually measuring all media. Your online marketing strategy today will most likely become your all-media strategy next year.

The Analysis Mandate

These four trends are beyond your control:

- The consumer revolution
- The shift from offline to online marketing
- Instant brand building (and destruction)
- Rich media and infinite variety

They have changed how we do business both online and offline, and the changes are just going to keep on coming. Marketing executives need new tools and new strategies to successfully navigate this changing landscape. Unfortunately, there are lots of ways to become overwhelmed or paralyzed by the changes.

Marketing has always been about creating value. From the earliest days of people in the village saying something nice about a butcher or tailor (this is what we now call *word of mouth marketing*, and whole books are dedicated to the subject) to the more modern practices of advertising and PR, marketing tries to create value. In many cases, it appears to be successful. A new product is launched, people read about it in the paper and then see the ad on TV, and sales for the product rise. If you stop running the ads, then sales drop. If you offer a coupon, then sales rise again. It's very much a cause-and-effect situation.

What if this is wrong? What if no relationship exists between marketing and outcomes? Perhaps hidden variables are driving demand up or down and just happen to be correlated with marketing efforts. What would happen if a company stopped doing all marketing?

For a long time, Starbucks essentially did no advertising at all. Even today, they don't advertise their core offering: the local Starbucks store. Yet Starbucks has been successful at making their product highly desirable to a large group of consumers. They manage to charge a huge premium for a product that was practically a commodity beforehand. Should Starbucks start running ads like McDonalds to drive people into their stores?

How can you know that marketing works? How can you create a culture of accountability in marketing and make ROI the single most important benchmark of success?

The major trends described here are creating a rich environment for you to create a new marketing paradigm. Every one of these trends demonstrates a shift from media and behavior that can't be measured to those that can be measured. Not just measured, but measured and tested and adjusted in real time. These trends should strengthen your hand when it comes to driving business value. They've created an analysis mandate and provided the opportunity to transform marketing into an ROI-driven discipline.

One of the keys to the success of your business in the face of these trends is having the right teams in place, both inside your organization and at your partners. Part IV of this book has a tremendous amount of detail on finding and selecting agencies (Chapter 12), staffing your own team (Chapter 14), and working with technology partners (Chapter 15).

ROI Marketing

"However beautiful the strategy, you should occasionally look at the results."

—*Winston Churchill*

Return on investment should be the three most important words in every marketer's vocabulary. Marketing is an investment, and in many businesses it's one of the single largest investments made. For a long time, the relationship between this investment and the outcomes were sketchy and assumed. We know of CMOs who looked at ROI as something the financial department managed, not something that should be core to their strategy. Programs were created and executed without much thought to the specific results they were driving. Frankly, this isn't a good way to run a business.

In this book, we'll spend considerable time discussing KPIs—key performance indicators—and illustrating how they can transform marketing into an ROI-driven discipline. KPIs allow marketers to rationalize their investments, normalize the results, and consistently report them to every department and executive in a company. A focus on KPIs is a significant step up the strategic ladder from doing web analytics. Chapter 6 will help you build specific goals and the KPIs needed to measure achievement.

The output of web analytics is data, and that data always needs to be put in some context. Running one tool or another to analyze the traffic on your site or the results of a specific demand-generation campaign is only the first step in the ROI marketing model. The analysts on the team (see Chapter 14 on how to identify and hire those analysts) are working to mine the massive data generated by your marketing activities and reduce it to reasonable abstractions. However, their work is essentially useless without a specific framework in which to act on this data.

That framework must include the ability to change. Simply reporting data, even the most positive of data, isn't sufficient. Every result is an opportunity to make the business better and increase ROI. If a specific website is working exceptionally well, how can the data from analytics help make it better? If a campaign drives conversion for products A and B, how can it be extended to product C? These are the questions the data has to answer.

Our own CMO has worked in organizations where reporting results was one of the most important tasks for every marketer. Senior management often required so many metrics delivered to them on a single page that the only solution was to use bigger paper. The discussions about these metrics—these KPIs—were usually heated and focused on what happened and what our goals had to be for the next reporting period. Very rarely was the focus on what had to change in order to achieve the new goals. Instead of using ROI marketing, he was part of a cycle of KPI marketing.

Your strategy must explicitly prevent both data overload and the data dead-end game. Zero in on a few key metrics, and work to create ongoing improvement. Make scorecards the basis of all discussions around performance of marketing initiatives, and focus on what you can learn and change based on those scorecards. Measure the dollar value of converting visitors into purchasers on your website, and weigh that against the cost of ongoing analytics, optimization, and redesign. This process will create a culture of analysis in your organization and make ROI marketing the only strategy you can take to the bank.

Innovation

New trends are emerging that will extend the models already discussed and cause new complexity to emerge. Some experts argue that we're as early in the evolution of the Internet as the Model T was in the evolution of the automobile. That can be a frightening thought or a liberating one; it's all a matter of perspective. Our perspective is that of extreme liberation and vast opportunity.

Returning to the thoughts of Peter Drucker that opened this chapter, we're going to propose that marketing has *become* innovation. Marketing can explore new tools and technologies and integrate them quickly into daily activity, but tools aren't the solution. Tools are the *sine qua non* of good analytics, and good analytics are good marketing hygiene.

Innovation is an exciting concept, and the Internet has made it part of our daily lives. Today you can create a little video on your personal camcorder and make it available to millions of viewers before the sun goes down. Essentially, you can create a commercial for your life. What is the ROI on that marketing investment? If you can do that, your business can do something amazing in the next 30 or 60 days, and your team can analyze the results in real time. That is the most amazing innovation of all.

Some Final Thoughts

This is a book about taking action. For the senior marketer and web business owner, it's a resource guide that will help inform and empower you to take action based on real data. For the web analyst, it will provide you with a set of strategic mandates to help drive your activities.

This is also a book about marketing and the fundamental changes that are occurring in this discipline. Being *actionable* means that there is something to act on and some reason to take those actions. The Web is the most interactive and measurable medium ever created, but realizing its full value requires significant effort and clear strategy. Building a website is the easy part, measuring your success is a lot more difficult, and taking action based on what you measure is even harder.

We wrote this book because we believe deeply in the Web and the analytics approach. We also believe that doing brilliant design and thinking deeply about brand are essential elements to website creation. The blending of these—the intersection of logic and design—has been the foundation of our success as a web agency, and we hope it can be the foundation of yours as well.

Performance Marketing

Like all good things, analytics is best when it's used with moderation and good judgment. When deployed properly, it's an invaluable tool for helping you make smart business decisions and choose communication strategies that will enable you to get the most out of your website.

In this chapter, we're going to look at the current state of web design and the strategies some companies are using to make decisions about how their sites should look and perform. We'll look at the kinds of sites that win awards, and why they may or may not be right for your business. Then, we'll tackle the problems that arise when companies deploy analytics to make design decisions independent of business goals. Finally, we'll give two examples of how we've used performance marketing to solve knotty problems in the field.

2

Chapter Contents

Data vs. Design

Throughout the industry, you'll find competing theories, interests, and, some would argue, ideologies about what a good website should be. There are those who talk about brand extension, usability, and experience design. They all have prescriptions for success and predictions of doom if you fail to follow their advice. Each sees web design as something that can be inherently good or bad.

Some web analysts would like to promote their field as yet another voice in this debate. This should not be so. Analytics isn't a design strategy; it's part of performance marketing, a business strategy that seeks to achieve maximum return on investment in all promotions. Analytics is the method by which the performance marketer measures a company's success.

We hope that, in the end, you'll agree with us that performance marketing is the goal, and analytics is a means to the end. Don't be tempted to use analytics for its own sake; that's largely a waste of time and money. You should use analytics to create insight into your processes. Then, take action on its findings so you can achieve your overall business goals.

Web Design Today

If you've ever attended a web meeting at a large company, you know that such a gathering can resemble a family dinner after a few too many cocktails. Behind the happy facade of a home page often lies a group of people who fundamentally disagree with each other. Product marketing managers argue with designers; financial officers clash with technologists; designers irritate editors; and information architects fight with everyone.

The problem is that each comes from a different place, and each has a set of beliefs about what's important on the Web and what isn't. Visual designers, for example, tend to take a brand-centric view. They believe that when colors and typography work well, a site produces a pleasing emotional experience that yields long-term benefits for a company. Marketers often focus on messaging. They believe that they will be successful if customers know enough about their product; and they're not above force-feeding if necessary. They believe that a site is most effective when it delivers users quickly to the content they want to see.

As we've said, analytics doesn't take a side in these debates. It's a tool that helps you make smart decisions about your website in the context of your overall business. When used properly, it doesn't increase click-through or raise the number of users visiting your site. As a result of your web-analytics efforts (especially those that lead to insight and action), you may see improvement in those areas, but only if they support your business goals.

In other words, web analytics is an important part in driving performance marketing. In essence, it takes marketing and holds its feet to the fire. When you become a true performance marketer, you'll realize that no one of the competing theories of web design is right for every application. Sometimes your site-design team wants what your usability team wants; other times, the crazy blue-haired kid in your creative department has the best idea.

To explain what we mean, we're going to look at examples of sites—ours and others—where performance marketing can come into play. We'll start with creative approaches and move on to more technical ones.

The Web Award Fallacy

Before we begin discussing performance marketing, we have to first confront a challenge to our theory. Many sites that excel from a performance-marketing standpoint don't win awards. They won't take center stage at Communication Arts or Cannes, and they probably don't win the usability kudos of gurus like Jacob Nielsen. They aren't what the industry as a whole sees as particularly "good." As you pursue performance marketing, you'll often find yourself on the outside of the party, looking in. Are we advocating bad design?

Far from it. Website awards are a bit like movie awards. Every year, they come out, and people in the industry pay a lot of attention to them, and they help careers move forward. Still, no one who watches the Oscars or the Golden Globes agrees with every outcome. We understand that movies are judged on criteria that sometimes add up to a movie we want to see. A particular movie—*The English Patient* comes to mind—may perfectly fit the industry's criteria and still be dreadful.

In the interest of full disclosure, we should admit that at ZAAZ, we've won our share of awards. And from a web agency's perspective, that's great. It motivates employees, it attracts quality prospects, and it impresses some of our potential clients. But what's good for a web agency isn't always what's good for a client. We've never set out expressly to win an award; we've won them only in the case of clients like Tazo Tea, whose fun branding and particular market needs neatly coincide with the criteria of certain web awards.

Although we enjoy winning awards, we'd far rather not win them, as long as we increase the performance of our clients' key performance indicator (KPIs) and drive their overall business goals. In an ideal situation, we not only achieve both, but we also ensure that their sites are top performers within the industry based on those KPIs.

When Visual Design Goes Wrong

The problem is that the desire for awards can overcome more rational urges, like accomplishing objectives. It's here that analytics can play an important role. It can be used to gauge the effectiveness of a site or campaign, identify what's working and what isn't, and tell companies what they should continue doing and what they should discard.

A good case of where analytics may have saved an award-winning site from the abyss of uselessness is whatamigonnadonext.com. This site was produced in 2005 for the United States Air Force, and we have few qualms about picking on it. As American taxpayers, we paid for it, and we're not satisfied with our ROI.

On the surface, the site is ripe for a performance-marketing approach. Its purpose is to ask graduating high school seniors to think about their future, and to convince them to join the Air Force. Web analysts love to build sites like this one, because it has a well-defined audience and a clear objective. Here they are:

Audience: Graduating high school seniors

Objective: Convert them to fill out a sign-up form to receive more information about Air Force careers

What could be easier to measure? We can look at the number of people the site reaches, see how many sign up, and measure the site's overall effect against that of other initiatives. Unfortunately, the site has failed both in understanding its audience and in reaching its objective. As you'll see, it never gave itself a fighting chance.

On the surface, it does well. Its interface consists of a popular notebook-doodle style, often seen on sites for youth brands such as surf and hip-hop companies. Using lots of Flash and uncomfortably heavy transitions, it asks users to select different career paths. Depending on what they choose, they learn the probable outcome. If they select something the Air Force approves of, they find an exciting career. If they choose something else, they find out that they'll end up living with their parents.

Has the site been effective? Although we have no numbers, we doubt it. Among other things, the site is roundly insulting to its audience. At every turn, it tells them they will fail at life unless they enter the Air Force. Bizarrely enough, it even discourages them from going to college. Colleges, it says, are either party schools or private institutions. A party school will turn you into a burnout and teach you nothing, whereas a private school will never accept you unless you have a name like Morton P. Throckmorton VI. Those are our tax dollars hard at work, saving America's youth from the dark cloud that threatens them all: higher education.

It's hard to imagine the audience swallowing this message. The Air Force, after all, has an ROTC presence at most universities in the country, including party schools, private universities, and the large number of public universities that fit in neither category. Although a creative director who judges an interactive contest may not be aware of this, the target audience—which is being talked down to—presumably does.

Leaving aside these problems, the site's design (see Figure 2.1) is also maladapted to its clearly stated objective. It's supposed to convince young people to fill out an application form to get information about careers in the Air Force. If so, the application should be easy to find. But it isn't. Not only does the homepage lack a link to the form, but the informational text about how to use the site is displayed in such a convoluted way that it's nearly impossible to read. And we could go on. The entire site, from its loading screen to it Flash transitions, is far too cumbersome to drive anyone to do anything.

Figure 2.1 The words "What am I gonna do next?" may well apply to the site itself. If the point is to drive users to sign up for the military, shouldn't there be somewhere they can actually do so? (whatamigonnadonext.com)

In other words, with its style, transitions, and humor, the site was perfectly aligned to win lots of awards for its web agency. But from a performance-marketing standpoint, it's a disaster. Because the Air Force failed to understand its audience and recognize its objectives, the site not only disparages its visitors but it also makes it nearly impossible to do the very thing it wants them to do.

Where Data Goes Wrong

At the same time, performance marketing doesn't mean you should always abandon a whimsical approach. After all, there are many places where a little silly fun is exactly what's needed. Branding sites for consumer products hardly need to convey information in a dry way. Flash can be a great tool for connecting emotionally with an audience. Even the dourest Fortune 500 company might, for example, use a fun microsite to inspire potential employees to apply or to educate others about its charitable efforts.

The examples in the previous paragraph are both fun and aligned with business objectives. And they can also be measured, although their benefits may not be as clear and straightforward as an improvement in a shopping-cart process. But when analytics becomes divorced from performance-marketing techniques, it can become dangerous to a company.

To explain what we mean, let's look at a certain practice that's become popular among the analytics-minded set. For lack of a better word, we'll call it *page-packing*. The technique rests on short-term understanding of business objectives. Let's say, for example, that an enterprise software maker, Company X, has identified a particular initiative as its number-one priority. This initiative involves getting as many people as possible to fill out a particular application so that a sales representative can contact them. How can you get them to do that?

Web analytics has taught us that there are always foolproof ways to get lots of people to sign up for something. One way is for Company X to offer an incentive, like an iPod Nano. Unfortunately, if the company does this, it will end up spending a lot of money to attract-low quality leads. Plenty of people sign up for any form that offers a shot at a prize. Is it really a good idea to pay sales representatives to talk to them?

Another more interesting method was discovered by web analysts who conducted a battery of multivariant tests. It involves packing a page with blocks of linked text, nearly all of which direct the user to the particular promotion.

Does it work? In a short-term sense, yes. If you do this, click-through rates will skyrocket, and the number of people signing up for your promotion will probably do so as well. Of course, if a supermarket owner wanted everyone to see their promotion on T-bone steaks, they could post strong men at the front door to grab every customer who came in and bodily drag them to the meat department. Chances are, the owner would not see a great increase in T-bone sales—and over time, they might lose all their customers.

In our more realistic example, if Company X packs its pages, it will probably see a great increase in signups. It will also irritate the large number of people who aren't interested in hearing from a sales rep. On top of that, the quality of the leads will probably diminish, meaning that the sales team will be forced to waste time making a lot of calls with no return. Page-packing may even end up costing the company money.

Just as with creative approaches, it's important not to get too excited about what analytics can do in the short term. Analytics without a comprehensive performance-marketing strategy is like a ship without a captain. The mates, sailors, and everyone else can run around making minor improvements to the ship's performance, but they may end up beaching it in the log run. Focusing exclusively on conversion rates and ignoring branding and other less quantifiable tasks can lead to disaster. Remembering that everything depends on your overall business objectives will help drive success.

Performance-Driven Design: Balancing Logic and Creativity

Most companies should look for a balance between numbers-driven and creative design. For every initiative, of course, this balance will be different. Your customer-service site doesn't need the same level of emotional impact as your home page. A site for bubblegum should not look anything like one for an insurance broker.

How can you know where your site should fall? The answer is a practice called *performance-driven design*. Another way of putting it is "create, but test." In the best scenario, you should try a number of different designs for each initiative, test them to find the best ones, and then optimize them from there.

If that's not feasible, then choose one direction, but be sure it's working the way you want it to. If you decide to unleash your imagination, check your conversion rates to ensure that you're accomplishing your goals. At the same time, if you're driving hard to push users down a particular behavioral path, you may also want to conduct an occasional attitudinal survey to find out whether you're annoying them and what impact this may have on the overall brand perception of your site. Every web initiative has a sweet spot between creativity and conversion, and analytics can help you find it.

Oddly enough, although your creative team may balk at first, you'll find there are benefits to using analytics as a touch point. Focusing on performance marketing can liberate creative people to do what they do best. Let's say you're a designer, for example, and you've come up with three comps: a wild one you really like, a conservative one you expect your client or boss to choose, and a middle-of-the-road one that you like least of all. With analytics, there's no need to make a Sophie's Choice every time. Instead, you can build them out, test them against objectives, and see which one wins. That way, you're free to make each one the best it can be, and you don't have to argue for your version or feel cheated because another has been chosen.

Other team members will see similar effects: An information designer need not spend hours trying to convince senior management that Option A is better than Option B. A simple test will suffice to put the matter to rest. Copywriters also tend to thrive, thanks to analytics. Historically, they've been left at the bottom of the bottom of the web hierarchy, and in many companies they're forced by marketing managers to produce reams of convoluted, jargon-filled prose. An A/B test will usually reveal what they already know: Jargon rarely pays.

And on it goes. When the creative design is submitted to a battery of tests, the best solution emerges. Each team member stops wasting time arguing for their perspective. Instead, they're free to concentrate on what they do best, and they can trust the numbers to ensure that they're doing well.

How does this work in the real world? Let's look at a few case studies, where our company encountered typical marketing problems and resolved them through performance marketing techniques.

Case Study: Dealing with Star Power

Several years ago, we were working for a shoe company that had an important relationship with a very prominent basketball star. Their marketing department loved him and had, frankly, invested a tremendous amount of money in him. He tested well with the public and was extremely popular among kids.

However, the company wasn't primarily in the business of selling basketball shoes. When we looked at their website, we saw that they sold a wide variety of shoes, the vast majority of which had nothing to do with sports. When we spoke with people throughout the organization, we soon realized that the company's focus on its star was producing a lot of grumbling in the ranks. Unrelated shoes were getting short shrift, and competitive analysis showed that online sales were lagging behind the company's competitors.

One side of the company wanted to reduce the star's presence and focus more on the variety of shoes. The other side felt that the star's presence brought in the right audience and encouraged them to buy. They advocated using the homepage of the e-commerce site to promote him and steer users towards branded minisites.

From our standpoint, this argument was easy to resolve. Click-path analysis clearly indicated that the people who came to the site by and large were not basketball fans. In the marketplace as a whole, the star did help the company's profile, but not on the Web. Visitors to the site were more interested in other things and tended to click around him. Worse still, the site generated substantially more revenue when his presence on the homepage was muted. When he was used in the proper way in the proper sections of the site, he was successful in increasing conversion.

The verdict? Well, it's not as simple as it sounds. In the end, the company didn't completely remove the star from their homepage. After all, he was important to their brand image, and he did help the company relate to younger customers. Still, by producing numbers that showed he wasn't effective on the home page by himself, we were able to restrain the more exuberant ideas of the marketing and branding team and focus more around overall revenue and impact to the brand based on the different views that different segments held.

Case Study: Forget Marketing at All

One of the most interesting things about performance marketing is that it can sometimes rule out spending promotional dollars. Most inexperienced—and some very experienced—marketers try to get their message out any way and anywhere they can. But if a marketer is genuinely concerned with getting the most out of their marketing buck, it can be just as valuable to know where marketing isn't effective as where it is.

A good example can be found in the tradeshow world. Many companies, for reasons of pride or the desire to penetrate new markets, have large and expensive booths at dozens of tradeshows each year. Unfortunately only a small percentage of these shows produce any revenue or prospects. On the Web, your initiatives may show similar failures.

For example, one of our clients is a credit union for whom we do a large amount of work. Like many financial institutions, they outsource their online banking operations to an outside vendor. If you've ever seen one of the sites that these vendors produce, you'll wonder whether a qualified visual designer ever laid eyes on it. The experience can be positively Neanderthal, with heavy blue buttons, dark backgrounds, and blocky links.

Our client wanted us to resolve two questions. First, was the experience so unappealing that their users wouldn't be happy with it, and what impact did that have on overall brand perception? Second, was it possible to reach out with cross-selling or community opportunities?

And so, we went to work. We tracked sign-ups and defection rates to see whether the experience was turning off customers. We also worked with the outsource vendor to enhance the branding and place promotions inside the experience. Then, we examined the performance of those initiatives.

The results were surprising. In the first case, the experience, as unappealing as it seemed, had no effect on customer retention, satisfaction rates, or brand perception. People seemed happy with the convenience of the service and were more than willing to put up with its unfriendly appearance. On the question of softening the experience, we were similarly surprised: Hardly ever had we seen a set of ads with a worse click-through rate. It turns out that when people are looking at the state of their finances, they're not interested in anything else.

As a result, we recommended to the credit union that they not only keep the antediluvian tool, but also not bother advertising on it. There were other places to put their money.

These aren't findings that we would automatically carry across to all other financial services clients. Instead, we'd use this as insight and past experience, but always be sure to determine what makes the most sense with different target audiences and segments.

Recap

In this chapter, you've seen that web analytics doesn't support or deny any particular theory of "good" web design. Instead, it's a central plank of a holistic business strategy called *performance marketing*. Simply put, performance marketing seeks to maximize the ROI of all web initiatives over the long term. As a result, it rejects creative branding projects that may win accolades in the industry but fail to take business objectives into account. It also rejects short-sighted tactics, such as page packing, which increase click-through rates while harming the long-term reputation of a company's website.

Rather than trying to go after awards or idealized theories of good design, we advocate performance-driven design. This process seeks to identity the ideal mix of creativity and data that drives long-term business benefits. This sweet spot is different for every company and every initiative, and you can find it only by monitoring and testing page performance and user satisfaction.

When used properly, performance marketing isn't a threat to designers, usability experts, or anyone else in your organization. Rather, it leaves them free to concentrate on what they do best, while allowing the company as a whole to monitor web activity and adjust it for the better.

Shifting to a Culture of Analysis

II

The first section of this book provided a general overview of the strategic issues that are impacting all businesses on the Web today and the place that web analytics can play in addressing those issues. This next section turns the focus "inward" to your business and provides some insights to the organizational changes necessary for addressing the larger strategic issues.

What "Culture of Analysis" Means

It's a great first step to implement some measure of analytics in your web channel. But to get the most out of your data requires a more comprehensive process: You're going to have to change many things from the ground up and build a culture of analysis in your company. In this chapter, we'll outline what that means and how it will change the way you make critical business decisions.

Becoming a data-driven organization won't happen overnight. Like any change in corporate culture, you'll need plenty of time, and you'll have to overcome significant obstacles to complete your transition.

3

Chapter Contents

What Is a Data-Driven Organization?

If you're trying to build a data-driven organization, it's a good idea to start by looking at the behavior of the best companies in the field. Over the course of our analytics practice, we've had the chance to examine a number of businesses that are doing a great job with performance marketing (as well as a much larger number that aren't). From this, we've been able to identify the major characteristics of companies with a strong culture of analysis:

1. They use business goals to drive decision-making One of the common problems with analyzing data is that companies look at their numbers without putting them in the context of their overall business. As a result, when they receive an analytics report (often in a handsome binder with attractive charts), they sift through it without knowing what it means to their bottom line. Data-driven organizations make sure that goals and metrics are defined and agreed on, and they communicate them to everyone according to role.

2. They avoid gut feelings Data-driven organizations never rely solely on gut feelings. Making educated decisions based on analytics-driven insight will help you meet your site goals quickly. Making them based on intuition may work sometimes, but it eventually results in a scattered and inconsistent strategy.

This doesn't mean you should throw your experience out the window. But you should be honest with yourself about what you really know and what it means. Because we all surf the Web, we often mistake our personal likes and dislikes for real insight into web behavior. If you can easily navigate a complex interface you've never seen before, great; but don't assume everyone else can. If you hate cute e-mail cards, fine; but realize that other people enjoy them. In other words, your experience can be a useful data point, but if you want to make smart decisions, you should combine it with solid analytics.

3. They invest around business goals Successful data-driven organizations spend money in the right places and in the right way. As a result, they can justify every marketing dollar they invest and tie it to business goals and key performance indicators (KPIs). Instead of putting millions of dollars every other year into a full site redesign, they target their spending according to where it will be most effective.

To do this, you first need to identify which aspects of your web channel are most important in driving your business. For example, let's say you have a lead-generation site that tries to get visitors interested in your offerings so they will request a meeting with a sales representative. Every upgrade you make to the site should improve the way it converts your visitors into high-quality leads. Your efforts may involve highlighting calls to action or streamlining request forms so that it's easier to separate good prospects from bad.

Companies that are serious about data also use analytics to maximize their ROI for online and offline initiatives. If you have an underperforming marketing campaign, you should pull the plug on it and increase funding in more successful areas. That way, you'll always be sure you're investing wisely and strategically in areas that drive your business goals.

4. They employ data-driven standards In data-driven organizations, every team, business unit, and individual operates under a unified, global set of standards. To do this, you first need to set overall business goals and metrics. Then, you assign different groups in the company their own targets and metrics based on how their work impacts the top-level goals. This process continues down the chain of command until it reaches individual employees. In the end, everyone is aware of how their actions contribute to the success of the company.

Once people and departments have clear and specific metrics to define their success, they tend to have an entirely different (and often much more motivated) approach to their work. We'll dig deeper into this subject in future chapters.

5. They segment users according to their needs and value Data-driven organizations often present different web pages and experiences for different audiences. There are a number of ways to do this, including personas, online behaviors, campaign drivers, and so on. And remember, a small change in traffic direction can have a large impact on a specific audience.

Data-Driven Decision Making

What exactly does it mean to use data to make decisions? Probably the best way to explain the process is to look at the traditional way web organizations work. Typically, they plan their long-term, strategic initiatives by using a project queue. Resources such as designers, developers, information architects, and so on work continually on this list. As a new project comes up, it's normally placed at the back of the line, and it gets done when its turn comes. A senior manager can intervene in the process and prioritize one initiative over another, but that is often done in a haphazard way.

Such organizations tend to schedule site releases far in advance. They plan updates on a monthly or quarterly basis and fully redesign their sites every year or so. Whenever they roll out a new page, the process is internal, with creative directors, information architects, and sometimes usability advisors weighing in on the changes. The new initiative is rarely tested live or benchmarked against its previous version. Instead, it goes out, and any shortcomings aren't addressed until the next redesign.

Interestingly enough, many companies perform these upgrades independent of the need for them. The redesigns are seen as "what everyone does" rather than as opportunities to drive better ROI.

Dynamic Prioritization

Considering how popular it is, the previous methodology ought to be effective. In fairness, it's not a bad way of doing things. Publications such as newspapers and magazines have traditionally worked that way. But the Web offers opportunities that good businesses can't afford to ignore. Because we can measure the performance of our sites so precisely and change them so easily, we can say goodbye to the traditional way of planning projects and replace it with something we like to call *dynamic prioritization*.

Whereas traditional companies make plans according to arbitrary notions of time and resources, data-driven organizations set priorities according to what will help their business the most. In other words, if you have a culture of analysis, you schedule and launch projects based on their value in your business. Some features of this approach are discussed in the following sections.

Prioritizing Based on Business Impact

Data-driven organizations assess the impact of all initiatives based on monetization models. (The practice of monetization is assigning dollar values to different site behaviors to understand and quantify the value of the overall web channel.) It doesn't matter whether the initiative involves branding revenue generation, lead generation, cost savings, or even a simple enhancement in site efficiency. All of these things can be assigned a dollar value and prioritized according to their potential impact.

This may sound easier than it is. In your organization, you'll encounter significant resistance when you try to delay initiatives. Although the marketing manager for a top priority may be happy, there are always people whose careers are tied to projects whose priorities are low. Strict prioritization may turn out to be so disruptive that you won't be able to implement it without mass resignations.

Take it slow. Start by conducting monetization exercises and using them to inform your priorities. Make sure you focus on initiatives that will have the highest impact, and try to deemphasize those that will merely cost you money. Above all, don't try to implement a draconian ranking process for every project at once. As time goes on, these exercises may change the way your organization evaluates potential projects. Your team may begin looking at assigning potential impact values to all items before it decides to put them on the schedule. In the meantime, be patient. Any prioritization you do will have a positive effect, so even small changes in your project queue can be considered big wins.

Optimizing Resource Planning

Along with prioritizing projects, you also need to organize your resources to cope with them. Data-driven organizations typically have staffs whose workload isn't dictated by a long-term project schedule. At the least, they can flexibly leave projects and form teams to take advantage of new opportunities or optimize existing initiatives as needed.

Avoiding the Big Dog Syndrome

The Big Dog Syndrome is a common problem in many organizations. It occurs when the person with the most seniority in a meeting makes decisions while everyone else nods in agreement, whether they agree or not. In the web world, this practice is extremely common, especially when reviewing design comps and selecting copy and image treatments. Because these decisions are largely subjective (who's to say whether blue or green is better?), strong leaders tend to dominate the discussion.

Who should select the best design option or copy direction? Unfortunately, those experts aren't in the meeting room (and they aren't sitting in a usability lab, either). They're the people who visit your site in its live environment. That's why you should always put a number of versions up on your site and see which one performs better based on your different audiences.

Typically, the big dog is fairly smart and will see the value of this kind of testing. Make sure you base your decisions on real data and avoid the Big Dog Syndrome!

You should build flexibility in your team. In traditional organizations, designers, developers, and information architects have their time booked long in advance. Data-driven organizations typically set aside some of these peoples' schedules so that they're always available to jump on opportunities when they arise.

Accelerating the Release Cycle

Does your business work on a quarterly or monthly basis? Outside of financial reporting, companies should be able to move and react flexibly. If you're truly a data-driven organization, you shouldn't have to hold yourself to arbitrary release cycles. Instead, your site releases should be small but common. You should continually be looking for opportunities using analysis and be prepared to make releases weekly, if not more often.

How do you know when to schedule a new release? Whenever a data-driven organization launches a page or other initiative, it tests a number of options using A/B and multivariate testing. These tests should allow you to quickly identify opportunities and optimize your site to get the best results.

Holding Initiatives Financially Accountable

Whenever a data-driven organization launches an initiative, it has already put together a forecast of the initiative's potential impact on the business and the bottom line. When these projects are complete, the organization also wants to know how the outcome of the project compared to earlier estimates. For this, you need to include a full post-launch analysis in your process. You should not only focus on the outcome but also use the opportunity to look at the forecasting process. Are you making accurate predictions? Does something need to change?

At the same time, the exercise will help you identify potential places for improvement. Depending on the value and effort required, you may want to optimize the initiative or perhaps feed it back into a queue where it's ranked according to its potential value.

Perking Up Interest in Web Analytics

Now that you understand how a culture of analysis works from an organizational standpoint, it's time to talk practically about building one. Unless you're a bureaucratic genius, you won't be able to wave your magic wand and suddenly have a fully functional data-driven organization. And so, for the rest of this chapter, we'll look at strategies for moving in the right direction.

If you're planning to dive into web analytics, you probably fall in one of two categories: either you're in a position to drive the transition or you're not. In the first case, you're a Chief Marketing Officer (CMO) or head of a web organization, and your job is to lead the charge. Over the next few pages, we'll discuss how you can do that. Then, we'll look at what you can do if you're not in a position of power in your company.

Establishing a Web Analytics Steering Committee

For CMOs and web leads, the first step is to set up a web analytics steering committee. It should be led by the marketing organization and including members from across the company.

Sounds easy enough, but how can you ensure such a committee will be successful? We've often noticed that even when organizations establish a web analytics steering committee, it often lacks the people, resources, and influence to make a difference. It's important that you start by gathering the right people.

Steering Committee Members

The committee's makeup is the single most important factor in its success. Not only does it require a diverse membership from across the organization, but also its members should be in positions of influence. We've seen excellent committees make great recommendations, only to have those ideas ignored or diluted by others.

The model steering committee should contain at least the following members:
CMO
Director of e-business
Director of technology
Senior web analyst

Steering Committee Mandate

The committee should also have a clear set of responsibilities. To some degree, these will vary from organization to organization, but at the minimum, every successful committee needs to accomplish these 10 tasks:

Set a schedule Establish a regular meeting schedule. Monthly meetings are a good target, especially when the committee is deciding on its goals and responsibilities.

Establish internal communication Create a method for sharing ideas and decisions with the rest of the organization. An intranet site is a great place to start.

Specify incentives Require that committee members' bonuses be tied in some way to website behavior.

Set goals Agree on success metrics and KPIs for your organization.

Define terminology Define the terms you'll use, and document them on your intranet site.

Agree on technology standards Agree on a page-tagging methodology, and document it.

Set a budget Set aside funding for web analysis, including headcount, in your organization.

Work with human resources Work with your HR department to integrate behavioral goals into your entire marketing and e-business organization.

Develop agency relationships Make sure your agencies have a financial incentive to report and achieve your behavioral goals. Remember, alignment between your organization and theirs is crucial.

Ensure data accuracy Your organization must be able to trust the integrity of its data. Pay close attention to conflicting reports from different data sources. Also, commission a quarterly third-party audit of your data accuracy.

Starting Out Small with a Win

Once your committee has completed its initial tasks, it's time to start getting others in the organization excited about it. That's why you should try to get a small, early win that you can share as a success story throughout the organization. With this, you'll not only start to show an ROI on your analytics software, but also be able to demonstrate its power to your web team and senior management.

How do you get that win? First, try to identify the highest-value behavior on your site, and try to monetize it according to KPIs (see Chapters 6 and 7). Then, dig in and understand everything you can about the desired behavior based on the web analytics data you collect. Where do people come from? Where do they drop out of the desired behavior path? Do they get to the key page? Do they start the process and then leave? How do different visitor segments on your site behave?

Now it's time to look for somewhere you can improve performance. If you're looking at a checkout process, for example, you should focus on the step or page that loses the highest percentage of people. At this point, you may decide to look at attitudinal or competitive data to help you understand why this drop-off behavior is occurring.

Next, it's time to act on the data. Redesign the page several ways, and roll them out in an A/B or multivariate test. If that's not feasible, create one redesign you feel confident about, split traffic between the new and old pages (or processes), and compare them side by side. Ideally, you'll show some progress. Then, plug the new numbers back into your monetization model, and show the ROI. Finally, go back to your team (and the rest of the company), and show how the changes impacted the site and your bottom line.

Empowering Your Employees

You should make sure every employee understands your KPIs and knows what they can do to improve them. Unfortunately, this isn't easy. Employees get plenty of reports. Many ignore the parts that don't matter to their jobs, so they need incentives to care about them, too.

What are we talking about?

Goal setting Part of having a successful website is working against benchmarks. If you have KPIs, you should also have realistic ways to measure your progress against them. It's not enough to say, "let's improve this." You must define success and work toward it.

Communication There's no point in collecting metrics that no one sees. Create a web-metrics dashboard: a single-sheet report that breaks down the relevant statistics daily, weekly, or monthly and presents them in a meaningful way. Also, hold regular meetings to discuss metrics, or include them as a running feature in other meetings.

Rewards What better way to get people to pay attention to statistics than to give them a real incentive to do so? Rewards needn't be large. A simple gift card to a coffee shop can do a world of good.

Managing Up

You may not be so lucky as to have a CMO who is committed to web analysis. In truth, web analysis remains a low priority at many companies. How do you direct your executives' attention to the problem? The answer is *managing up*, or creating a strategy to inform them about the importance of web analysis. We usually advise these six simple steps:

Speak English Web analysts use a rich jargon, full of KPIs, log files, and conversion rates. As much as we love it, it makes no sense to outsiders. For them, you need to take the time to explain things simply. As they become more aware of web analysis, you can create a glossary of terms to get them up to speed. We've included a few key definitions and descriptions at the end of the book to get you started with the basics.

Be willing to take risks Set specific performance goals for yourself and your team based on web analysis. At first glance, this may not seem prudent, particularly if your manager doesn't require it. But managers come and go, and tracking and achieving these goals will help you weather the inevitable corporate storms.

Empower your CMO Provide your CMO with data and analysis on the correlation between online and offline advertising spending. Typically, a well-run advertising campaign generates highly predictable and effective results in the web channel. If your CMO has these figures in hand, they will be better able to understand the importance of web analytics.

Speak holistically Speak holistically about the business. Remember that the web channel is only one part of your company's overall strategy. Your executives have other responsibilities and will understand your arguments better if they know where they fit into the bigger picture.

Demonstrate benefits Demonstrate the benefits of multichannel customer measurement and analysis—don't restrict yourself to the Web. Show how the web channel can help reduce costs and improve performance in other channels, too.

Contact your CEO Write an e-mail to your CEO suggesting that web performance become part of your company's overall strategic goals. Oddly enough, this simple step can be quite effective. Most companies have a way for employees to make suggestions directly to the CEO. Although they may not be the first person to read your proposal, if it's well-written and intelligently reasoned, it may be the best way to get attention.

By managing up, you can guide your company's decisions in the right direction and, we hope, create a fulfilling job for yourself. Remember, your efforts may not bear fruit immediately. But companies often change their policies. When that time comes, your ideas will be on the table.

Impact on Roles beyond the Analytics Team

Because moving your company to a culture of analysis involves a fundamental shift in policies and procedures, it will impact everyone in your organization. To help you along, we've put together a list of all the usual players on a web team and how their roles will change as you make the transition. You probably won't want to read this list exhaustively (which would be a bit tedious), but you can use it as a handy reference:

CMO:
- Ensures that site goals are understood by all team members
- And that targets for all goals are understood by all team members
- Understands the ROI of all online marketing expenditures
- Has confidence that dollars and resources are being allocated based on the greatest impact to the business

Web team manager/leader:
- Ensures that site goals are understood by all team members
- And that targets for all goals are understood by all team members
- Sets a review and bonus structure tied to the performance of the web channel against overall goals

Designer:
- Understands and commonly discusses the goals and targets for the web channel
- Has reviews and bonuses based on meeting targets for site goals
- Deploys multiple design concepts for testing rather than a single one agreed on by the organization
- Is committed to learning what works well for different audiences based on feedback and reporting of success
- Has the ability to test ideas that are out-of-the-box and less conservative
- Can produce more frequent releases, rather than one or two big pushes per quarter

Information architect:
- Understands and commonly discusses the goals and targets for the web channel
- Has reviews and bonuses based on meeting targets for site goals
- Understands how effective their work really is
- Has the ability to test less conservative ideas
- Continually fine-tunes the information architecture based on feedback

Usability expert:
- Understands and commonly discusses the goals and targets for the web channel
- Has reviews and bonuses based on meeting targets for site goals
- Is able to combine attitudinal insights with behavioral feedback to truly understand how site changes impact business goals
- Gets involved in the analysis of pre- and post-launch testing

Copywriter:
- Understands and commonly discusses the goals and targets for the web channel
- Has reviews and bonuses based on meeting targets for site goals
- Produces multiple versions of text for each deployment
- Understands the impact of specific copy changes

Developer:
- Understands and commonly discusses the goals and targets for the web channel
- Has reviews and bonuses based on meeting targets for site goals
- Makes more frequent site updates and changes based on key business goals

Web analyst:
- Understands and commonly discusses the goals and targets for the web channel
- Has reviews and bonuses based on meeting targets for site goals
- Constantly measures and analyzes new initiatives
- Evaluates performance, and creates forecasting tools

Strategist:
- Understands and commonly discusses the goals and targets for the web channel
- Has reviews and bonuses based on meeting targets for site goals
- Is willing to test new and off-the-wall ideas
- Understands the impact of specific ideas and concepts

Channel manager:
- Understands and commonly discusses the goals and targets for the web channel
- Has reviews and bonuses based on meeting targets for site goals
- Compares the performance of the web channel to other channels

Segmentation lead:
- Understands and commonly discusses the goals and targets for the web channel
- Has reviews and bonuses based on meeting targets for site goals

Online advertiser:
- Understands and commonly discusses the goals and targets for the web channel
- Has reviews and bonuses based on meeting targets for site goals
- Conducts real ROI measurements of campaigns, not click-through analysis
- Has a process to move quickly on opportunities to improve conversion of goals once campaigns drive traffic to landing pages

SEM/SEO (Search Engine Marketing/Search Engine Optimization):

- Understands and commonly discusses the goals and targets for the web channel
- Has reviews and bonuses based on meeting targets for site goals
- Focuses efforts on terms that benefit the business the most
- Has a process to move quickly on opportunities to improve conversion of goals once campaigns drive traffic to landing pages

We've left one person out of this list, and they're probably the most important to your success: the CEO. In addition to fully supporting the effort to transition to data-driven practices, CEOs should also benefit from them, receiving regular reports and updates to see how the overall business is performing against its objectives.

Cross-Channel Implications

In all the hard work of building a culture of analysis in a web organization, it's important not to let cross-channel considerations fall by the wayside. As your team aligns itself to support business goals, you should be sure to measure *all* the ways that it does so, not merely the obvious ones.

Web organizations, although they may not produce much revenue on their own, can have a significant impact on call centers and even brick-and-mortar operations. Last year, for example, our team worked with a large company that sold consumer goods. The company received 95 percent of its orders through their call center. They knew that a portion of those calls came after people visited their website, but they weren't sure of the exact number who did and whether they behaved differently.

We worked with the company to set up unique toll-free numbers for different sections of the site. That way, we knew whether a call came from a person looking at a catalog or visiting the company through the Web. By analyzing traffic through the call center, we learned some interesting things. First, the number of people who placed orders through the call center after visiting the website was 10 times larger than those who placed orders through the Web. In other words, the Web was driving significantly more business than its online sales figures suggested.

Because the call center was a far more expensive sales channel, the numbers also showed us that there was a significant opportunity for cost savings if we could convert more of the users to buying through the Web.

After further analysis we learned a few even more interesting facts. It turned out that people who went from the site to the call center

- Closed at a higher rate than the non-web calls to the call center.
- Closed faster than the non-web calls into the call center. This meant their calls cost the company less on average.

- Booked significantly higher average order sizes than other calls coming into the call center.
- Booked higher average orders than those placed through the site.

In other words, the call center people were doing a good job of cross-selling. Although at first we thought it would be a good idea to move call-center calls back to the Web, in this case, the overall benefit to the company was greatest for specific segments of the target audience if the customers did their research online and then called and ordered.

The lesson in this story is that being a data-driven organization requires you to measure indicators across all your channels, especially when customers are continually moving from one to another.

Questionnaire: Rating Your Level of Data Drive

Still wondering how data-driven your organization is? For each of the following questions, rate your organization on a scale of 1 to 5. (Give yourself 1 if you've never considered doing such a thing, or 5 if your organization has been doing it for years.) Come back regularly, and test yourself to find improvement:

1. Do you have agreed-upon success metrics for your web channel?
2. Can most people identify the overall success metrics the same way?
3. Have you monetized your key site behaviors?
4. Do you prioritize projects and initiatives based on potential financial impact?
5. Do you evaluate all projects post-launch to determine their impact on your business?
6. Do you commonly use web analytics to identify opportunities to improve your site?
7. Do you conduct attitudinal surveys to identify opportunities to improve your site?
8. Do you use competitive data to benchmark success and identify best practices?
9. Do you analyze behavioral, attitudinal, and competitive data in conjunction with one another to drive greater insight?
10. Do you include success-metrics in statements of work and RFPs for both internal teams and outside agencies?
11. Do your creative briefs include success metrics and behavioral, attitudinal, and competitive benchmarks?
12. Do you employ an ongoing testing and optimization methodology based on insight generated from data?
13. Do you segment your site to customize experiences and determine the best page solutions for different audiences?

14. Do you measure the offline impact of the web channel?

15. Do you reward employees based on performance against specific KPIs?

16. Do you regularly take action on data to improve site performance?
    Total your score, and see how you're doing:

0–32 Don't worry; you're in the same boat as most Fortune 2000 companies today. Yes, there is plenty of room for improvement, and we hope this book will give you a few ideas to get started.

33–64 Pat yourself on the back. You're off to a good start, and you have plenty of room to take it to the next level.

65 and over Congratulations: You're one of a few companies that are leveraging the power of data. You're probably continuing to push your efforts and have plenty of ideas of ways you'd like to do better.

Interested in seeing how you compare to others who answer these questions? If so, visit the online version at www.zaaz.com/AreYouDataDriven.asp, and read additional tips and success stories related to the questionnaire.

Recap

In this chapter, we've examined the main characteristics and tendencies of data-driven organizations. Above all, they use data to inform smart business decisions and drive measurable success. This is a holistic process that affects everyone in your web organization, from your CMO to the individual designers. Rather than relying on gut instincts or competing design theories, data-driven organizations align web-team initiatives with business goals and measure them against agreed-upon benchmarks.

Such an effort should not be a straitjacket to a creative organization. Rather, it should free the individuals in your organization to do the best they can to drive success.

Getting there, however, is a long process, and we examined two ways to start building a data-driven organization. The first is a top-down approach, with a web analytics steering committee that oversees the transition. The second, managing up, involves using data and regular communication channels to convince management of the need for change. Both approaches focus on starting out with small wins to prove the value of web analytics internally, before tackling large-scale change.

You also saw the impact that moving to a culture of analysis has on job types and cross-channel operations. Finally, we left you with a questionnaire that you can use to benchmark your organization's success in adopting data-driven processes.

Think it'll be easy? In the next chapter, we'll look at some of the problems—real and perceived—that you may encounter in transforming your organization. Remember that pushing organizational change is never a seamless project. By taking small steps and consolidating your success, you'll eventually be able to move your marketing team to modern processes.

Avoiding Stumbling Points

Sometimes things go wrong. In web analytics, "going wrong" often means just going halfway. Many companies have made significant investments in web analytics tools and processes over the years, but they never get the full value of that investment. There may be lots of reports floating around the office that say "web analytics" on the cover, but they may be missing the point. This chapter will help you determine if you need an intervention and, if so, how to recover successfully.

4

Chapter Contents

Do You Need an Analytics Intervention?

In recent years, companies have spent hundreds of millions of dollars on web-analytics tools, software, support, and personnel. But surprisingly, only a small percentage of those investments have translated into positive returns.

It's not that companies aren't compiling web data. In fact, they're gathering and storing it at a record rate. But somewhere between data extraction and business improvement, something gets lost. Perhaps the company isn't collecting the right data. Or they may lack analysts with the skills needed to turn the data into actionable insights. Or they may not be sharing those insights with the right people. And even if the company is doing all those things, they may not be tying their analytics efforts to business goals in any meaningful way.

With most of our web engagements, we look at the first phase of the work as a kind of intervention. In psychology, an *intervention* occurs when someone has a destructive behavior that they're unwilling to control. Instead of dealing with the issue, they find excuses and justifications for continuing it. Finally, a group of friends and family get together and confront the person. They discuss the problem in detail and (they hope) convince the person to change for the better.

The job of web-analytics consultants is similar. The destructive behavior we see is that companies aren't using data to improve their websites. Some of them have analysts. But too often, the analysts' job involves little more than issuing reports that are as thick as phone books and not quite as interesting. If anyone bothers to read them, they see them as a report card on web activity rather than a means for streamlining their operations and getting more out of their web channel.

This is a dysfunctional way of approaching web analysis. In order to get a solid return on their analytics investments, companies need to transform themselves into data-driven organizations. They need to start using the information they collect to transform their sites and, ultimately, improve their bottom lines.

Analytics Intervention Step 1: Admitting the Problem

The first part of any analytics intervention is to get companies to admit that they aren't using web data effectively. In most cases, this is easy. In previous chapters, you've seen that across different industries, many companies are already dissatisfied, if not completely disillusioned, with the state of their analytics.

But even though they admit they have a problem, too often they blame it on the wrong things. They have many imaginary culprits, but over the years we've heard two of them so often, they're worth mentioning:

- Our web-analytics tool can't deliver the data we need.
- Our website is built in such a way that it can't be tracked properly.

To an untrained eye, both of these reasons make sense. If a web-analytics tool is delivering subpar data, it's all but useless. And if a company's website "can't be tracked properly," there is little value in analyzing data from it. Luckily, these issues probably aren't keeping your organization from realizing the promise of web analytics. Unless your site has substandard tracking tools or a strange web technology, it's unlikely they're hindering your ability to acquire actionable intelligence.

Still not convinced? Let's look at these perceived gaps in detail.

Perceived Gap: Inadequate Analytics Tools

Because web-analytics software is the messenger that brings companies their data, many of them think the easiest solution is to take the software out and shoot it. It's rare that we go into a web engagement without hearing that the client expects us to recommend a change in tracking solutions. Often the idea comes from an otherwise rational manager who is convinced that somehow, somewhere, there is a magic tool that can be plugged into a website and instantly yield top-quality data.

"We don't have the right solution," they tell us. "Our analytics tool doesn't give us the data we need," they may say, with slightly more reason on their side. But when they're at their most self destructive, they say, "If we had Analytics Tool X, we could do so much more."

This isn't surprising. After all, most companies learn about web analytics from vendors of web-analytics solutions. And, naturally, it's in their interest to differentiate their products. Salespeople for Tool A gladly point out the scenarios in which its capabilities vastly exceed those of Tool B. In doing so, they haul out a brilliantly colored chart with columns indicating all kinds of useful information: "Here is how analysis should work." To back it up, they can even produce "telling" statistics about speed, efficiency, and usability.

Such marketing has been convincing over the years. In a 2005 survey by Forrester Research, only 23 percent of all respondents reported that they'd worked with the same web-analysis tool for the last five years. An astonishing 48 percent had worked with three or more tools in the same time period. And 11 percent were such optimists that they'd tried out five or more.

Of course, in some scenarios, a new analytics tool is essential. Certainly you should upgrade your systems if you're working with eight-year-old software that primarily accesses data from log files. And you also most likely need a new tool if you're using the one provided by your ISP for free. (In web analytics, you sometimes do get exactly what you pay for.)

Over the years, we've worked with all the top-tier tools and found that although they have differences, those differences aren't usually significant enough to make or break a company's success. Every tool is capable of providing the insight companies need to optimize site performance. On the other hand, no provider offers a solution that can automatically improve site performance. That's not possible. Selecting and configuring your tool to produce data is only the start of a long process. Unless your organization commits to the full scope of web analysis, you'll never see the ROI the field can offer.

In other words, don't shoot the messenger. By changing your web-analytics solution, all you're likely to get is a bill from a different company—and the same data and the same problems you already had.

Perceived Gap: Inability to Track a Site

The second most common perceived gap we hear from companies is that their sites—by the nature of how they're built—won't allow analysts to get the data they need. Such sites are said to be "untrackable."

Untrackable sites are a myth, but the myth is widely believed. The notion originates with IT departments and web-development teams. If you poll them, they'll say that certain common types of technology cause this problem.

This is untrue 99 percent of the time. As of today, no site is fundamentally untrackable. There are rare cases in which the amount of work needed to add tracking code to a site exceeds the amount of work it would take to completely rebuild the site. But statistically, such instances fall into nearly the same category as lightning strikes and winning lottery tickets.

If your developers are telling you that your site is untrackable, it's more likely that they lack the time, knowledge, or training to configure the analytics tools properly. Every advanced tool requires that your site contain snippets of tracking code. Whatever you want to test has to be tagged with this code. If your developers don't know how to do this for particular technologies, or they're so busy with other things that they don't have time to research the problem, they will return that most common of IT answers: "We can't do that."

All leading web-analytics tools can work with almost every possible development scenario. They can track many sites out of the box, and for the rest, they have plug-ins or other applications to help retrieve data. It doesn't matter if your site is dynamic, is Flash-heavy, relies on a content-management system that scrambles URLs like eggs, or even uses a cutting-edge technology like Ajax. It can be tracked.

That said, depending on how your site is built, you may need to spend extra time and money to get the kind of data you want. Should you take the trouble? In the coming chapters, you'll see that you have many opportunities to improve site performance through a better understanding of customer behavior. Even if you have to make a few technical changes, you should find it well worth the effort.

Analytics Intervention Step 2: Admit That You Are the Problem

If you look closely at the two perceived gaps we just described, you'll notice that they put the blame on something other than the organization trying to implement the analysis. Their culprits are inadequate tools or the technology used to create the website.

In reality, the case is exactly the opposite. Today's analytics tools can deliver far more information about website behavior than most companies can use. We're only now beginning to understand what various site behaviors mean. The real issue is that companies aren't using the tools to gather actionable insights, and they're not prepared to act on those insights when they do obtain them.

Instead of blaming outside factors, companies need to look within themselves to find out why their web-analytics initiatives are failing.

Analytics Intervention Step 3: Agree That This Is a Corporate Problem

Part of the process is realizing that analysis doesn't exist in a vacuum. It should never be the sole responsibility of one isolated department to deliver intelligence to "customers" throughout an organization. Rather, analysis should be integrated in the decision-making process of many people in your organization, as shown in Figure 4.1.

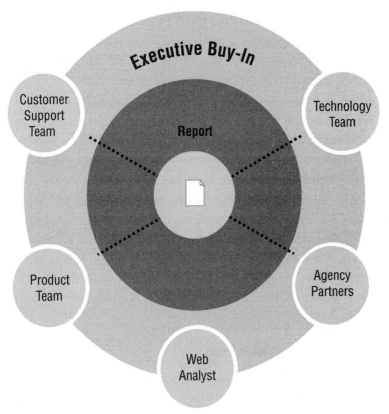

Figure 4.1 Analysis should be tied into every level of your organization, from your executives to your agency partners.

Of course, some companies don't see themselves as the problem. They still want to blame their tools, their websites, or even their employees. For them, we have constructed an "Are You Data-Driven?" test. If you can answer yes to every question, congratulations: Your organization isn't holding you back from the benefits of web analysis. Otherwise, you probably have some work to do:

- Do you establish success metrics for your web initiatives?

  Data-driven organizations rarely make a change to a page of their website without agreeing on the goals for the project. These goals are then measured against the outcome to determine if the project was a success or if further enhancements are needed.

- Do you have confidence in the accuracy of your data?

  Even if you do collect data, you should properly account for things like internal traffic, spiders, robots, and spam. If you don't, you can't trust the data you're receiving.

- Do you identify problems and opportunities based on your analytics data?

  Your organization may be collecting and analyzing its data. But if you aren't using it to identify areas of opportunity, you aren't getting any value from it.

- Do you conduct A/B or multivariable testing based on data?

  Many web designers and usability experts believe they can use their experience or qualitative data to judge the efficacy of their web pages. Some of them are indeed gifted at delivering results, and no one says you should do away with these disciplines. But data-driven organizations trust what they can measure.

- Do you use data to set employee and team goals and incentives?

  If you collect and use data to improve your website, you can also use it to set goals for individuals and teams in your organization. If they hit their targets, they should be rewarded for it.

When we pose these questions in our analytics interventions, most companies answer no to the majority of them. At that point, they should begin to see that the problems they're having with web analysis aren't technological. Rather, they're organizational issues that need to be addressed over time.

The Road to Recovery: Overcoming Real Gaps

Once a company has accepted that it's not data-driven, the next step is to tackle the real problems that are holding it back. In our practice, we've seen a great many issues that can stand in the way of getting solid returns on a web-analytics investment, but 12 of them seem to crop up over and over again. The following sections look at these issues in detail:

1. Lack of established processes and methodology
2. Failure to establish proper KPIs and metrics

3. Data inaccuracy

4. Data overload

5. Inability to monetize the impact of changes

6. Inability to prioritize opportunities

7. Limited access to data

8. Inadequate data integration

9. Starting too big

10. Failure to tie goals to KPIs

11. No plan for acting on insight

12. Lack of committed individual and executive support

Issue #1: Lack of Established Processes and Methodology

At most companies, the web-analysis process is relatively simple: A tool collects data. The data is collated and reported by an analyst. The analyst then distributes it for reading to various members of an organization. And there it ends.

Unfortunately, this isn't a process for improving a company's web channel; it's merely a procedure for creating web-analytics reports. There's a big difference between the two. To benefit from analysis, companies need a comprehensive methodology for collecting and using data to drive their businesses. At ZAAZ, we've developed a four-step process that we recommend to our clients (described in detail in Chapter 5).

Whether you decide to use our process or not, you should have clear steps that take your company from the initial gathering of data and identification of opportunities to the making of changes and evaluation of results. Whenever you decide to run a test and compile a report, you should know what to do with its conclusions. If you're testing your home page, you should be ready to implement whatever changes the analysis suggests. And once you've made those adjustments, you should also be prepared to evaluate their success.

Part 3 of this book deals extensively with setting up and implementing a web-analysis process.

Issue #2: Failure to Establish Proper KPIs and Metrics

In our web engagements, we often find companies measuring and comparing the wrong things. It's important to set key performance indicators (KPIs) that are relevant and specific to your organization. From the most basic standpoint, a KPI is a measurement of performance based on your most important business and web goals. That definition leaves out a lot of detail, but it's a good way of thinking about the problem.

To go a bit deeper with KPIs, the best definition probably comes from Webopedia.com:

> *KPIs… help organizations achieve organizational goals through the definition and measurement of progress. The key indicators are agreed upon by an organization and are indicators which can be measured that will reflect success factors. The KPIs selected must reflect the organization's goals, they must be crucial to its success, and they must be measurable. Key performance indicators are long-term considerations for an organization.*

This definition contains a few key phrases:

"KPIs…must reflect the organization's goals" Goals that an organization sets must be *specific* to its particular needs. Many companies tie their KPIs to goals that are standard in their industries. But no two companies are exactly alike, even competitors. They all use the Web in slightly different ways. Rather than adopt the same KPIs as others, you should develop ones that reflect your own requirements.

"long-term considerations" It's important to measure KPIs over time. As you make changes to improve your site performance, the value of those initiatives must be measured against your KPIs. Did the changes make a difference, and, if so, was the difference enough to justify the effort?

"agreed upon by an organization" Probably the biggest mistake companies make is assuming that data-gathering and analysis can be done in a vacuum. Nothing could be further from the truth. An analyst may produce reams of telling data, but if decision makers don't agree that it's relevant and that it should dictate a change in course, analysis is a worthless exercise. People with different functions in your organization should work together to construct and agree on your KPIs.

KPIs are a big part of ensuring web-analysis success, and we'll continue with them in Chapter 6.

Issue #3: Data Inaccuracy

In some ways, data inaccuracy is the hidden killer of all web-analysis initiatives. Imagine that you want to sail to the Bahamas. You spend a great deal of money on a fancy GPS device, you chart your course, and you provision your boat with food and water. Finally, the big day comes, and you set sail with confidence. Yet somehow, in spite of all the data you gathered, you find yourself in Nova Scotia instead of Nassau. At that point, you may want to chuck the GPS overboard and revert to dead reckoning.

Many companies that are inexperienced with gathering and interpreting their web-analytics data find themselves in a similar situation. First, they purchase the most expensive tool on the market. Then, they engage a well-respected web-analysis consultant. The consultant produces a report with recommendations, which the company zealously follows. Finally, they measure their progress using new data. The result? They learn that the changes they made have produced a random outcome, often at odds with their goals.

Why does this happen? Because they aren't collecting accurate data to start with. One of the first things we do with every web-analytics engagement is to perform an accuracy audit. In most cases, the audit reveals a 10 to 30 percent discrepancy between reported and actual metrics.

Some of our findings border on the comical. One well-respected Fortune 500 company overestimated its site visits by 400 percent. The owners of a certain e-commerce site didn't know that 40 percent of their "visitors" had never viewed a single page. And a lead-generation site underreported its traffic by nearly 30 percent.

Many issues can cause data inaccuracy. A few common ones follow:

Inaccurate cookies Analytics software tools primarily use cookies to track users. These are snippets of code—entirely harmless—that tell the tool who is visiting the site, what they're doing, and if they've been there before. If the tool fails to set this information correctly or deletes it at the wrong time, problems result. The most common is that the site thinks a user is new to the site every time they visit. Because analysts need to segment behavior between people who have never visited a site and those who are repeat customers, this issue leads to faulty reporting.

Internal visitors People inside a company use their website to look up information, find URLs for customers, or evaluate its design. But because such visitors aren't customers and use the site in nonstandard ways, they should be automatically excluded from analysis. Surprisingly, many websites fail to make this distinction.

Caching servers Caching servers are a more insidious way to produce inaccurate data. Large organizations sometimes deploy these servers to cut down on the amount of bandwidth they use. Every time an employee visits a site and downloads a page, the caching server automatically saves a local copy. If another employee decides to visit the same page, the caching server delivers the page it stored, rather than pulling down another from the Internet.

If you're not careful, caching servers can depress results on certain pages, especially commonly used ones like home pages. Oddly enough, measured per visit, this can make it seem as though your site is performing better than it is. For example, if caching servers cause your tool to undercount page views of your home page, users appear to be clicking through to secondary pages at a higher rate than they are. As a result, you may conclude that your site is performing well but that you need to purchase ads to attract more traffic. Accurate data may not support this conclusion.

Incomplete or incorrect tagging When tags are incorrectly implemented on a site, a tracking tool can miscount traffic and produce reports with incorrect page names, confused paths, and muddled conversion metrics.

Inaccurate filters within the tracking tool Last but not least is your tracking tool. Every tracking tool has filters that help it determine how you want to track your visitors. If those filters aren't set properly, you experience problems with your data.

In some cases, an accuracy audit won't result in major changes to top-line metrics, such as unique visitors and overall traffic. Even so, the underlying data may provide better insight about visitor behavior.

Problems with data accuracy can lead to the following:

- Tracking false visits. The tracking tool reports visitors who never looked at a page on the site.

- Missing site visits (or portions of visits). The tracking tool doesn't record the entirety of a real visit.

- Recording false paths. In this case, the tool tracks visitors who appear to jump from one page to another, even though there's no way to navigate between those two pages without typing in a URL.

- Gathering incorrect information for high-level metrics. These include visits, unique visitors, page views, page views per visit, and other data.

- Miscalculating conversion metrics.

- Falsely identifying drivers to key pages.

From a strategic standpoint, data inaccuracy can lead to the following:

- Poor decision making. Based on your faulty analytics data, you may decide to make unnecessary changes or focus efforts on an area of the site that is performing well.

- Lack of faith in web analytics. People in your organization will begin to question every data point and distrust your reports. Over time, they will ignore web analytics entirely because they feel they can't count on it.

Data inaccuracy can undermine everything you do with web analytics. Companies should always be vigilant about the accuracy of their data. They should review their reporting methodology and check the configuration of their tracking tool on a regular basis. Like experienced navigators who consistently check and adjust their course, data-driven organizations continually verify and modify their tactics to adapt to external circumstances that affect the integrity of their data.

Issue #4: Data Overload

Nowadays, the sheer volume of available information has become a danger. In an influential 1997 book, David Schenk coined the term *data smog* to refer to the condition that results when people are overloaded with input. Schenk's work dealt with the social, medical, and psychological effects of this condition, but organizations need to cope with it as well.

Web analysis data smog occurs when you collect so much data that you're unable to make any sense of it. In corporate America, this is a common condition. In addition to web-analytics data, which by itself can be overwhelming, companies compile a huge range of other information:

- Attitudinal data from surveys and user studies
- Customer-satisfaction data
- Competitive insight
- Customer-segment information
- Industry research reports
- Customer data
- Transaction data
- Campaign data
- Affiliate information
- Call-center data

Avoiding data smog involves several steps. First, focus on the most important metrics and behaviors on your site. Web-analytics solutions can deliver reams of data, but only part of it is business critical. The executives at your company may be interested in knowing how often their biographies are viewed, but this data speaks far more to their egos than your bottom line. On the other hand, if your e-commerce site is losing users in its check-out process, that's an area of grave concern that should be addressed.

Second, start small with your optimization tests. Dig into one issue to determine the best way to use data to solve the problem. Once you've identified an opportunity and forecast the results, move on to A/B or multivariable testing.

Third, focus on actionable data. You can learn many interesting things by analyzing data. But you should only spend your time looking at information that identifies opportunities for improvement.

The bad news is that data smog will only increase in the future. Analytics tools are evolving, and people are continually looking for new ways to combine behavioral with attitudinal and competitive data. Don't get caught up in the hype. Conduct only the analysis that provides insight that helps improve your business.

Issue #5: Inability to Monetize the Impact of Changes

One of the most persistent problems on the Web is that managers can't accurately gauge its value to their organizations. Most look at it as a fuzzy channel, one that is necessary but whose real impact is hard to know. As a result, websites (and their budgets) are often fixed entities that are seen more from a cost-management perspective than as opportunities to be exploited.

To ensure that upper management buys into the web-analysis process, companies must develop monetization models that measure the positive effects of making changes to websites. Analysts should estimate the impact of every proposed initiative and assign it a dollar value.

Some of the possible benefits of this process include the following:

- Increased revenue
- Increase profitability
- ROI on campaigns
- Increased lifetime value
- Reduced customer-service costs

Monetization is a major factor in building a successful analysis initiative, and we'll look at it in detail in Chapter 6.

Issue #6: Inability to Prioritize Opportunities

The inability to monetize changes goes hand in hand with the inability to prioritize opportunities. Once a company gets up and running with web analysis, their tools start returning data that identifies areas that could use improvement. If things go well, companies find that they have more opportunities than they can address at one time. With limited budgets, deciding which ones to pursue can be difficult.

Analysis can lead the way out of this pitfall. You can prioritize changes by creating a list of all your opportunities and monetizing the potential value of each one. After you assess the upside of each change and subtract its cost, you can rank it against the other possibilities. From there, it becomes easy to see which opportunities you should act on first.

We'll discuss prioritizing changes in greater detail in Chapter 7.

Issue #7: Limited Access to Data

Recently, ZAAZ met with a company that was spending over $150,000 per month on their web-analytics tool. To increase communication among users, the company had set up more than 100 accounts. But when we looked at the logs, we found that over 85 percent of the users hadn't even logged in during the previous six months. Unfortunately, this lack of interest is all too common.

Even so, by opening up such access, the company had done better than most. In most organizations, web-analytics information isn't shared. A limited number of executives may look at a short list of high-level metrics, but otherwise, analytics information rarely ventures beyond the analysts.

Nothing is more important for improving your web channel than making sure everyone has access to this data. Information architects need know where users are going and what their most popular searches are. Copywriters should always understand what calls to action are important and what cues are prompting people to convert. Designers need to understand what types of pages, callouts, or visual images are helping drive interest.

The following people should always have access to web-analytics data:

- Web product managers
- Designers
- Executives in upper management
- Developers and technical leads
- Merchandisers
- E-marketing group members
- Salespeople and business developers
- Information architects

You shouldn't stop at merely providing these people with access to data. You have to train them properly and work with them so they understand how to interpret it properly. Such an effort requires up-front education as well as ongoing support.

Issue #8: Inadequate Data Integration

In spite of the drive toward integration, many companies still find themselves compartmentalized into isolated silos. They collect and analyze data on their own activities but rarely share it with the rest of the organization or take advantage of information gathered by other business groups.

Web data should not be looked at in a vacuum. Rather, it should be integrated into a company's total business process. Other sources of data include the following:

- Surveys
- Usability studies and expert reviews
- Customer and prospect panels
- Competitive information
- Additional usability information
- Customer profile information
- Campaign information
- Research reports
- Customer care information

To facilitate data sharing, companies should set up a team to focus on the best ways of delivering information to those who need it most. To begin, they should take an inventory of the different data types collected by the company. Then, they should look at how that data is currently being used and how it could benefit other parts of the organization. Finally, they should set up a process for gathering and disseminating this information.

This task sounds easier than it is. Most organizations need time to implement an integrated system that houses and delivers information. Still, there are ways you can get started today:

Building awareness

- Understand what data types and information are currently available within your organization. Investigate how other departments are using that data to make decisions.
- Identify holes in the types of data you have. Then, look for solutions and providers that may be able to provide that information.
- Determine which data types can help you understand site performance and make better decisions.

Making comparisons

- Arrange to make information accessible to the necessary people based on its usefulness.
- When you identify a problem on the site using web analytics, collect information from the other data sources that correspond to the problem to better understand behaviors.
- As you become more comfortable with the data, you may want to integrate it into your reporting using a scorecard or other means.

Depending on your current needs and data-sharing infrastructure, you can start building a more sophisticated system that ties your web channel to other metrics. This system can include information from data-warehousing tools, Customer Relationship Management (CRM) applications, Enterprise Resource Planning (ERP) analysis, and more.

Issue #9: Starting Too Big

If you look at marketing brochures today, you'll get the impression that everyone wants to do everything at once. Companies tout out-of-the-box solutions for everything from office furniture to ERP software. They promise big changes and big results. However, anyone who's ever tried to implement one of those ready-made solutions knows they're not all they're cracked up to be.

Web analysis is no different. If you talk to a salesperson from a web-analysis solutions provider, you'll hear that everything in the way your organization handles data can be changed in an instant. With Tool X, they'll say, you can start getting actionable information tomorrow. But leaping into web analysis is much the same as jumping into a cold pool. If you ease in step by step, you may get a refreshing swim; but if you jump too fast, you could end up with a heart attack.

Most organizations aren't data-driven and require plenty of work before they get there. Businesses shouldn't try to do too much at once. Our most successful clients start their evolution with small steps and slowly roll out the process across their organization.

Sometimes it's best to start with a simple project to get buy-in from others in the organization. Pick an underperforming page or promotion and look for ways to improve it. You can start with a basic A/B or multivariable test. Set goals and KPIs, and try the process. After the first successful optimization steps, others will come much more easily.

Issue #10: Failure to Tie Goals to KPIs

Setting proper KPIs is a great step toward building a data-driven organization. But often that initial effort turns out to be temporary. A few months later, companies lose sight of those goals. Soon, web-analytics reports become just pieces of paper (or e-mails) that float across desks on their way to oblivion.

To keep your organization thinking about its KPIs, you should make them part of your individual and group goals. As any manager knows, nothing can focus employee attention quite like the promise of financial rewards (or the possibility of a bad performance review). By holding teams and individuals accountable for web performance, you'll drive them to improve it.

But if you're going to tie goals to KPIs, you should also distribute data effectively. The best way to do this is through customized scorecards that highlight individual and group goals. Figure 4.2 shows an example. Any decent analyst or tool provider should be able to set up this kind of reporting for you.

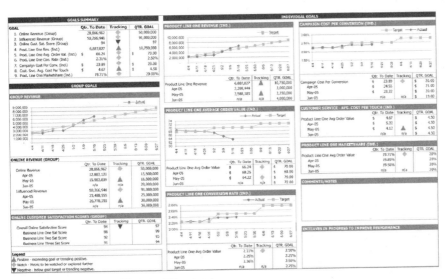

Figure 4.2 Analytics scorecard featuring KPIs and goals

Issue #11: No Plan for Acting on Insight

In 2005, Forrester Research asked web professionals what they found to be the hardest part of using analytics in their organizations. Surprisingly, as shown in Figure 4.3, only 24 percent replied "pulling together the data." By contrast, 53 percent said "acting on the findings."

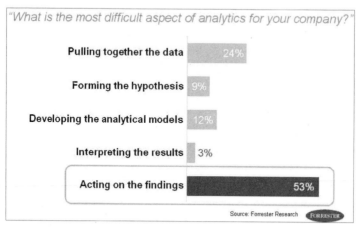

Figure 4.3 Forrester—web analytics' most significant barrier

This is a big problem. An organization that fails to act on its analytics findings is like a marathon runner who completes 25 miles in record time and then walks home without completing the race. By itself, compiling information won't help your organization. The surest way to achieve a 0 percent ROI on web analytics is to look at the data you collect and then do nothing with it.

To get the most out of analytics, you should plan to dedicate about 5 percent of your overall web budget to optimization. That should be enough to take advantage of the opportunities your analytics effort identifies without depriving your organization of the funds it needs for ongoing operations.

Of course, setting aside even such a small percentage of the overall budget to a new line item will raise objections. But any opposition you encounter should be easy to overcome. To justify the expenditure, pick two or three of your top KPIs, and look at their performance over the past 12 months. Next, model the financial impact that would result if you improved their performance by a small amount. Present the benefits of this change, and you should have little difficulty convincing others in your organization to provide the resources needed for optimization.

Issue #12: Lack of Committed Individual and Executive Support

Unfortunately, web analytics isn't a pressing day-to-day concern. It's a long-term process whose benefits accrue over time. As such, it can easily slide to the back burner when other fire drills arise.

To avoid this pitfall, make sure you have one person in your organization (or one consultant) expressly dedicated to your web-analytics effort. They should champion the use of the data and provide insight to other team members on how to use it properly.

Because ongoing site optimization involves a paradigm shift for a lot of organizations, you also need executive support to get (and keep) the ball rolling. Many otherwise excellent web-analytics efforts have failed because they lack interest from the top. You can't force the executives in your company to take an interest in analytics, but you can make a strong case by modeling the analytics' financial impact. Executives are rarely excited by the intricacies of design and information architecture. On the other hand, they respond well to dollars and cents.

Recap

This analytics intervention demonstrates the basic steps an organization needs to take to start moving toward data-driven solutions. First, you need to admit you have a problem with web analytics. Most companies find this easy. But then, you have to admit that the problem isn't your tools or the technology behind your website.

The real problem is that most organizations fail to deploy analytics in a comprehensive manner. They don't set proper KPIs, they collect too much of the wrong data, they don't share information, and they don't follow up on the opportunities their analytics solutions identify. By overcoming these stumbling blocks, your company can start moving toward a data-driven world, where analysis leads to better ROI and a more effective web channel.

Proven Formula for Success

III

It's easy to be skeptical of a "proven formula for success," but we really believe this will help you grow your business successfully. Over the last decade, we've helped dozens of businesses, many of them Global 500 firms, focus their web efforts and reap the benefits of a data-driven strategy. In this section of the book, we'll drill down into the details and give you a clear roadmap for success.

Preparing to Be Data-Driven

5

In this chapter, we'll outline the methodology we've developed over the years at ZAAZ. Obviously, all web organizations are different, so you shouldn't look at this plan as a straitjacket but as a basic roadmap for using data. For the record, we've deployed it at more than 50 Fortune 500 companies, and none of them have complained too loudly.

Chapter Contents
Web Analytics Methodology
Results and Starting Again

Web Analytics Methodology

In order to succeed at web analytics, you need a comprehensive and well-defined methodology for using data. The good news is that the plan doesn't need to be complex. It merely needs to provide a blueprint for collecting information and putting it to work to achieve tangible business results.

Like all successful web analytics methodologies, this one keeps its eye on the big picture. It consists of four steps that revolve around an analytics platform. In order, they are as follows:

1. Business metrics

2. Reports

3. Analysis

4. Optimization and action

When we talk about this process with our clients, we often show them the graphic from Figure 5.1 to explain it from beginning to end.

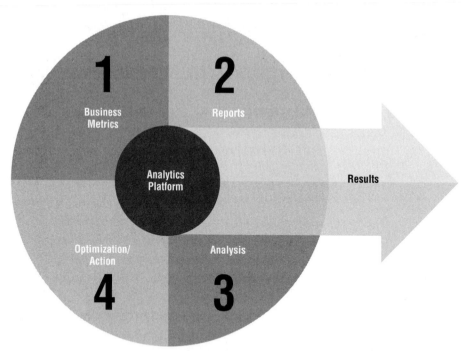

Figure 5.1 The ZAAZ methodology sees web analytics as a cyclical process focused on delivering results.

This process may seem a little foreign at first, but the beauty of it is that it's quite intuitive. It isn't all that different from what you may have already done without thinking about it.

For example, let's say you're planning a party. For the purposes of argument (and to make it work better as a web-analytics story), let's also say you decide to use a service like Evite to send out 50 invitations. To make your party a success, you know that at least 40 of these people need to attend. Congratulations: This is your *business metrics*.

A week later, you log in to Evite. The service tells you that 38 people have replied yes, 7 have said no, and the remaining 5 haven't replied at all. This is your *report*, and it shows you how you're performing against your business metrics.

Your next step is *analysis*. You look at the names of the five people who haven't replied. You realize that you don't know two of them that well, so you imagine they're not likely to come. But the other three are good friends. One runs a small business, another juggles a career and a family, and the third is an amateur triathlete preparing for an upcoming race. By analyzing this list, you realize that they're all busy. Perhaps they haven't had time to reply to your invitation—or, worse, they may have forgotten about it.

And so, you take *action*. You give them each a call, and, as a result, you manage to cajole two of them into attending. The good news is that you now have the requisite 40 people coming to your party, just as you wanted.

Without even thinking about it, you've gone through every step of our methodology. You've set up metrics for success, you've received a report on them, you've analyzed the report, and you've taken action to improve turnout at your party.

The Four Steps of Web Analytics

Of course, when it comes to the business world, web analytics can get much more complicated than this example. Let's take a closer look at the different phases of the process.

Defining Business Metrics (KPIs)

The first step of the analytics process is to define your business metrics, which are typically called key performance indicators (KPIs). In doing this, remember that KPIs go well beyond your website. Site-centric statistics, such as hits, number of visitors, or average visit length, aren't business metrics. They're merely ways of measuring activity on your website, and in most cases they can't tell you anything meaningful about your performance.

To get real business metrics, you need to look at your website in the context of your overall business strategy. Your business is the foundation for everything you end up doing with web-analytics data. And so, you need to determine how the behavior of users on your website relates to your overall business goals.

This isn't as difficult as it may sound. The easiest way to think about user behavior is to ask yourself what you want people to do on your site. In web analytics, we refer to these actions as *desired behaviors*. They include such things as the paths you want users to take, the marketing initiatives you want them to come into contact with, and the products you want them to buy. Desired behaviors may be as simple the movement of customers from your home page to a specific initiative. Or, they may be complex. For example, a content site may want its users to explore particular site areas that have higher ad-conversion rates than others. There are as many possible desired behaviors as there are business objectives; the important thing is to isolate what you want users to do.

The second step is to monetize these desired behaviors. In other words, you should figure out the value of each behavior to your business. For example, if you're trying to drive customers to a particular offer, you should be able to define the likelihood that each new prospect will take you up on it and how much each conversion is worth to your company.

Note: If this sounds complicated, don't worry. In Chapters 6 and 7, we'll go into plenty of detail about the first step of our methodology.

Reports

Once you've defined your business metrics, you have to collect the data you need. To do this, the first step is to configure your analytics tool. You want to collect two kinds of data: the KPIs you've identified and the contributing metrics that can help you to better understand the details behind your performance.

Sound difficult? It's really not. For a simple example, let's say you're trying to generate more leads on your website. You have a call to action on the home page and throughout your site that says "Request More Information." One of your KPIs may be visitor-to-lead conversion (for example, 3.2 percent of all site visitors request more information). Following is a sample of some of the supporting data metrics you may want to understand:

- What pages drove people to the Request More Information page?
- What percentage of people that got to the request form completed it?
- Where did the people go if they left the form without completing it?
- When people successfully submitted a request, what else did they do on the site?

At the same time, you should consider gathering other data outside of pure web analytics to round out your analytics story. This may include data from call centers and retail stores, attitudinal surveys, or information about your competitors.

Finally, you need to determine how to distribute the reports. To do this, you have to answer the following questions:

- Who needs what data?
- How can they leverage it?
- How often do they need to see it?
- In what form should it be delivered?

Note: Reporting is obviously a crucial step in the process, and we'll examine it in detail in Chapter 8.

Analysis

Once your goals have been defined and your tools (analytics and otherwise) have been leveraged to collect and distribute the data you need, it's time to analyze it.

You may wonder what exactly this means. Haven't you used an analytics tool to collect and report data? Haven't you put the information in the hands of people who can use it? The answer to these questions is yes, but reporting merely tells you what people are doing on your site. It gives you a description of their behavior. Although gaining this knowledge puts you miles ahead of many companies, it won't make you succeed with analytics.

Instead, you need to understand why people are behaving the way they are. In the invitation example given at the start of this chapter, your reporting told you that five people hadn't responded to your invitation. Your analysis told you that three were busy people and that they might not have answered because they might not have read the e-mail. Analysis involves looking at the factors driving your performance so you can identify opportunities for improvement.

But analysis doesn't end there. In a perfect world, you could address every opportunity you identified. But when properly done, analysis always presents more opportunities than you have the resources to address. When this happens, you need to be prepared to monetize the financial impact of those opportunities and prioritize them.

Note: We'll go into much greater detail on these topics in Chapters 9 and 10.

Optimization and Action

Sadly, until now, even if you've done every step perfectly, your entire analytics investment hasn't paid off. It's a complete loss. But oddly enough, in our long practice, we've found that only a very small percentage of the companies that use analytics tools advance beyond the reporting stage. To truly realize the power of web analytics, you must have a plan in place to act on the results of your findings.

In our earlier Evite example, optimization was straightforward. You took the information received from your analysis and decided to pick up the phone and call your tardy friends. In true web analysis, there are a large number of ways you can take action and optimize a site, with the most common being A/B and multivariate testing. You can make changes to the design, information architecture, the structure of your promotions, and much more.

 Note: In Chapter 11, we'll dive into these options and explain how to turn your insights into action.

Results and Starting Again

The final part of our web-analytics process is obviously the best: results. Once you've optimized your site, you can sit back, knowing you've done a good job. Or can you? Actually, there is one final step: You need to check your business metrics again and see what you've achieved by going through the process.

The good news is that successful results give you a powerful tool in your efforts to build your company into a data-driven organization. When you achieve great results, don't forget to tell everyone in your organization about them. That way, they will understand how important your web-analytics efforts are and what you're achieving from them.

If you look at our methodology diagram again, you'll see that it goes in a circle. That's important: Web analytics is a cyclical activity. It doesn't begin and end with a single application. Once you've gone through the entire process of determining business metrics, compiling reports, identifying opportunities, and then taking action, it's time to start looking at your business metrics again. Are you satisfied with the results? Has your business changed such that you need to focus on new KPIs? It's time to define new business metrics. And so it goes.

Recap

In this chapter, you've seen a basic methodology for web analytics. It consists of four steps:

- In the first, *business metrics*, your organization defines the KPIs that will drive success in your web channel. Above all, make sure you take your overall business objectives into account when creating KPIs.

- In the second, *reports*, you configure your tool properly to deliver the data that is relevant to your business. In this stage, don't forget to create and distribute personalized reports to everyone in your organization who can benefit from them.

- In the third, *analysis*, you must determine what this data means to your business. That includes identifying opportunities for improvement, monetizing them, and prioritizing them based on their potential effect on your business.
- In the fourth step, *optimization and action*, you take action based on your analysis. Don't forget, if you don't use the results of your analysis to optimize your site, you won't see any tangible benefits from your analytics efforts.

Finally, once you've gone through the process, it's very important to start it again.

In the following section of this book, we'll examine each of these steps in much greater detail.

Defining Site Goals, KPIs, and Key Metrics

In Chapter 5, you saw that the first step in the web-analytics process is to define your business metrics. In the following pages, we'll explain what that means and show you how to set the right kinds of goals to drive your success. In particular, we'll examine how to define both overall business goals and web-specific ones, as well as how to construct and set targets for KPIs.

After we've covered the subject in general terms, we'll look at some of the more common site categories, including branding, e-commerce, customer service, lead generation, and ad-supported commerce, and outline some of the major KPIs used to evaluate them.

Chapter Contents

Defining Overall Business Goals

If you look at the field of web analytics as a whole, you'll find that many of its practitioners are interested in research for its own sake. They try to understand how people interact with the Web at an abstract level, and they construct generalized rules for predicting human behavior. Their work often reveals fascinating insights into how people interact with interfaces and machines. Even so, businesses should leave purely scientific research aside and take a practical approach with analytics.

Part of that involves constructing web goals that are meaningful to your overall success. In the early Internet boom, for example, it was common to regard the web channel as something that stood apart from the rest of your business. Companies never tried to relate website goals to their bottom line. Instead, CEOs would tout numbers of users and hits without explaining why such traffic mattered. In those days, it was good enough to have something to talk about. Nobody cared what it meant.

Obviously, this approach is no longer feasible. As it has matured, the Web has become a primary outreach tool for some companies; for others, it's the sole contact point with customers. People now use the Web to make early decisions about where they want to work, whether they should visit a retail store, and whether they'll recommend a company to friends and colleagues.

As a result, before you determine the metrics you collect on your website, you have to understand the goals of your business as a whole. What makes your company successful today? What will contribute to its long-term viability and the value of its stock price? At the same time, you should also think about what might hurt your business in the long term. As you saw in Chapter 2, you can use heavy-handed techniques to produce near-term increases in conversion rates. But the user experience will end up overwhelmingly negative, and although you'll realize a short-term success, you'll find that fewer and fewer customers return.

What are your overall business goals? If you're lucky, your company has already defined and documented them. They include everything from key current initiatives to the overall health and branding of your company. In most cases, they're composed of a number of competing interests woven together into a single mission statement. If your business has already defined its goals, you're off to a great start. Just make sure you understand them thoroughly. Talk to as many people as possible, and gather as much information as you can. Goals can sometimes be vague, but if you ask enough questions, you should be able to establish what they are.

In some cases, however, even large corporations fail to define their overall objectives or communicate them in a way that's easily accessible to all their employees. That problem lies outside the scope of this book. Besides, if your business goals aren't defined well, your company probably has bigger problems than the success or failure of its web-analytics initiatives. In that case, you need to work with the right people—including all levels of leadership—to establish concrete goals. Then, you can start working with analytics.

Defining Site Goals: The Conversion Funnel

Once you understand your overall business goals, it's time to find out how your web channel can support them. In doing this, it's useful to break the sales process into discrete steps. Over the years, marketing researchers have come to define that process as a series of stages known as a *conversion funnel*. The typical funnel has four stages:

1. Awareness
2. Interest
3. Consideration
4. Purchase

To understand how this works, let's look at a simple purchase: a boy who walks into a store to buy a soda. By the time he reaches the store, the awareness stage may have already occurred, especially if he has seen commercials touting different beverages or talked to friends about them. The interest phase occurred when he became thirsty. And so, he stands in front of a drink cooler and reviews his options. This is a rudimentary consideration phase. Finally, he selects one, pulls it off the shelf, and purchases it.

To understand the supporting roles the Web can play in a typical marketing funnel, let's look at a hypothetical real-estate developer who sells upscale homes and condos. At the highest level, this business has a simple goal: to sell as many properties as possible. Most people don't buy expensive homes over the Internet, so it may seem unlikely that online marketing could have a significant impact on a purchasing decision. Even so, you'll see that an intelligent, targeted website can have positive impact on the business.

Awareness

The awareness phase of a marketing funnel involves bringing the product to the customer's attention. During this stage, the real-estate developer naturally focuses on traditional media, including newspaper and magazine ads. But the Web can also contribute. Using search-based ads or even a guerrilla blog campaign, the company can try to drive users to its site, where it can show off properties in an attractive way. Web analytics can help them determine the effectiveness of these activities and their value to the overall business. Analytics can also identify opportunities to improve performance.

Interest

In the interest phase, a company tries to get consumers excited about their products. For our real-estate developer, the web channel can have a significant impact if the site encourages visitors to explore its offerings. The purchasers of expensive real estate are typically busy people, and they tend to appreciate multimedia presentations that allow them to investigate a property from the comfort of their offices.

The Web's contribution to the interest phase doesn't stop there. A real-estate developer's site isn't the only online location where customers can research their offerings. Customers can also look at blogs, reviews, and comments that other customers have posted in forums. As a result, the developer should build a strategy that goes beyond the website and engages users across the Internet. The company may, for example, sponsor a site for people interested in luxury travel. Or they can place immersive banner ads on financial portals.

Web analytics can assist in the interest phase by measuring the effectiveness of a site in attracting and retaining customers, as well as assessing the value of other initiatives.

Consideration

Marketers define *consideration* as the process of evaluating a purchase and either accepting or rejecting it. Typically, websites assist in this phase by providing information (often flattering) about products and services. In the real-estate developer's case, the site should offer an educational but friendly experience that encourages multiple visits and provides information easily on request. It can also facilitate contact with agents and help turn prospects into valuable leads.

Web analytics can help evaluate the effectiveness of these efforts by measuring things like conversion rates and identifying which keywords and other drivers convince people to pick up the phone and make contact with the developer.

Purchase

Purchase is perhaps the simplest of all the phases of marketing. The Web's role in purchasing can range from relatively insignificant to crucial. E-commerce companies, for example, handle the entire process online. As a result, they invest heavily in making sure their checkout flows are smooth. In our real-estate example, this phase may seem irrelevant. But still, a website may help the developer reach their business goals.

Many businesses, for example, have found that their websites can help drive repeat purchases. In real estate, that's a remote consideration, but a positive or negative purchasing experience can help drive or depress word-of-mouth advertising. In addition, a poor post-sales experience may depress the overall value of your properties.

Website Goals and the Marketing Funnel

By going through your own marketing funnel step by step, you can see how the Web intersects with your overall business goals. A careful examination of how it contributes to each phase should enable you to isolate the places where it can make the most impact.

For example, our real-estate developer has a straightforward business goal: Sell more properties. However, their website goals are a little different:

- Raise awareness about the properties.

- Create an inspiring, emotional experience to drive interest.

- Provide easy-access information to assist in customer consideration.

Notice that we left out the purchase phase. Although the website may help there, its potential value in that phase is probably slight and shouldn't be factored into overall goals.

Understanding Key Performance Indicators (KPIs)

Once you've decided on your web goals, it's time to identify the measurable ways in which your online efforts support them. For that, you have to construct key performance indicators (KPIs).

Over the last few years, KPIs have generated a lot of controversy in the analytics industry, most of it centered on what they are and how they should be used. Before we dig into how to create KPIs, we should define them clearly. Basically, a KPI is a measurement of performance based on your most important web goals. That definition leaves out a lot of detail, but it's a good way to think about the issue.

In a previous chapter, we mentioned that Webopedia.com has a slightly more in-depth definition:

> KPIs or key performance indicators help organizations achieve organizational goals through the definition and measurement of progress. The key indicators are agreed upon by an organization and are indicators which can be measured that will reflect success factors. The KPIs selected must reflect the organization's goals, they must be key to its success, and they must be measurable. Key performance indicators usually are long-term considerations for an organization.

At that time, you saw how this definition emphasizes that KPIs are

- Tied to your organization's unique goals, not industry standards or individual goals.

- Measured over time, not just once. If you make a change to a site, you should determine whether it's driving KPIs in the right direction.

- Agreed on by an organization. It's important that everyone in your company contributes to the creation of KPIs and agrees on their importance.

We believe these are the key points to remember about KPIs, whatever definition you prefer. Most of all, don't forget that websites aren't merely a bundle of statistics. KPIs are only as good as the business behind them. You can construct terrific KPIs, but if you don't have a good process for evaluating them, or if people within your organization don't agree that they're important, your analytics efforts won't be successful.

Constructing KPIs

KPIs should flow directly from your business goals. Usually, they're expressed as numbers or percentages, and they shouldn't be complicated. Top-line revenue, for example, is one of the most basic and important KPIs, and it's a number. Your web channel's direct contribution to that revenue is also a common KPI; it's a percentage.

The majority of your KPIs will be financial in nature: increased revenue, better conversion rates, higher average revenue per purchase, and so on. However, KPIs should also look beyond web data. To round out your understanding of the impact of the channel, you should include financial, attitudinal, call-center, and competitive measurements.

The most effective way to define KPIs is to first set them at the executive level and then allow them to cascade through the other departments. At the departmental level, the KPIs should support the executive ones according to the function the particular department performs. From there, the department can set individual KPIs based on the role a person plays in supporting the group's goals.

Depending on an individual's role in an organization, they may have five to eight KPIs. For, example if your focus is e-commerce, your KPIs will include average order value, total revenue, items per order, and conversion rate. Other individuals may have different KPIs. They can be anything, as long as they're tied to the most important aspects of your business.

To ensure success, you must monitor your KPIs continually (or at least on a weekly basis). That way, you'll be able to see how you're performing against your goals and also identify trouble spots whenever they arise.

Tips on Building KPIs

by Eric T. Peterson

When the practice of web analytics was young, most people relied completely on basic reports—essentially, single dimensions like "pages" or "referrers" providing counts or summaries of the "holy trinity" metrics: page views, visits, and visitors. Sometimes these lists were delivered via applications like WebTrends, HitBox, and Urchin; other times, these lists were exported into Microsoft Excel. Either way, the basic unit of web-analytics consumption was the list. Unfortunately for the nascent field of web analytics, few businesspeople seemed to see great value in these lists; they were long, they were hard to interpret, and understanding them often required knowledge of a specific vocabulary. So, more often than not, these lists went ignored.

Tips on Building KPIs *(Continued)*

Then, some time around 2003, bright folks began to use an old concept to help people better understand the data contained in these lists: key performance indicators (KPIs). According to Wikipedia:

Key Performance Indicators are financial and non-financial metrics used to quantify objectives to reflect strategic performance of an organization. KPIs are used in Business Intelligence to assess the present state of the business and to prescribe a course of action. The act of monitoring KPIs in realtime is known as business activity monitoring. KPIs are frequently used to "value" difficult to measure activities such as the benefits of leadership development, engagement, service, and satisfaction. (From http://en.wikipedia.org/wiki/Key_performance_indicator.)

As widely used in the web-analytics arena, the first and last sentences in the Wikipedia definition are the most relevant. Key performance indicators are an excellent strategy to translate visitor activity into the context of a site's primary business objectives, and KPIs are often used to evaluate otherwise complex ideas by providing a relative framework.

In my first book, *Web Analytics Demystified*, I described the relationship between any website's business objectives, the activities that visitors engage in to help satisfy those objectives, and the KPIs that could be used to describe relevant activities. In a nutshell:

- Business websites exist as a channel to foster interaction between visitors and customers. Given this, there is a series of *business objectives* the site is designed to support.

- Each of these business objectives is achieved as visitors to the site engage in any number of *activities*. These activities can be as simple as a single link click or page view, or as complex as an ordered series of clicks and page views that compose a multistep process.

- For each of these activities, a set of metrics and ratios can be defined to describe the rate at which visitors engage in the activity, the rate at which visitors complete the activity, and a series of heuristic measures for the activity. These metrics and ratios form the basis for the site's KPIs.

To make this more concrete, let's think about the Best Buy web site (www.bestbuy.com):

- Best Buy's high-level business objectives for their web site are likely Sell Products and Services and Provide Customer Support.

- Some of the activities that visitors must engage in to help Best Buy sell products and services include Search for Products, View Products, Add Products to the Shopping Cart, and Complete the Checkout Process.

- Some of the KPIs that describe visitor engagement in each of these activities include Percent of Visitors Who Search, Browse to Buy Ratio, Cart Add Rate, Checkout Start Rate, Checkout Completion Rate, Order Conversion Rate, and Average Order Value.

Continues

Tips on Building KPIs *(Continued)*

I hope you can see a natural progression from business objective to tangible measurement. Often, KPIs are percentages, rates, or ratios—a strategy that is powerful in that it simultaneously provides relative context to the calculation *and* mitigates the temporal effect often associated with web-analytic data. Consider the following:

Page views is a commonly used metric in the web-analytics field, perhaps the most popular of all. But the number of page views generated by a website is a complex function of marketing expenditure, site visibility, brand awareness, visitor engagement, and site design. As marketing spending waxes and wanes over time, site visibility and brand awareness follow, directly impacting the number of pages viewed on the site.

Page views per visit, on the other hand, is a ratio that describes the average number of pages viewed when any visitor comes to the site. This ratio mitigates many of the external forces impacting page views, leaving the reader with a metric useful for understanding visitor engagement and site design.

By putting numbers in a relative context, you can more easily compare the indicators over time. I strongly recommend that everyone using KPIs track them over time, either by making day-over-day (or week-over-week) comparisons or by trending the indicators against upper- and lower-control limits. See Avinash Kaushik for a good explanation:

http://www.kaushik.net/avinash/2007/01/excellent-analytics-tip-9-leverage-statistical-control-limits.html

The free worksheets I provide with every copy of my third book, *The Big Book of Key Performance Indicators*, are designed to let readers examine their indicators as they change over time:

Key Performance Indicators	This Period	Last Period	% Change	Warning
Average Order Value	$128.54	$109.20	17.71%	
AOV - New Visit Customers	$123.96	$112.57	10.11%	
AOV - Repeat Visit Customers	$130.56	$107.83	21.07%	
Revenue per Visitor	$3.55	$2.20	61.12%	
Revenue per Visit	$3.11	$1.94	60.03%	
Percent Orders from New Customers	30.55%	28.79%	6.10%	
Percent Orders from Repeat Customers	69.45%	71.21%	-2.47%	WARNING

Traffic Metrics

	Today	One Week Ago	% Change	
Page Views:	13,814,892	12,347,523	11.9%	▲
Visits:	6,030,778	7323112	-17.6%	▼
Unique Visitors:	3,663,210	3235998	13.2%	▲

Creating Targets for KPIs

After defining KPIs, you'll probably make changes to your site to move them in the direction you want them to go. But how can you set realistic targets for their movement?

The first step is to take into account a crucial fact about gathering statistics: They tend to fluctuate over time. For example, if you're studying the effects of global warming on ocean levels, you need to measure those levels over several years in different places around the world. If you measure from one spot for too short a time, you may be thrown off by an ebb tide or two.

With web analytics, the same thing can happen. Traffic on most sites varies throughout the year. For example, visits to corporate sites tend to fall off during the holiday season, whereas those to e-commerce sites greatly increase. And it's natural to see random fluctuation from week to week. So, before you begin constructing targets for you KPIs, you should establish thresholds to determine what is or is not a significant change. To do this, you must observe the regular variations in your KPIs over time and discount them.

Beyond that, there are several methods for determining reasonable targets for KPIs. One way is to look at levels of standard deviation. Another is to assess how far a specific KPI needs to move to fulfill a certain business goal. But one of the most effective ways to set targets is to conduct a competitive audit of different companies in your industry using data from companies such as ComScore and HitWise. By comparing your KPIs to those achieved by others, you can see where you stand. If you're at the bottom of the range of your competitors, you have plenty of room to improve. If you're at the top, you may want to moderate your expectations or focus your efforts on another KPI where you have a greater potential upside. At the same time, you should also establish thresholds that tell you when you should move your KPI target again.

One word of caution: Having worked with a number of Fortune 500 companies, we know from experience that it can be hard to get people to agree on targets for KPIs. Nobody wants to sign on to something that may not be realistic. On the other hand, having targeted KPIs is a great way to encourage people to pay attention to them.

Common KPIs for Different Site Types

The rest of this chapter will deal with the KPIs for common types of sites. As we've said before, most sites don't fall completely into one of these categories. A content site may also sell merchandise, and a lead-generation site typically includes a large branding component. Whenever you construct your own KPIs, be sure to mentally divide your site accordingly.

E-Commerce

The objective of nearly every commerce site is the same: to drive site visitors to purchase products, services, or subscriptions. As a result, commerce site metrics are usually the easiest to understand. They track purchases, checkout paths, and total revenue. Even so, they can sometimes become complicated if you try to get in-depth information about buying behaviors and channel tracking. For that, you have to look not only at your web channel but also at catalog and in-store buying. Overall, however, e-commerce sites offer a model platform for web analytics and optimization.

For the most part, you should find it easy to construct and track commerce KPIs. Top ones include the following:

Overall purchase conversion This is a basic calculation in which you divide orders by site visits. Every e-commerce site should track this metric whenever changes are made.

Average order size (AOS) This metric tracks the amount that the average user buys when they make a purchase. This metric can be extremely important. Online music stores, for instance, have margins that are directly related to the dollar value of a purchase. For them, increasing AOS is a primary concern.

Items per order (IPO) This KPI measures the success a site has in cross-selling and product recommendations. It's an important number for most online stores. A different but related metric is *conversion by campaign*, which looks at how visitor segments are attracted by different initiatives and converted into buyers. By studying the differences in campaigns, a company can fine-tune its messaging and improve its results.

Agenda Blending

Great relationships are built on healthy, two-way communication and mutual respect for each party's needs. The same principles apply to your website and how you use it to communicate with your customers. Effective use of web analytics can help you create a site that fulfills your business goals while meeting your customers' information-gathering and transactional needs.

Look at the Drivers

In many cases, when companies define their site KPIs, they focus too much on the final goal and ignore drivers that motivate visitors to take the desired actions that will contribute to it.

You have an agenda, and everyone who visits your site has an agenda. In most cases, the visitors' agenda differs from yours; and a lopsided focus on one or the other will impede the site's ultimate success.

When defining site goals, KPIs, and metrics, you should take into account not only your own objectives but also your visitors' purpose for visiting your site. This process is called *agenda blending*.

A Balancing Act

Let's consider a lead-generation site that uses the Web to encourage visitors to make a phone call to a sales representative. (Such sites are common in the enterprise software, real estate, and life insurance fields, among others.)

With such sites, you can follow two possible extremes. Some sites provide the absolute minimum needed to produce a phone call. They post a form on a page, and ask visitors to submit information to learn more about their offerings. Although this may seem to be an unlikely road to success, many large corporations lean strongly in this direction. They have sites or sections of sites that ask for information without providing anything in return.

On the other end of the spectrum, some companies have sites that offer a great deal of information but are shy about asking their visitors to contact them. With lead generation, convincing visitors to pick up the phone is the goal, so an overly informative site could negate the need for the visitor to talk to someone. As a result, it may prevent sales reps from talking to genuinely qualified leads.

How Analytics Helps

Agenda blending helps companies understand and anticipate visitor needs and use this information to create a site that drives the desired visitor behavior.

Web analytics can help identify what drives site visitors to make contact or submit a form. Analytics can also help determine the type of contact people find most (or least) helpful. By looking at which pages drive site exits and comparing them to those that drive people to make contact, a company can determine which pages should be more aggressively pushed.

Make sure you blend your agendas. A successful site requires meeting your goals as well as your customers'. If you focus only on one or the other, you're leaving opportunities on the table.

Step-by-step purchase conversion in the registration process During every purchasing process, online stores lose customers. As a result, they should try to identify where people are dropping out and focus on improving the experience at those points. Although such improvements may seem unrelated to your core business, they can lead to a significant increase in orders and revenue.

Analysis of purchase-funnel defectors When people drop out of the purchase process, it's useful to know where they went and why. They may, for example, simply be looking for additional information before they return to the process. If you find out what they're looking for, you can provide it at the right time and optimize your checkout process.

Effect on offline sales Many sites list toll-free numbers or direct customers to retail stores as purchase options. In this scenario, the online channel can play a key role in a sale but not receive credit for it. You can solve this problem by offering unique toll-free numbers that appear only on the site. That way, you can more easily track sales from your online channel. You can also study this issue through an analysis of your store locator.

First-time versus returning buyers You can improve your site experience by understanding behavioral differences between first-time and repeat buyers and offering unique experiences for both.

The insight to be gleaned by focusing on a commerce site's top-level KPIs is also relatively easy to monetize. Because every customer behavior can be related to purchases, finding out what each one is worth usually involves a simple calculation. And remember: Don't ignore the value of small changes. A 0.5 percent improvement in a conversion rate can lead to a significant increase in revenue.

Lead Generation

Lead generation is the most common corporate activity online. It involves attracting potential customers and informing them about a product or service. The sale for these items doesn't occur online; rather, the customer is encouraged to pick up the phone and arrange a face-to-face visit with a salesperson. Examples of lead generation include enterprise software vendors like SAP and Oracle. Such companies offer complex, customized services that are unique to every buyer. They're also very expensive.

For such companies, websites provide a valuable lead-generation tool. They should offer enough information to prod a potential customer to contact a sales representative (or, in many cases, the sales representative of an implementation partner). To be successful, these companies need to track online leads and understand how they ultimately convert into offline sales. That way, they can establish the average web-lead value based on the average close rate and the value of the services purchased. Then, they can work to optimize site conversions and ultimately improve their bottom lines.

The key to a lead-generation site is to capture information about a visitor to use in future communications. Different types of lead generation include the following:

- Forms that request information
- Online applications
- Newsletter sign ups
- Registration to download products and information
- Referrals to partner sites

When you're constructing lead-generation KPIs, a number of important metrics can help you understand the behaviors that drive success. Here are some of the most common:

Overall conversion This is a calculation that divides leads by site visits. No matter what changes you make to your site, you should always pay close attention to this metric.

Conversion by campaigns This metric tracks how visitors from different campaigns or visitor segments convert to leads. By comparing them, an analyst can fine-tune messages for different audience segments.

Drivers to the registration process This metric examines the effectiveness of content in driving visitors to the registration process, where they will (you hope) register and become customers.

Step-by-step conversion analysis via the registration process This metric is especially important for longer registration processes. It looks at where visitors drop out of the process, so that you can focus on improving the conversion rate.

Analysis of registration-process dropouts When people drop out of the registration process, you should find out where they go next. That will tell you what other information people are looking for in the registration process. By presenting that information in context, you can optimize the process.

Conversion of leads to actual customers In addition to knowing what types of lead-generation options drive the most visitors to register on your site, you should also understand if and how those visitors ultimately convert into customers.

Lead-generation sites are often undervalued. In many cases, they drive significantly more revenue to their owners than e-commerce sites. Recognizing this is the first step toward maximizing the ROI of your online investment with the help of web analytics.

Customer Service

Customer-service sites focus on reducing expenses and improving customer experiences. Their particular value lies in the high cost of other support options, such as call centers. If a company can shift even a small percentage of its customer-service requests to a website, it can save millions of dollars per month.

Unfortunately, these pages aren't sexy, and companies often underestimate their value and dedicate few resources to improving them. But if you're looking for the best way to increase your overall ROI through your web channel, this is probably it.

A customer-service site's main task is to quickly and successfully answer customers' questions and problems. As with anything in web analytics, you should first assess the impact of your site in dollar terms. To do this, you need to begin by looking at the average cost of every service option you offer. These options can include the following:

Call-center service This is normally the most expensive service option; in 2007, costs range from $3.50 to well over $10 per instance.

E-mail service Here, costs are somewhat more reasonable but still run from about $1 to $3.

Online chat These costs are roughly the same as e-mail, but because service issues can be resolved more quickly, they're usually a little cheaper.

Online self-service This is the cheapest support option by a wide margin. Because your customers answer their own questions, your only cost is maintaining the site.

Needless to say, the objective of any customer-service site should be to move visitors from more expensive support options to less. There is a big caveat here: You have to provide acceptable service. In the early days of the Web—and even on some less reputable company sites today—customer-service phone numbers were often buried under masses of self-help options. Although this practice certainly cuts down on the number of requests that go through your call center, it won't win you any friends or word-of-mouth customers. In designing a site, you should concentrate on optimizing the quality of your online service—not on making it impossible for people to call you if your site fails to answer their questions.

To increase the ROI on your service site, you should look at the following KPIs:

Percent of support touches served online Here, you measure the total number of customers served by each method and calculate the percentage of each option. Obviously, the object of this KPI is to track the movement of users to less costly options.

Average cost per touch The average cost per touch (that is, service engagement) is a good way to track the effect of changes over time. Driving the average cost per touch down by a few cents per month can have a significant impact on total customer-service costs.

Drivers to other support methods With this KPI, you want to understand if people are finding what they want on your site or if they're being forced to try another method. A good way to do this is to place unique toll-free support numbers. That way, calls originating from the site can be tracked separately from other calls to your call center.

Onsite search effectiveness A well-tuned customer-support search tool can help reduce the number of people who turn to offline support options. To measure the effectiveness of your search, look at searches per visit and exits from the search return page. The first of these numbers tells you how effective your search engine is. If visitors need to search three or four times, they're not finding what they want easily. The second shows you how many times a person views the results of a search, gets frustrated, and leaves the page to look for another way to resolve a problem.

Survey results Surveys are a good way to determine whether visitors have found what they were looking for during their online support experience. Two common types are exit surveys and page-rating surveys. The first asks visitors about their online support experience when they leave the site. The second is usually embedded in a page and asks users to rate their experience as it's happening. You can use this information to optimize the way you present support content.

As we've said before, support sites have a great potential for cost savings to any organization. Improving the way you present your customer-service information can reduce expensive calls to your call center and have a significant impact on your bottom line.

Content Sites

In discussing content sites, it's important to begin with an observation: Almost all sites provide some amount of content. Many corporate sites, for example, maintain large editorial staffs whose primary job is to provide information about the company's products and organization. But this isn't what we mean by the term *content site*.

Content sites derive their revenue by offering games, audio, video, articles, or some combination. They don't provide information about a company that makes its money elsewhere. Instead, they rely on advertising support, a subscription base, or sometimes both for their revenue. To succeed, these sites must attract repeat visitors who explore the site in depth.

When you're constructing KPIs for a content site, it's important to know how it generates its revenue. There are two main types of content sites: subscription-based and advertising-based. The first asks users to pay a weekly or monthly fee for using the site; they're common in the financial industry. Advertising-based sites are usually free, and they generate revenue by displaying ads.

The KPIs for these two sites can differ greatly. At its most basic level, an advertising-based site makes money when people click ads and leave. A subscription-based site is the opposite: It generates additional revenue when its users not only stay, but also explore and find content that's intriguing enough that they invite more friends to the party. Let's look at the standard KPIs for each.

Advertising-Based Content Site KPIs

Here are some typical KPIs for advertising-based sites:

Visits per week This metric looks at how often visitors come to the site. Because ad-based sites rely on traffic numbers to support advertising, it's important that their visitors return frequently.

Page views per visit A good portion of ad pricing is based on *impressions*, or the number of times an ad is displayed. As a result, advertising-based sites try to move people through multiple pages. However, more page views aren't always better. A site can go too far in promoting page views, leading to a poor visitor experience. When this happens, visits per month are often negatively affected.

Visit length This metric looks at how long people stay on the site. The longer they're there, the more likely that they'll click an ad.

Advertising click ratio Because revenue from this site type is generated from advertisers, it's important to measure traffic to advertisers based on ad formats (banner, skyscraper, intra-content placements, and so on). Understanding which types of ads are the most effective and drive the most clicks can help keep advertisers happy and set appropriate expectations. As a site tests new ad formats, this metric also helps benchmark their effectiveness.

Ratio of new to returning visitors Understanding the ratio of new visitors to returning visitors is important in that it offers insight into how effective you are in retaining visitors. If your site has 100,000 monthly visitors, it makes a big difference if most are new or returning. Ad-based sites always want loyal and reliable audiences; high turnover rates raise a red flag that something is wrong.

Recency and frequency These common measurements look at the last time a visitor came to the site and how frequently they come back.

Subscription-Based Content Site KPIs

Subscription-based content sites have a much harder initial sell, but they also have the advantage of being able to generate a loyal and stable user base. Their KPIs include the following:

Conversion of nonsubscribers to subscribers This family of metrics is similar to what you find on e-commerce or lead-generation sites. Content sites should pay particular attention to what drives users to the subscription sign-up process and where they tend to abandon it. Understanding user behavior in these areas can help you identify what may hold people back from subscribing. As a result, you can optimize the signup process and increase conversion.

Active subscriber base What percentage of current subscribers are active on a weekly or monthly basis? If a given subscriber's use drops off, the risk of defection increases.

Average subscription length Understanding how long different visitor segments maintain their subscriptions can be helpful when you're trying to increase subscription longevity. Site owners can examine behavioral differences between longtime subscribers compared to those who cancel early.

Branding Sites

Branding-based sites and initiatives typically involve experiential content that doesn't directly drive a transaction. Examples include microsites, online games, and sites for a wide variety of low-cost consumer products.

Traditionally, companies have found it difficult to determine success metrics for such sites. Even so, a web experience can have a significant impact on either the positive or negative side of overall company brand perception. A positive experience can lead to repeat site visits and more positive feelings, whereas a negative experience may keep visitors from coming back to the site or impact their behaviors offline.

Branding can also be a key goal on sites that have e-commerce components. For example, if a site has a sales conversion rate of 7 percent, what's the monetary value of the other 93 percent of visitor activity? This other category of behavior, which represents *online brand value*, offers a great opportunity for measurement.

In the world of consumer electronics, for example, data shows that consumers leverage the Web for product research and pricing comparisons but make the majority of their purchases at local brick-and-mortar stores. Top retailers' exit surveys have shown that as many as 60–70 percent of in-store purchases now originate online. Traditional online conversion metrics wouldn't capture this behavior's overall value and its impact on the business.

Based on this trend, branding sites or those with significant branded content should try to determine the following:

- The value of their online branded content, including movies, podcasts, interactive games, and rich media brand campaigns
- The frequency and length of visits, and their relationship to total sales
- The keywords visitors use in searching to find information about the company's products and services
- Which customers are its brand cheerleaders, how they're driving traffic, and how they're influencing others about the brand within their social networks

To measure the value of your online branding efforts, you can look at a number of specific KPIs:

- Page views per visit.
- Average time spent on the site.
- Visits per visitor over a certain period of time. This metric indicates how often people come back to your site to interact with your brand.
- Average order value per person who visited branding content compared with those who didn't.

- Customer satisfaction surveys conducted by companies like ForeSee. These surveys offer insight into what drives brand impact.
- Brand-perception lift. By comparing entry and exit surveys, you can sometimes gauge the effect your site is having on your brand.

Recap

In this chapter, we've taken an in-depth look at how you can define site goals, KPIs, and key metrics. We began by explaining that you must start with clearly defined business goals. Once you determine and fully understand them, you can examine your marketing funnel and see how it relates to your web channel.

From there, we looked closely at KPIs. First, we defined them as a measurement of performance against your key web goals. You saw that they aren't usually complex equations; rather, they're simple numbers or percentages that allow you to carefully monitor your progress against your goals. We also discussed ways to set comfortable targets for KPIs, in particular by using competitive data to see how much room exists for improvement.

We looked at the KPIs for a number of different kinds of sites: content, branding, commerce, lead generation, and customer service. Because most large sites combine a number of these, we stressed the need to be flexible in creating your KPIs.

In the next chapter, we'll delve deeper into specific analytics for your site. In particular, we'll discuss how you can construct monetization models that will help you assign dollar values to specific site behaviors and KPIs. Being able to construct KPIs is a good thing, but knowing what they mean financially is also crucial to your success.

Monetizing Site Behaviors

7

It's all about the money. For many businesses, the only "action" that matters is driving revenue into the company and profit to the bottom line. Fortunately, web analytics can have a significant impact on monetization of online initiatives. Instead of trying to guess how valuable a change to the site will be, monetization models show you exactly what will happen. When someone in the organization says "show me the money!" show them this chapter instead.

Chapter Contents

The Monetization Challenge

The first time you try to put data to work to make a positive impact on your site, you may be surprised at the reaction. Web teams are typically overwhelmed with projects and have limited resources to complete them. The last thing they want is a new assignment, even one that offers the potential for a significant improvement performance.

How do you get the ball rolling? Web analysts often have a hard time being heard if they stick to jargon like "average conversion rates" and "click-through paths." Managers roll their eyes, not least because they don't understand what these things mean. But if you can take those same issues and put them into real dollar terms, you'll find people are much more likely to get excited about them.

The process of assigning values to site behaviors is known as *monetization*, and it's one of the most important tools a web analyst has. Monetization isn't hard to understand at the basic level. For example, the act of making an online purchase is easy to monetize. If every T-shirt you sell makes a $5 profit after expenses, then that behavior is worth $5 to you. Obviously, most types of monetization are a good deal more complicated; we'll go into the nuts and bolts of the process later in the chapter. Before that, however, let's look at how monetization can motivate an organization to embrace the idea of identifying opportunities and improving site performance.

Case Study: Monetization and Motivation

To see how monetization can help prompt a manager to take a close look at optimization, we'll use a fictional example: an enterprise software company. The company's site tries to educate potential customers and drive them to pick up the phone and call a sales representative. It gets many of its prospects over the Web, and for each sale it closes, it sees a profit of between $50,000 and $1 million.

The company has recently hired a web analyst, not because it understands her value, but because all its competitors are doing so. The analyst decides to look into how many of the site's visitors are being converted into leads. She learns that the conversion rate is extremely low when compared to the company's competitors. She isn't sure why, but she suspects that visitors aren't seeing enough calls to action, or that the ones they do see aren't compelling. In addition, the analyst learns that even when people make it to the site's registration page (where they leave a phone number so that a salesperson can call them), they fill it out at a low rate.

As any web analyst knows, these are important findings. And so, she decides to take them to the head of the web organization. Depending on whether the analyst monetizes the effect of these issues, they will have one of two different conversations.

Conversation A: An Unmonetized Argument

If the web analyst goes to the executive without a monetization model, we can almost guarantee difficulties. Let's imagine that she knocks on his door while he is busily immersed in e-mail. The conversation might go something like this:

Web Analyst: Do you have a moment?

Head of Web (without taking his eyes off his computer screen): Sure, make it quick. I've got a meeting.

Web Analyst: I was looking through our web-analytics data and found a few problems with the site.

Head of Web: Is it down? [This is a common misunderstanding of what analytics can and should do for you.]

Web Analyst: No, it's a problem related to visitor behavior.

Head of Web: Oh, OK. You should talk to Pam in usability.

Web Analyst: Actually, I wanted to share it with you. I think it's important.

Head of Web: OK—what is it? [Still looking at the computer screen]

Web Analyst (speaking quickly and excitedly): By analyzing click-through patterns, I found that only a few people were converting from the top-tier pages to our request form, and those who did convert exhibited a further subpar form-conversion ratio. I think there is ample room for improvement.

Head of Web (looking up from his computer for the first time, probably dazzled by the polysyllables): Interesting...

Web Analyst: When I compared our data with clickstream reports from third-party sources, I learned that... [A few long, dull minutes pass as she continues, using every word in the web-analytics dictionary] ...And in conclusion, with a few simple adjustments, we might be able to fix everything.

Head of Web (a long pause follows until he realizes she has stopped talking): OK, we could look at your recommendations in release 34.

Web Analyst: When do we get started?

Head of Web: We're just about to launch release 32 in three weeks. And release 33 functionality is locked down and is scheduled to launch the end of next quarter. That means that in about two months we'll start working on the requirements document for release 34. I'll make sure I invite you to the kick off. [Makes a mental note to ensure that he doesn't]

Web Analyst: Uh...

Head of Web: Thanks for letting me know about this important, er, thing, er... [Tries for a moment to remember her name] buddy.

Conversation B: Monetization Changes Everything

In our previous example, the web analyst broke several rules, the most obvious of which was that she forgot to speak in plain English. But she could also improve her chances if she spoke in a more universal language: that of money. Let's suppose that rather than identifying the problems the site was having in converting its visitors, the analyst also forecast the financial impact of the lost opportunity on the business as a whole. The conversation might go something a little more like this:

Web Analyst: Do you have a moment?

Head of Web (without taking his eyes off his computer screen and still typing): Sure, if you can make it quick. I've got a meeting.

Web Analyst: I was looking through our web-analytics data, and I noticed that we're having some problems we can improve. We could easily increase the number of visitors who sign up for calls from our sales reps.

Head of Web: Really?

Web Analyst: Yes, and it's a lot of money too. We analyzed the performance of this, which is our number-one desired behavior, and found that each lead we get from our site is worth $682.

Head of Web: You mean every person who fills out the form is worth $682?

Web Analyst: Statistically speaking, yes. And here's the problem: We're not turning enough visitors into sales leads. Not many people are getting to the sign-up form, and the ones that do are submitting it in low numbers. Our competitors do much better.

Head of Web: They do?

Web Analyst: Yes. I think this represents a significant opportunity. I won't bore you too much with the details, but we compared our web-analytics data with attitudinal survey results from our site. We also looked at the performance of our competitors' sites. Anyway, to make a long story short, we should be able to generate between 750 and 1,250 more leads per month. Based on a value of $682 per lead, that's between $500,000 and $850,000 per month or $6–10 million per year to our bottom line.

Head of Web: Wow—great job. How sure are you that we can hit that range of increased leads? Is it reasonable?

Web Analyst: Yes. Based on what we're seeing from visitor behavior and what others are doing in our industry, I think the range is quite realistic. I think we could make a significant impact if we run a few tests and optimize our registration form and calls to action.

Head of Web: Release 32 is scheduled to launch in a few weeks. We talked about A/B and multivariate testing a few weeks ago; let's leverage some of our testing partners and try to get this rolling within the next two weeks.

Web Analyst: Perfect. I'll pull together a team for a meeting tomorrow. It would be great if you could join us.

Head of Web: You bet. I'm open all afternoon. Anything else?

Web Analyst: Well, I was afraid you were going to tell me we'd have to push this to release 34.

Head of Web: Don't be silly. And, one other thing, Mary: I'm meeting with the board at the end of the month to talk through our overall web strategy and plan. I'd like to include some of the work you're doing and some of the improvements we're looking at. Please schedule a meeting for us to dig into this further.

Web Analyst: Sounds good—thanks!

Although this is a fictional conversation, it's similar to many we've witnessed over the years. Even if your discussion doesn't make you an instant favorite with the head of your web group, they will always be more receptive and willing to act when you can tie opportunities to real financial impact.

One other point. If talking about potential upside doesn't get the attention of your managers, try phrasing it in a different way: Tell them what they're losing by not acting. In the previous case, the web analyst might have pointed out that if they delayed action by six months, they would leave $3 million to $5 million on the table. That would certainly have gotten his attention.

Web-Monetization Models

Web-monetization models assign dollar values to desired site behaviors, most often those directly involved in driving your overall business. The behaviors they quantify are different for every type of company and range from easy-to-measure e-commerce sites to more difficult ones like consumer-product-branding sites. For example, the enterprise software company in the earlier example probably has five ways in which its site can significantly contribute to making or saving money:

Online lead-generation form This allows individuals who visit the site to request more information.

Phone inquiries generated online Potential customers can call a unique toll-free number they find on the website.

Customer service savings The site's online self-help pages can save the company money by reducing the number of calls to its customer service representatives.

Upgrade offers Current customers can buy more licenses or additional products or services.

Prospect education The site can weed out or otherwise educate prospects so that sales reps only contact high-quality, well-informed leads.

As you've probably noticed, these five things are all different. Some involve sales, others service, and still others education. In reality, most websites have many opportunities for improvement. How do you choose one over the other? The only way to get beyond comparing apples with oranges is to find a least common denominator—in this case, a monetization model. Without one, you have to guess the impact of every possibility and will probably guess wrong. By creating monetization models, you can compare initiatives using a framework that everyone understands.

The models you create don't have to be accurate down to the last penny. It would be nice to have that kind of precision, but it isn't practical or necessary. In creating monetization models, you need to make assumptions and educated guesses. That is perfectly OK. All you're trying to do is to create a general model that the key players in your organization agree on.

Above all, the measure doesn't always have to be absolute. For most initiatives, you need a relative measure. Imagine, for example, that you're running a ski race and using a certain piece of equipment to time downhill skiers. Just before race day, you find out that your radar gun is off somewhere between 5 and 10 percent, and you don't have time to get a new one before the race. Do you cancel the race? Of course not. You go ahead with it and use the faulty radar gun. Although its speeds may not be perfectly accurate, it will tell you that skier 1 was faster than skiers 5 and 6. The same thing is true with monetization models. As long as you know that Initiative A has a greater potential upside than Initiative B, you're usually fine.

Top 10 Ways Monetization Models Can Help Your Company

The advantages of using monetization models revolve around understanding the potential impact of initiatives and making decisions based on this knowledge. Used correctly, they can help you allocate your resources properly. When we introduce this concept to our clients, we usually give them the following list so they can understand why they should adopt the practice.

Monetization models help you:

- Understand the impact of following through on opportunities.
- Prioritize opportunities based on impact. (In chapter 10 we'll explain different methods for prioritizing opportunities.)
- Eliminate time-wasting projects.
- Transform your team from one that pushes pet projects to one that drives the business.
- Measure the impact of site changes, launches, updates, or tests after they're rolled out.
- Determine the real value of campaigns using a common framework.
- Understand your site's true ROI.
- Focus your team on the things that matter in real dollar returns.

- Justify your web-channel spending, and support additional budget requests.
- Evaluate the performance of different teams based on a standard measurement that supports the overall business.

How to Create Monetization Models

Monetization models aren't terribly complicated, as long as you understand a few basic principles. First, there are ultimately only two ways in which your site can impact your company's bottom line: additional revenue and reduced costs. In addition, two kinds of visitor behaviors can affect your business: direct and indirect.

Direct Behaviors

Direct visitor behaviors are those that occur on the site, triggering a primary conversion that should lead to the future success of the business. We'll also touch on indirect conversions, which are generally a little earlier in the overall conversion process and often occur as a result of a site visit, but not necessarily on the site.

SALES

Sites sometimes generate revenue through direct sales. Within this are several measures you should look at. First is top-line revenue: How much do you generate though sales? Second, you should look at your gross online margin to understand how it compares to the cost of offline sales. Does it make sense to try to push more sales into the online channel, or offer bigger discounts or free shipping? Finally, you estimate the lifetime value of new customers who find you via the Web. Many customers begin a relationship with a small buy, but they return once you know they're there. Understanding this value is crucial to gauging the effect of online marketing efforts.

LEAD GENERATION

When you're looking at leads, don't be taken in by their raw number. Lead quality is also important. As a result, you should always try to track what happens to leads after they're generated, and quantify their value. Solid offline tracking can show you close rates as well as average sales values of online leads. To calculate lead value, use the following formula:

(leads closed × average revenue per sale) / total leads = avg. lead value

For example, if your site generates an average of 1,000 leads per month, and 200 of them end up in sales averaging $5,000 each, each web lead's value can be calculated: (200 × 5,000) / 1,000 = $1,000 per lead.

CUSTOMER SERVICE

The web channel can typically service customers at a much lower cost than other options. Many of our client organizations want to calculate the impact of the web channel on overall customer service costs. To do this, you first have to know your baseline costs.

Average per-call call-center costs, for example, can range from $3.50 to well over $10; answering an e-mail can cost $1.50 to $3.50 or more. The cost of a site-based service transaction is usually well under $1.

To find out the value of each option, you must multiply the volume of each type by its related cost. For example:

- Call center: 100,000 calls × $5.00 per call = $500,000

- E-mail: 50,000 e-mail messages × $3.00 per e-mail = $150,000

- Web: 80,000 help visits × $0.30 per visit = $24,000

- Total support costs: $674,000

- Average cost per touch: $2.93 (total costs divided by total support touches)

These are just a few examples of direct values that are fairly easy to quantify for many sites. There are, of course, others, and we'll look at some channel-specific monetization models later. But first we'll focus on the indirect value a site can add and how a web team can claim credit where it's due.

Indirect Behaviors

Unfortunately, calculating indirect value means focusing on visitor behaviors that are harder to track, value, and quantify. Not surprisingly, many companies don't even try. They simply say, "Oh, we don't sell products on our site, so we can't come up with a dollar value for what our visitors are doing." Or if they do sell online, they only allow the web channel to take credit for the direct revenue it generates and ignore the influence it has on purchases made elsewhere.

These companies are short-changing themselves. If direct value is the only valid value, then what's the point of all those glossy automotive sites? They don't sell cars; they only display them. Bettycrocker.com doesn't sell Hamburger Helper. Pampers.com doesn't sell diapers, but it does generate high value in the business-to-consumer (B2C) world. Even if you're not selling or capturing leads online, you can still quantify your site's indirect value.

REFERRALS

Many organizations use their sites to steer referrals to partners or resellers who handle the ultimate transaction. (In case you're interested, this is what automotive sites do.) If your site performs this kind of service, it should get credit for it. We've often heard managers of such sites say, "Our site is there to educate potential customers about our products and answer any questions." In reality, their site's business role is to drive qualified customers to partner sites.

It's important that you track your referrals carefully, counting your handoffs to partner sites and working with them to learn what happens next. You'll want to know what percentage of them buy, what their average revenue is, and what that means to your bottom line. Your site is, after all, driving that revenue.

OFFLINE SALES

People regularly use websites to research products or services and then go to a brick-and-mortar store to purchase them. Nowadays, the numbers of these kinds of interactions has risen dramatically. One of our clients, for example, conducts fewer than 3 percent of its sales online. Even so, over 30 percent of its new customers conduct online research before making a purchase. A persuasive website can assist your enterprise well beyond the narrow confines of the Internet. How can you gauge this? Here are a few common methods:

Dedicated e-mail This method involves inviting users to contact you by e-mail using a unique address for different channels. The address that appears on your website shouldn't appear anywhere else. That way, you can track the exact number of e-mail leads that come from your site.

Dedicated phone numbers This method involves the same tactic, but with phone numbers. If you want to isolate which customers contact your call center after a visit to your website, set up a unique phone number that only appears online. Our clients are often shocked at how many leads originate there.

Web-only offer codes or coupons You can give customers an exclusive, nominal premium offer on your site and then see how often it's redeemed in other channels.

CUSTOMER SATISFACTION

A good website can help improve overall satisfaction with your organization. If you regularly conduct customer-satisfaction surveys after a sale, add a couple of website-specific questions. You could also consider running surveys or questionnaires on the site itself, although because you'll be using self-selected respondents, the data won't be as accurate.

Assembling a Monetization Model

In the beginning of this chapter, you saw that Mary, our intrepid web analyst, was able to say with some confidence that each lead her company's website generated was worth $682. How did she do this? Usually, the best way to start building a monetization model is to look at the overall business goals first and then determine the role the web channel plays in them. In Mary's case, it was clear that one of the keys to the company's success was to sell as many enterprise software licenses as it could. To do so, the sales reps need to have people to sell to. The web channel could drive leads to them.

From there, Mary had to determine what each lead was worth. To do this, she gathered a few data points:

- The number of leads from the website for a given period
- The number of sales closed by reps from these leads
- The dollar value of closed sales from these leads
- The profit based on closed sales from these leads

She found that the site generated 8,000 leads per month. Analyzing those leads, she learned that 2.96 percent (237 deals) were closed within 6 months of getting the lead from the web channel. The average dollar value of those leads was $100,000 each. With a profit margin of 23 percent, the average sale contributed $23,000 to the bottom line. Working the math backward, she found that each lead was worth $682 profit on average.

Using Monetization Values to Create a Pro Forma for Your Web Channel

Pro forma statements contain the projected effect of business initiatives. In other words, if a company decides to implement changes to its website, it can create a financial pro forma that lays out, in dollar terms, how those changes can improve the bottom line.

We almost always begin a web engagement by asking our client what the financial goal of the initiative is. The question doesn't always make them comfortable. We find that marketing professionals can be intimidated by terms like *pro forma*, particularly because they involve math. But although they can be complex to implement, these documents aren't tough to understand.

Defining ROI

The heart and soul of a financial pro forma involves calculating the ROI of an initiative. Basic ROI is a key financial metric that determines the value of business investments and expenditures. Mathematically speaking, it's a ratio of net benefits divided by costs and is usually expressed as a percentage:

$$ROI = [(\text{monetary benefits} - \text{cost}) / \text{cost}] \times 100$$

Let's say a company's e-business team wants to implement web-services technology, which will cost $75,000. They believe the initiative will result in a 10 percent increase in software automation. What does that mean to the company as a whole? Does the implementation make financial sense?

At this point, the e-business team has the web-analysis group look at other data. They learn that each 1 percent increase in software automation increases overall annual profit by $25,000 per year. This implementation would yield $250,000 in profit—a 10 percent increase. The company can calculate this investment's ROI as follows:

$$[(\$250,000 - \$75,000) / 75,000] \times 100 = 233 \text{ percent}$$

Payback-Period Analysis

ROI is merely a percentage, however. To get real visibility into ROI, you also need to look at the *payback period*. This is the time it takes an investment to pay for itself. For example, if a $100,000 investment in web-services technology generates $400,000 a year in profit, it pays for itself its three months.

Using Monetization Values to Create a Pro Forma for Your Web Channel *(Continued)*

Payback periods are important. What if you make an infrastructure enhancement that will pay for itself in four years? Chances are, the change you make may be replaced by other systems before it has a chance to pay for itself. In that case, you'll realize a net loss rather than a gain.

The best way to understand the value of an initiative is to use payback-period analysis. This methodology looks at the entire effect an initiative will have on every aspect of a company's bottom line. It then calculates the length of time it will take for the initiative to yield enough returns to pay for the initial investment.

To do this, you have to look at the initiative's direct and indirect benefits. Direct benefits measure the cash flow generated by the initiative. Indirect benefits include such things as overall brand impact; they're more much more difficult to measure.

Some examples of direct benefits include the following:

- Visit-to-purchase conversion
- Online media units
- E-mail conversions to purchase
- Articulation and measurement only moderately difficult
- Self-serve via the Web vs. higher-cost channels, such as retail or phone systems (IVR or Interactive Voice Response)
- Automation of services, such as account access in financial services and airlines
- Account tracking

Indirect benefits include the following:

- Word of mouth
- Brand affinity
- Increased visit length
- Product consideration
- Branded entertainment
- Positive community buzz and activity

Of course, other metrics can be useful in payback-period analysis. Customer lifetime value, value of leads, and value of cost savings can all contribute to overall ROI.

Conclusion

With an insistence on financial pro-forma reporting, you'll be able to understand the financial impact of every web initiative your company undertakes. That way, you can focus on things that help the bottom line—and shelve those that don't.

Monetization Models for Different Site Types and Behaviors

So far, we've tried to explain in general how you can create monetization models. As with many things in analytics, however, you'll be able to understand the process better by looking at real-world examples. In the following pages, we'll show how our company created specific monetization models for four different kinds of sites.

Each example is fictional but similar to a real-world project we did for a Fortune 2,000 client. Some of the monetization models may be obvious, but we've selected a few that show how companies often find unique measures to be important. And although we describe only one monetization model for each company, we usually create 5–15 of them for any engagement.

With each model, we also forecast the potential impact of specific changes we might make on the site. For the purposes of explanation, the examples assume that you move one conversion rate without affecting any other measure. For example, we're assuming that if we increase the lead-conversion rate, the quality of the additional leads is the same as the initial ones. Obviously, this is unlikely, but we're trying to keep the examples straightforward. In the real world, you'd also want to consider the possibility that making changes in one metric often has a domino effect on others.

E-Commerce Opportunity

Normally, when analysts think of e-commerce sites, the first thing that pops into their heads is the checkout process. In this example, however, we'll look at something else. The company in question is a manufacturer of consumer goods that are sold through a number of different channels:

- Its website
- Its call center
- In brick-and-mortar stores
- Its catalog
- Other websites

Because the Web is its most efficient channel, the company ideally wanted all of the sales of its products to occur on its site. Of course, that was an unrealistic wish, and in reality only a small percentage of its revenue came from online purchases.

We knew from studies about the company's industry done by publishers like Forrester and Gartner that its customers did most of their research online and then made offline purchases. On top of that, we knew that detailed product pages were key to triggering purchases in the industry. If a customer navigated down into product details, it greatly increased the likelihood that they would make a purchase. We decided to focus on that behavior.

The Monetization Model

We undertook a series of studies. By combining them with educated assumptions, we were able to determine that for each site visitor who visited one or more detailed product pages, the manufacturer ultimately received a profit through sales from all the different channels of $0.38. In other words:

Monetized site behavior, value of visits to detail product information:
$0.38 (profit)

Was that measure completely accurate? Probably not. It failed to take into account the particular products people were buying and the sales channels they used to do so. But in this case, we were just getting started with the engagement, and we wanted to provide a baseline so our client could better understand the impact of changes.

From there, we created a chart (Figure 7.1) that looked at what would happen if we were able to increase the number of people looking at detailed product pages. At the time, the company was able to drive only 42 percent of its visitors to look into greater detail on the site. The chart forecast the potential impact on the business if we enticed more of them to do so.

At first, 38 cents doesn't seem like it would have a significant impact on a large company. But as the model shows, even these small values can add up quickly.

COMPANY NAME REMOVED WEB SITE VALUE MODEL

Visit-to-Product Detail Visit

Monthly Site Visits	5,000,000
Visits that Access Product Detail Content	2,100,000
Current Visit-to-Product Detail Conversion Rate	42.00%
Value of Product Detail Visit	$ 0.38
Current Monthly Value (Profit) from Behavior	$ 798,000

Future Conversion Rate:	Product Detail Visits	Incremental Prod. Detail Visits	Monthly Profit Impact	Annual Profit Impact	Lost Opportunity - Delaying 3 Months
42.00%	2,100,000	-	$ -	$ -	$ -
43.00%	2,150,000	50,000	$ 19,000	$ 228,000	($57,000)
44.00%	2,200,000	100,000	$ 38,000	$ 456,000	($114,000)
45.00%	2,250,000	150,000	$ 57,000	$ 684,000	($171,000)
46.00%	2,300,000	200,000	$ 76,000	$ 912,000	($228,000)
47.00%	2,350,000	250,000	$ 95,000	$1,140,000	($285,000)
48.00%	2,400,000	300,000	$ 114,000	$1,368,000	($342,000)
49.00%	2,450,000	350,000	$ 133,000	$1,596,000	($399,000)
50.00%	2,500,000	400,000	$ 152,000	$1,824,000	($456,000)
51.00%	2,550,000	450,000	$ 171,000	$2,052,000	($513,000)
52.00%	2,600,000	500,000	$ 190,000	$2,280,000	($570,000)
53.00%	2,650,000	550,000	$ 209,000	$2,508,000	($627,000)
54.00%	2,700,000	600,000	$ 228,000	$2,736,000	($684,000)
55.00%	2,750,000	650,000	$ 247,000	$2,964,000	($741,000)
56.00%	2,800,000	700,000	$ 266,000	$3,192,000	($798,000)
57.00%	2,850,000	750,000	$ 285,000	$3,420,000	($855,000)
58.00%	2,900,000	800,000	$ 304,000	$3,648,000	($912,000)

Figure 7.1 E-commerce: product detail conversion

Some of the key points on interest in this example include:

Monthly Site Visits This is the total number of site visitors. For forecasting purposes, this number is assumed to be constant.

Visits that Access Product Detail Content This number doesn't look at the total number of product-detail pages accessed by users. It counts the number of visitors who request that content. For example, if a visitor views six different product-detail pages, they're counted only once. Here the number is 2,100,000.

Current Visit-to-Product Detail Conversion Rate This is the percentage of site visits that access the product-detail content. You can see that it's 42 percent.

Value of Product Detail Visit This is the profit we judged that was generated by the impact of the desired behavior.

Future Conversion Rate This column shows the current rate of product-detail visits and the projected rates if improvements are made.

Incremental Product Detail Visits If we manage to increase the conversion rate, this is the number of extra visitors who will access product-detail content.

Monthly and Annual Profit Impact These numbers show the amount of additional profit that will presumably be generated by the additional visits to the product-detail pages.

Lost Opportunity—Delaying 3 Months This column shows the negative impact to the business based on the different potential conversion-rate improvements if it takes three months to act on the opportunity. We find that this metric is particularly useful in convincing reluctant managers to act.

Target Conversion Rate We derive this number by looking at attitudinal and behavioral data as well as through comparisons to competitors in the space. Here, the targeted conversion rate is 50–55 percent. This shows an annual profit impact potential of somewhere between $1.8–3.0 million.

Such charts are especially useful to people like our earlier web analyst, who is trying to convince her Head of Web to act on an opportunity. It's important to note that the company may not see these exact improvements in its bottom line. This is a method to *estimate* the potential impact of different initiatives and forecast their financial impact in terms that are easy to understand. It isn't an iron-clad prediction.

Lead Generation

For this example, we'll look at another enterprise software company, but in a different way. This company uses free webcasts as a tool to generate leads and start the sales process with potential prospects. They produce (and heavily promote) a series of informational videos and animations on different topics relevant to their product line. Interested customers can sign up and attend a session on the featured topic. Afterward, the company's sales representative contacts the prospect and asks if they have additional questions or (ideally) would like to talk about how the company's products might help them. As a result, we believed that the time a session took place and the topic were important.

Thanks to a series of studies, some analysis of the company's sales process, and a few educated assumptions, we were able to determine that for each person who attended a webcast, 0.10 percent ultimately purchased from the company within 6 months, for an average profit of $83,333. As a result, we came up with the following monetization model:

Monetized site behavior, value of webcast attendees = $125.00 (profit)

With that information, we were able to produce the chart shown in Figure 7.2.

COMPANY NAME REMOVED WEB SITE VALUE MODEL

Visit-to-Web Cast Sign Up

Monthly Site Visits		2,000,000
Web Cast Sign Ups		45,000
Current Visit-to-Sign Up Conversion Rate		2.25%
% of Sign Ups that Actually Attend		60.00%
Actual Attendees		27,000
Est. Profit of Web Cast Attendee	$	125.00
Current Monthly Value (Profit) from Behavior	$	5,625,000

Future Conversion Rate:	Product Detail Visits	Incremental Prod. Detail Visits	Monthly Profit Impact	Monthly Profit Impact	Lost Opportunity - Delaying 3 Months
2.25%	27,000	-	$ -	$ -	$ -
2.30%	27,600	600	$ 75,000	$ 900,000	($225,000)
2.35%	28,200	1,200	$ 150,000	$ 1,800,000	($450,000)
2.40%	28,800	1,800	$ 225,000	$ 2,700,000	($675,000)
2.45%	29,400	2,400	$ 300,000	$ 3,600,000	($900,000)
2.50%	30,000	3,000	$ 375,000	$ 4,500,000	($1,125,000)
2.55%	30,600	3,600	$ 450,000	$ 5,400,000	($1,350,000)
2.60%	31,200	4,200	$ 525,000	$ 6,300,000	($1,575,000)
2.65%	31,800	4,800	$ 600,000	$ 7,200,000	($1,800,000)
2.70%	32,400	5,400	$ 675,000	$ 8,100,000	($2,025,000)
2.75%	33,000	6,000	$ 750,000	$ 9,000,000	($2,250,000)
2.80%	33,600	6,600	$ 825,000	$ 9,900,000	($2,475,000)
2.85%	34,200	7,200	$ 900,000	$ 10,800,000	($2,700,000)
2.90%	34,800	7,800	$ 975,000	$ 11,700,000	($2,925,000)
2.95%	35,400	8,400	$ 1,050,000	$ 12,600,000	($3,150,000)
3.00%	36,000	9,000	$ 1,125,000	$ 13,500,000	($3,375,000)
3.05%	36,600	9,600	$ 1,200,000	$ 14,400,000	($3,600,000)

Figure 7.2 Lead generation—webcast sign-up conversion

Some of the key points on interest in this example include:

Monthly Site Visits This is the total number of site visitors. For forecasting purposes, this number is assumed to be constant.

Web Cast Sign Ups This counts only the people who sign up for webcasts during a visit to the website. If they sign up for more than one at a time, they're still counted only once.

Current Visit-to-Sign Up Conversion Rate This is the percentage of site visits that sign up for a webcast.

% of Sign Ups that Actually Attend In this example, only 60 percent of the people who signed up for a webcast attended it. Our assumptions needed to take this into account.

It wouldn't be accurate to forecast profit from clients who didn't attend. Another model could look at what would happen if the company increased the rate at which people who signed up attended a webcast.

Estimated Profit of Web Cast Attendee Based on our analysis, we estimated that each webcast attendee generated on average a $125 profit.

Future Conversion Rate This current rate appears in bold, along with a range of better conversion rates.

Incremental Product Detail Visits This is the number of additional people who will attend a webcast if we're able to reach the increased conversion rates.

Monthly and Annual Profit Impact If we achieve the improved conversion targets, this is the projected financial impact on the company.

Lost Opportunity—Delaying 3 Months This shows the negative impact to the business based on the different potential conversion-rate improvements if it takes three months to act on the opportunity. We find that this metric is particularly useful in convincing reluctant managers to act.

Target Conversion Rate We derive this number by looking at attitudinal and behavioral data as well as through comparisons to competitors in the space.

There are also a few additional points of interest in this example. First is the rate of change we predicted. The current conversion of visit to sign-up was 2.25 percent, and we only forecast our ability to increase it to 2.50–2.75 percent. At first, this doesn't seem like a big change; but based on the value of these behaviors, even a small increase could potentially increase annual profit by $4.5–$9.0 million.

This process included two key conversion rates. The first was the conversion of site visits to webcast sign-ups. We believed that if we were allowed to conduct A/B tests and make incremental improvements to the site, we could have a significant impact on the company's bottom line. The other important rate involved the percentage of people who signed up and attended a webcast. We didn't look at improving that in our example, but in the real world, you would definitely want to consider that as well. There would be a number of interesting ways to try to affect this rate, some of which might not directly involve the website. For example, the company could put an Add to Outlook link on the confirmation page so the webcast would show up on people's calendars. Or it could explore the possibility of sending reminder e-mails or making automated phone calls the day before the webcast. In other words, you should consider both the onsite and offsite drivers for such behaviors.

Customer Service

This example looks at the relation between the help section of a company's website and its customer support call center. To understand this relationship, we placed a unique support toll-free number in the website's help section. That way, when a call came into the call center, we knew it was prompted by a visit to the site.

From data collected by the call center, we were able to monetize the cost of a call at $12 (in some circumstances, this would be considered a low number):

Monetized site behavior, cost of call-center calls from the support site: $12.00 (a conservative estimate of the cost of a call-center call)

With that information, we were able to produce the chart shown in Figure 7.3.

Support Section Visits to Call Center Calls

Monthly Support Section Visits	500,000
Calls to Call Ctr. (from Support Section of Web)	115,000
Current Support Visit to Call Ctr. Conversion Rate	23.00%
Cost of Call Ctr. Call from Support Site	$ (12.00)
Current Monthly Call Center Cost from Support site	$ (1,380,000)

Future Conversion Rate:	Calls from Support Site	Reduced Call Ctr. Calls (From Support Site)	Monthly Incremental Savings	Annual Incremental Savings	Lost Opportunity - Delaying 3 Months
23.00%	115,000	-	$ -	$ -	$ -
22.50%	112,500	2,500	$ 30,000	$ 360,000	($90,000)
22.00%	110,000	5,000	$ 60,000	$ 720,000	($180,000)
21.50%	107,500	7,500	$ 90,000	$ 1,080,000	($270,000)
21.00%	105,000	10,000	$ 120,000	$ 1,440,000	($360,000)
20.50%	102,500	12,500	$ 150,000	$ 1,800,000	($450,000)
20.00%	100,000	15,000	$ 180,000	$ 2,160,000	($540,000)
19.50%	97,500	17,500	$ 210,000	$ 2,520,000	($630,000)
19.00%	95,000	20,000	$ 240,000	$ 2,880,000	($720,000)
18.50%	92,500	22,500	$ 270,000	$ 3,240,000	($810,000)
18.00%	90,000	25,000	$ 300,000	$ 3,600,000	($900,000)
17.50%	87,500	27,500	$ 330,000	$ 3,960,000	($990,000)
17.00%	85,000	30,000	$ 360,000	$ 4,320,000	($1,080,000)
16.50%	82,500	32,500	$ 390,000	$ 4,680,000	($1,170,000)
16.00%	80,000	35,000	$ 420,000	$ 5,040,000	($1,260,000)
15.50%	77,500	37,500	$ 450,000	$ 5,400,000	($1,350,000)
15.00%	75,000	40,000	$ 480,000	$ 5,760,000	($1,440,000)

Figure 7.3 Customer service—call center calls

Some of the key points on interest in this example include:

Monthly Support Section Visits This is the total number of site visitors. For forecasting purposes, this number is assumed to be constant.

Calls to Call Center (from Support Section of Web) This is the number of calls generated by the unique 1-800 number in the site.

Current Support Visit to Call Center Conversion Rate This is the percentage of people who visit the support section and then call the call center.

Cost of Call Center Call from Support Site As we said, this is $12.

Future Conversion Rate This shows the current rate in bold as well as a range of better conversion rates. In this case, we want the conversion rate be lower so that we can reduce call-center costs.

Reduced Call Center Calls (from Support Site) This is the number of calls we can eliminate if we achieve the decreased conversion rate.

Monthly and Annual Incremental If we achieve the improved conversion targets, this is the projected financial impact on the company.

Lost Opportunity—Delaying 3 Months This shows the negative impact to the business based on the different potential conversion rate improvements if it takes three months to act on the opportunity. We find that this metric is particularly useful in convincing reluctant managers to act.

Target Conversion Rate We derived this number by looking at attitudinal and behavioral data. Here, the targeted conversion rate is between 20 and 22 percent. This shows an annual profit-impact potential of somewhere between $720,000–$2.2 million.

A Warning About Conversion Rates and Support

We intend this example to show what would happen if you improved your online help section. Naturally, you could reduce your Web-based call-center calls to nearly zero if you left out the phone number. Many companies in the early days of the Web tried to buy phone numbers and force people to try to use poorly designed help sections. In most cases, this caused many more problems than it was worth.

Whenever you make changes to a support site, you should also survey people who visit it to determine whether they're getting their questions answered—or if you're driving them away. Ideally, you should be making it a lot easier for people to solve problems. That way, it's a win for everyone. Customers resolve their issues quickly and easily, which results in a positive experience; and calls to the call center are reduced for the company, which saves money. Be sure to consider the impact of all aspects of changes—your customer is the most important part of the equation.

Ad-Supported Content Sites

In this example, we we'll look at a potential opportunity for a site that is primarily supported by advertising revenue, which we naturally want to increase. To do this, the site needs to increase the number of ad impressions it makes (it may also need to increase the volume of ads it sells, but that's a separate question). There are a number of ways you can increase impressions, including more ads per page and increasing site visits; this example looks at ways to keep people on the site longer so they view more pages.

Here, the monetized behavior is easy to derive, because it's the same as the cost per thousand impressions (CPM) that the site charges its advertising customers:

Monetized site behavior, CPM of ad impressions that the company sells: $15.00 CPM

With that information, we were able to produce the chart shown in Figure 7.4. Some of the key points of interest in this example include:

Monthly Site Visits This is the total number of site visitors. For forecasting purposes, this number is assumed to be constant.

Page Views Per Visit This measurement is crucial, because the more pages a person sees, the more ad impressions the company can serve.

COMPANY NAME REMOVED WEB SITE VALUE MODEL

Ad Supported Sites

Monthly Site Visits	10,000,000
Page Views Per Visit	6.37
Avg. Ad Impressions Per Page	3.00
Average Ad CPM	$ 15.00
Ads Served Monthly	191,100,000
Current Monthly Ad Revenue	$ 2,866,500

Future Page Views Per Visit:	Monthly Ad Impressions	Incremental Ad Impressions	Monthly Est. Incremental Revenue	Annual Est. Incremental Revenue	Lost Opportunity - Delaying 3 Months
6.37	**191,100,000**	-	$ -	$ -	$ -
6.40	192,000,000	900,000	$ 13,500	$ 162,000	($40,500)
6.50	195,000,000	3,900,000	$ 58,500	$ 702,000	($175,500)
6.60	198,000,000	6,900,000	$ 103,500	$ 1,242,000	($310,500)
6.70	201,000,000	9,900,000	$ 148,500	$ 1,782,000	($445,500)
6.80	204,000,000	12,900,000	$ 193,500	$ 2,322,000	($580,500)
6.90	207,000,000	15,900,000	$ 238,500	$ 2,862,000	($715,500)
7.00	210,000,000	18,900,000	$ 283,500	$ 3,402,000	($850,500)
7.10	213,000,000	21,900,000	$ 328,500	$ 3,942,000	($985,500)
7.20	216,000,000	24,900,000	$ 373,500	$ 4,482,000	($1,120,500)
7.30	219,000,000	27,900,000	$ 418,500	$ 5,022,000	($1,255,500)
7.40	222,000,000	30,900,000	$ 463,500	$ 5,562,000	($1,390,500)
7.50	225,000,000	33,900,000	$ 508,500	$ 6,102,000	($1,525,500)
7.60	228,000,000	36,900,000	$ 553,500	$ 6,642,000	($1,660,500)
7.70	231,000,000	39,900,000	$ 598,500	$ 7,182,000	($1,795,500)
7.80	234,000,000	42,900,000	$ 643,500	$ 7,722,000	($1,930,500)
7.90	237,000,000	45,900,000	$ 688,500	$ 8,262,000	($2,065,500)
8.00	240,000,000	48,900,000	$ 733,500	$ 8,802,000	($2,200,500)

Figure 7.4 Ad-supported content sites—ad revenue

Average Ad CPM This is the average cost that advertisers pay for 1,000 ad impressions. In this case, it's $15.

Ads Served Monthly The number of ad units able to be served from the site during the month.

Current Monthly Ad Revenue Revenue generated from onsite ads.

Future Page Views Per Visit This column shows the current rate in bold as well as a range of improved page views per visit.

Incremental Ad Impressions This column shows the number of additional impressions the site will have, based on the increased page views per visit.

Monthly and Annual Incremental The estimated incremental revenue for the time period based on the potential site change.

Lost Opportunity—Delaying 3 Months This shows the negative impact to the business based on the different potential conversion-rate improvements if it takes three months to act on the opportunity. We find that this metric is particularly useful in convincing reluctant managers to act.

Target Conversion Rate We derived this number by looking at behavioral data as well as data collected about competitive sites. Here, the targeted rate is between 6.7 and 7.5 pages per visit. This shows a potential profit impact of somewhere between $1.8 and $6.1 million.

Again, this example shows that making a small improvement in a key metric can have a significant impact on your bottom line. In the real world, however, it would not be this simple. The company could run into problems if it ended up having trouble selling out its advertising or had to significantly reduce its CPM in order to do so. If so, it might not make sense to look in this direction.

The company could also take this metric too far. If it were a news site, for example, it could take articles that normally ran on two pages and split them into three. It could even take the same two-page article and split it into eight pages, requiring site visitors to click ahead every other paragraph. Obviously, this approach wouldn't work. There is generally a sweet spot where you can maximize your side of the equation while still serving your audience and not frustrating them. This is where attitudinal surveys can come into play.

Recap

In this chapter, we've looked at the all-important task of making monetization models. First, you saw how valuable they can be when you're trying to convince upper management to undertake optimization projects on your site. The advantages of monetization models are many, but most often they revolve around understanding the potential impact of initiatives and making decisions based on this knowledge.

From there, we examined how you can isolate key behaviors and create monetization models to express them. It's important to remember to look at both direct behaviors, such as purchasing and lead generation, and indirect ones, such as referrals and offline sales. Only by looking at all of them together can you gauge the true impact of your web channel.

Finally, we looked at specific examples of monetization models that we've created for our clients. They include applications for e-commerce, lead-generation, customer service, and ad-supported content sites. The examples showed that by moving a key KPI even in a small direction, companies can see a substantial impact in their bottom lines.

In the next chapter, we'll focus on another use of monetization models: prioritization. You'll see how you can use the forecasting processes explained in this chapter to make smart decisions about where to allocate your resources when you're trying to improve your site performance.

Getting the Right Data

8

In this chapter, we're going to look at common data types that can help you better understand your web business and, more important, your customers' interaction with your business. In particular, we'll focus on behavioral, attitudinal, competitive, and transactional data. We'll explain how they're used, and what they can and can't do. We'll also examine how you should compare performance both inside and outside your organization.

Chapter Contents

Primary Data Types

In previous chapters, we've talked at length about leveraging data to make smarter business decisions. Along the way, we've primarily focused on web-analytics data, which—naturally—is important. Even so, the information you pull from a web-analytics tool is only one of many types of data that can help you improve your website. That data can be organized as follows:

Behavioral data Rather than learning an overly complex definition of behavioral data (there are plenty), you should think of it as data that tells you exactly *what* visitors are doing on a site. It includes things like what links they're clicking, where they're going, what they've looked at, where they came to your site from, and so on. Behavioral data is normally collected with a web-analytics tool.

Attitudinal data The easiest way to think about attitudinal data is that it tries to tell you *why* people are exhibiting the behaviors they are. Behavioral data may tell you that someone exited the site from the shopping-cart page. A well-constructed attitudinal study can help you understand why those people exited from that page (cost of shipping might be a reason, for example).

Competitive data Competitive data has many different flavors, including behavioral data, demographic data, and even heuristic reviews of competitors' sites. This data can be powerful when used correctly. We'll go into detail about it later.

Secondary data types We refer to these data types as secondary not as an indication of any lesser importance, but because fewer companies leverage this type of data to impact their websites and overall web strategy. This category is a catch-all for other data types that are available to your business. Some of the many things that fall in the secondary data type's bucket include the following:

- Call-center data
- Customer data
- Transaction data
- Third-party research
- Usability benchmarking
- Heuristic evaluation and expert reviews
- Community sourced data

Warning: Avoid Data Smog

Throughout this chapter, we'll dig further into each of these data types. We'll provide examples of what each can offer and, more important, how you can leverage them to generate insight into your customers and your web business.

Even so, we can't finish this chapter in clear conscience without mentioning one of the most common problems facing companies today: *data smog*, or data overload.

Few companies are short on data to look at, but nearly all are short on insight that can drive their businesses. As we explore other types of data you can consider leveraging, you should focus on the most important ones for your company and not become paralyzed by the sheer volume of data.

The best way to avoid data overload is to start small and focus your efforts on the most important portion of your website. You'll be tempted to look at everything and try to understand every aspect of every part of your site. Doing so can quickly lead to frustration and won't allow you to take full advantage of the opportunities you have.

Behavioral Data

So far, most of this book has focused on behavioral data. As explained earlier, behavioral data tells you what visitors do on a site. Sources of behavioral data include web-analytics tools, advertising-reporting tools, and others tools or software that report on user behaviors.

Using common analytics tools, you can understand things such as the following:

- Where people go when they're on a site
- What page drives them to request more information
- How they enter a site
- Conversion rates for key behaviors
- At what point people abandon the purchase funnel
- Which calls to action are most effective

Behavioral data does a good job of telling you what is happening on a site. It allows you to understand and aggregate data about visitors' behaviors. It can even tell you how to segment users to maximize opportunities.

However, there are several things that behavioral data can't tell you. One is why people are doing what they're doing. Did they drop out of the purchase funnel because they were frustrated, or did they suddenly realize they wanted more information before they decided to buy? Behind any behavior lie many potential reasons why people aren't performing the way you want them to. It's important to know that.

Behavioral data also can't tell you if a particular conversion rate or other metric is good or bad. It can tell that you have a 2.5 percent click-through from your home page to a key initiative. But is that effective or not? This common question can lead to a lot of frustration.

In the standard web-analytics process, it's best to start with behavioral data and then use it to leverage the other types of data. You can use behavioral measurements based on your overall KPIs to identify areas of opportunity where your site can be improved. By using behavioral data, you can hone in on the most promising possibilities; then, you can look to other data types to deepen your understanding of the problem and suggest potential solutions.

Attitudinal Data

As we explained in the first part of this chapter, attitudinal data can help you understand the *why* behind problems or specific site behaviors. Two common categories for attitudinal studies are surveys and focus groups:

Surveys These are an excellent tool to extend your understanding of user behavior on your site. However, most companies restrict their use of this tool to collecting customer feedback on their own sites. If customer satisfaction is extremely important to you, you may want to consider using a company like Foresee, which can conduct a survey on your site and then compare the results to a relative satisfaction index. This approach will allow you to see how your site is doing relative to other, similar sites in the marketplace.

Focus groups These offer a quick and effective way to gather high-level perceptions about your products and brands. You can use them in a competitive context to explore new concepts, find out what others are doing, and gain insight into how users perceive your brand. Focus groups have a particular place in the product-development cycle; you should consult experts when considering the web implications of this option.

Balancing Behavioral and Attitudinal Data

Mac or PC, Ford or Chevy, VHS or Betamax? These are all debates that have elicited strong opinions. The choice between behavioral and attitudinal data is another such controversy, common in the web-analytics world.

In reality, it shouldn't be. Neither type is inherently superior to the other. Just as Macs and PCs have their particular marketplace sweet spots, behavioral and attitudinal data are both great tools. What's more, when you put them together, the sum is much greater than the parts.

Pure behavioral data shows the impact a problem has on all visitors, not just a core sample. It's an unvarnished, unedited, macro view of site traffic patterns. On a site built to generate leads, for example, it may show that most visitors find a crucial contact page but quit before completing it. Behavioral data will give you the exact drop-off rate and the defectors' entry and exit routes.

That's much more useful than vague survey data that tells you visitors think your sign-up process is poor. But it's only half the story. Unfortunately, behavioral data won't tell you why so many people aren't filling out the form, or why they exit the site in a huff.

After you use behavioral data to isolate a problem, you should move on to attitudinal analysis. Surveys, follow-up e-mails, customer sessions, and feedback-form submissions can often tell you why a problem is occurring. Perhaps the form is too long, or users think it's too invasive. Perhaps the form is fine, but the copy in the link to it may be misleading. Maybe the site doesn't offer enough orientation information before asking personal questions. Or it could be that your target leads prefer phone contact and abandon your site when they can't find a number. Behind every behavioral *what* may lurk a dozen attitudinal *whys*.

If you use attitudinal data alone and talk with only a sample of customers, it can be difficult and time consuming to connect their complaints to degraded site performance. (Customers will give you all kinds of issues to wade through. Although many of these issues are important to them, they can distract you from what's really driving your site performance.)

Once you address the whys behind your data and optimize your site, you should move back to behavioral analysis and determine whether your efforts were effective. Weigh the new analytics figures against the old baseline to see if the changes improved site performance.

And so, attitudinal data and behavioral data lovers alike, relax. Used in complementary ways, they can lead to maximum site-change effectiveness. The market wasn't big enough for Betamax and VHS, but in the growing field of web-data analysis, there's no need to make a choice between one and the other. Not only can you accommodate both attitudinal and behavioral data, you need both, too.

Competitive Data

You've seen that web analytics can give you great insight into how people arrive at, utilize, and then exit your site. But inevitably, you'll also want to look over your competitors' shoulders and see how they're doing. How many visitors are they getting? How is their site performing? Is there an industry benchmark for performance, and are you hitting it?

Obtaining competitive data for its own sake isn't necessarily a good use of your time and resources. But if you use the data in the context of your overall web strategy, it can help in a number of ways: from generating ideas to enabling a deeper understanding of how your customers react to your brand. Especially when it's based on large sample sets, it lets you compare at a high level the way visitors view your site and those of your competitors. It can also provide information about search-engine effectiveness, campaign conversion rates, and visitor demographics.

The central weakness of competitive data is that it's nowhere near as complete as the data you can collect on your own site. In a perfect world, you would have access to comprehensive information about how your competitors are doing (and they would know absolutely nothing about your performance). In the real world, you can never measure your competitors' sites with the same precision as your own. Still, there are a number of ways you can gather valuable information to use in other ways, as we outline later in this chapter.

Types of Competitive Data

Let's look at a few different kinds of competitive data and how to use them.

THIRD-PARTY PRIVATE NETWORKS

Third-party networks are probably the most useful of all sources of competitive data. They're companies that collect and collate massive amounts of data about Internet usage. For a fee, you can purchase their services, which often come with online tools that you can use to create reports.

In choosing a third-party network, you should know that they aren't all the same. They use different methodologies to measure Internet usage, so you should know the strengths and weaknesses of each approach in relation to your own needs.

USER-CENTRIC NETWORKS (COMSCORE, NIELSEN//NETRATINGS)

User-centric networks work much like the Nielsen ratings you find on television (in fact, Nielsen//NetRatings is one of the better known providers). They rely on a community of users who agree to install software on their computers, often for a small fee or the promise of a prize. This software records the users' surfing habits and compiles the data into reports.

To ensure the quality of the data, the networks select millions of potential users at random. They come from all demographic segments of the online population, in large enough pools that their surfing habits are statistically significant.

The biggest advantage of these services is that they can provide intimate details about users' lives. Because the participants have provided a wide range of information about themselves, the tools can isolate, for example, high-income users from those between the ages of 18 and 21. By using all the information from their panels, these tools can also approximate conversion metrics (such as purchasing patterns) for different sites.

Because of the quality of the soft data (age, sex, income) these services provide, we typically advise our clients to use them in an advertising context. They can tell you where to make media buys, what kinds of ads to deploy, and what to expect in terms of conversion rates. That way, you can get crucial insight on the effectiveness of your campaigns and know whether they're performing well or need to be optimized.

NETWORK-CENTRIC (HITWISE)

Companies that offer network-centric services work more passively than their user-centered counterparts. They typically have agreements with Internet service providers that allow them access to the anonymous log data the ISPs collect. As a result, they can test and analyze an enormous amount of data about actual Internet users. By combining those findings with the same kind of opt-in panels that user-centric networks employ, they offer a rounded picture of Internet usage.

Network-centric services can provide deep insight into things such as search-term analysis as well as click-stream reports that analyze how visitors move from one site to the next. They can also look at differences in geographical areas and the kinds of sites people surf at work and at home.

One clear advantage of this methodology is that it looks at all Internet usage rather than that of a group of people who don't mind having their information tracked. We view these tools as particularly effective for marketers and e-commerce sites. They can measure the effectiveness of your campaigns, compare them to how well your competitors are doing, and suggest ways to acquire new customers.

Leveraging Competitive Data

There are three major ways to leverage competitive data to drive insight. Each can offer significant value and help you solve problems, depending on the issues you're facing:

Comparing specific site performance against competitors Earlier, we talked about how to know if a specific metric is performing well. Is a 2.5 percent conversion rate good or bad? Competitive data allows you to look across your industry and measure your site against others in your space. That way, you can establish realistic goals for where you would like to be.

Finding out what's working well on your competitors' sites This one can be tricky. If you identify something on your site that you want to improve, you can use competitive data to understand what's working well for others. Often, competitive-analytics tools can't do this exactly, so it can take some work to gather the data. If you can find out what's working best for your competitors, you can use that insight to create options for A/B or multivariate tests. When you examine your competitors' sites this way, you're looking for successful ideas to test on your site. You should never take what works well on a competitor's site and *assume* that it's also the best solution for you. It's imperative that you test what works for your competitors against your audience and site offerings.

With competitive data, you can also try to understand what types of campaigns drive the most traffic to your competitor's site as well as where its visitors spend their time online. That can help you better target your test campaigns.

Understanding demographics of site visitors on both your site and your competitors' Many competitive tools can provide solid demographic data about your site visitors as well as your competitors'. This can help you a number of ways by deepening your understanding of how people respond to your messaging in relation to others in the space. Typical data includes information about age, sex, income, education, and geographic location. All these things may provide insight that can help you better understand or solve a problem.

Later in the chapter, we'll explore a case study that will illustrate how this is done.

Getting Started with Competitive Data

Before you start looking at competitive data, you need to come up with a plan. Many types of data are available, and only some of them will be valuable to you. You may benefit from third-party network analysis, or from independent research reports, or even from in-house focus groups. (Descriptions of these follow.)

Your first step should be to decide which types of data will be most useful to you. You shouldn't look for a scorecard by which you evaluate your efforts against your competitors; all businesses are different and use the Web differently. Rather, you're looking for insights that will drive your business.

Next, create a formal process for evaluating and reporting the data. Unlike information about your own website, not everyone in your organization needs to be concerned with competitive data; but you should establish a process for distributing it. In addition, you should plan to check most data sources on a regular basis. One of the main advantages of using competitive data is that it allows you to spot emerging trends—and that requires continual monitoring. Above all, try to look at the data dispassionately. It's hard sometimes to see your site compared with another, but it can yield valuable insights that can help you improve your online efforts.

Secondary Data Types

As we said before, this category is a catch-all for the rest of the data that can help your business. In this section, we'll give just a small sample of the endless possibilities.

Customer Interaction and Data

Some examples of customer interaction data include:

Call-center data By understanding what your customers and prospects are looking for when they call in to your call center, you can better tune your site to meet their needs. Better yet, by using a unique toll-free phone number that is only listed on your site (or different numbers for different sections of your site), you can not only understand what all callers into the call center inquire about, but also determine what site visitors inquire about when they call the call center. By providing them with this information on your site, you can eliminate those costly calls.

Customer data Many companies have collected information about their customers' interests, behaviors, and demographic characteristics. You can sometimes leverage that information to segment your audience and better investigate and analyze site behaviors for different groups.

Transaction data You may be able to leverage previous purchases or interactions with your company in both online and offline (retail, call center orders, catalog) channels to help you understand visitor behavior.

Third-Party Research

If you want to quickly get up to speed on the latest web trends and strategic thinking in your field, a wide range of third-party research firms would be happy to help you. These companies produce affordable reports that contain a great deal of useful information about everything from projected sales to effective interface practices. Although this information will never come tailored to your particular business problems, it can save you time and money if you can live with a less than perfect fit.

The focus of these studies varies by source. Some providers, such as Forrester and J.D. Power, segment their reporting by industry. Others, such the Nielsen Norman Group, Pew Internet, and American Life Project, concentrate on best practices and usability findings for online experiences. By taking their advice into consideration, you may find many opportunities to improve your site.

The major weakness of third-party research is that it can't bring you a unique competitive advantage. Such reports are available to anyone who wants to buy them, and in some industries they're taken as a blueprint for good web strategy, rather than a tool for informing a company's marketing efforts.

A good current example is the automotive industry. A quick survey of carmakers' websites reveals that many are relying on the same resource: J.D. Power. That company provides binders full of information regarding user needs and desires in the online vehicle-buying process. The information is, of course, valuable. But over the last few years, the industry has seen a homogenization of its websites. Most of them feature remarkably similar content, navigation, information design, and functionality. Although these sites may all be following good practices, they aren't differentiating themselves from one another. Such a situation probably won't be good for their brands in the long run.

Usability Benchmarking

Usability testing, which looks at how people interact with websites and other interfaces, is an important field in web design. And it can provide valuable insight into how well your competitors are doing.

To compare your own site's usability to others in the field requires a benchmark usability study. To do so, you first hire a usability expert (or engage the one already on your team). Then, you put together a focus group, and the expert (or team of experts) observes them as they perform a similar series of tasks on your site and those of your competitors. Comparing interfaces this way provides insight into which specific features of the interface are working and which aren't.

The value of such studies is that you can find out how you're doing in comparison to others who are trying to do the same thing. There is one warning, however: You may find that your site's usability is about the same as that of your competitors. Such findings shouldn't be surprising. As the Internet matures and best practices become more established and validated, companies are finding it increasingly difficult to pioneer concepts that lead to improvements in efficiency, effectiveness, and satisfaction. Even so, you'll lose nothing (except the cost of the study) if you learn that that your site is just as usable as your competitors'. At least you'll know that you should focus your efforts on other factors, such as brand perception, credibility, and customer loyalty.

Heuristic Evaluation and Expert Reviews

One big drawback of usability benchmark studies is their cost. They require you to engage users to come to a central location and have experts analyze their reactions. Done well, such studies can involve a substantial investment. Because there's always a chance that you may not learn much, you may want to consider a lower-priced option: engaging an expert trained in heuristic evaluation.

Essentially, heuristic evaluators do a usability study of your and your competitors' sites without in-person testing. The theory is that they have such good training (and, you hope, experience) in the usability field that they can—without the help of actual users—conduct a formal and structured review of the different flows and processes on a website. This approach costs much less than a usability benchmark study, but you must be cautious.

First, don't try to do heuristic analysis yourself. Many companies go through ad hoc exercises of this kind. An executive, for example, may like the way a particular checkout flow works without understanding how the item that is catching their fancy is performing. In many cases, in our practice, clients have requested specific widgets for their sites because they saw them somewhere and liked them. Subsequent testing proved that the innovations weren't worthwhile. This is something you should leave to an expert.

What do you look for in a heuristic analyst? The most important thing is experience. We all feel that we can understand usability instinctively, and to a certain degree, that's true. But when it comes to more complex applications, there's no substitute for a good education or a long tutelage in the subject. If you can afford it, try to find someone with a good reputation in the field, and make sure you test their results afterward if you plan to use the analyst again.

Community Sourced Data

Are you interested in knowing what your customers think of you and your competitors? Why not listen to what they have to say? All across the Web today, people have gathered in communities. Whether they collect stamps, trade stocks, buy lipstick, or are interested in the Napoleonic Wars, sites and communities are geared to their interests, however bizarre they may be. Unless your business runs a concession stand in Antarctica (and maybe even then), there's probably a community that in some way addresses your products or services.

This doesn't mean your brand, like Apple, needs to have a community of users devoted to it. Even if you have only a modest online presence, there are places where your customers gather. They read blogs and newsgroups, visit support sites, or take part in content communities. Of course, the community in question may cover much more ground than your market niche. We doubt, for example, that there is an independent site devoted to cabinet hinges, but there's certainly one for people who make their own furniture.

Finding such sites isn't difficult. A simple web search will quickly uncover some of the important community venues where your company is discussed. Reading through those sites will reveal others. If you're interested in the blogosphere, you can use sites like Technorati and blogsearch.google.com to search for your products. It may take some time to understand the community ecosystem around your brand, but it will be worth it.

When you find the right sites, you'll have the pleasure (such as it is) of learning what your most devoted, discerning, and occasionally cranky customers are saying about you and your competitors. Because people tend to be honest on such sites, they can be a crucial tool in measuring relative brand perception. For example, if you ask customers what they think about Sony electronics on Sony's site, you'll get one answer. If you listen to them sharing insights, opinions, and advice on a third-party site, you'll get a much more accurate picture of what they really think.

Unfortunately, to do this kind of analysis, you need to steel yourself against bluntness and even rudeness—and be ready to learn the hard truth about what's missing from your survey data. If you can, however, try to resist the temptation to answer criticisms, no matter how unjust. You'll only end up adulterating a good source of information; and chances are, you'll end up annoying the participants.

Just like all other types of data, don't just look for every piece of data you can and then dive in and look at every metric. Go into it with a plan and a problem you're trying to solve. That way, you can focus your efforts and ensure you're spending your time wisely. Remember, you won't always find what you're looking for or what you need to know to understand your problem fully.

Leveraging These Data Types

Typically, when we start working with a new client, we discover within the first few days that they have access to and have reported on a few of the different data types. Unfortunately, they often stop at reporting. Even if a company has more than one of these types of data, it's often kept in discrete silos and isn't leveraged by the same people or compared in any way.

Here is where the real value of these data types comes into play. All of these types can help you better identify opportunities that can improve your site, but you'll see their true benefit only if you can leverage them together. By themselves, some of these data types aren't terribly valuable. But combined with other types, they can give you deep insight.

We've experimented a lot with the different types of data and have found ways that each of them can be used to complement the others. Sometimes you have to think outside of the box to figure out which types can be combined to give you the information you need to solve a particular problem. It's also good to occasionally step away from the data and think about what your customers are experiencing based on what you're seeing.

One last word about data. It's a common misconception that all the insights provided by these sources are easy to interpret. Although some of the data can be manipulated and put into tables using Excel, it often takes the form of customer quotes or expert reviews of competitive sites in your industry. Don't get caught up trying to tie all your data together in an automated, easily repeatable fashion. That would be ideal, but it isn't realistic. When leveraging different data types, you should roll up your sleeves and look for trends, common factors, and explanations for some of your problems. Think of it more as putting together a story about your site's spot in the overall web universe, rather than a hard and fast set of facts. This isn't always easy, but it's well worth the effort.

Comparing Performance with Others

Once you've made the commitment to create a culture of analytics, you'll begin to wonder what's happening outside your team and outside your company. You'll ask yourself and your team some obvious questions: How does this work compare to what's being done by others in our organization? How does our marketing performance on this demand-generation campaign compare to campaigns in the past? Is a 3 percent visit to e-mail registration rate good or bad? What about that 1.4 percent visit to purchase conversion? If you know you're getting a much smaller conversion rate in direct mail, is that a fair and reasonable comparison benchmark?

The answers to the fundamental questions about how your performance compares to that of others don't jump off your analytics report. You can only know how well you're doing compared to your own past performance based on your own data. You want to be able to take that data and find the key drivers for performance on your sites. The folks down the hall or down the street may have better answers to the questions than you do, and you may not know that. Your competitors may have passed your 1.4 percent conversion rate six months ago. There are many questions you can't answer, but this chapter will help you make some comparisons to help your business. As we discussed in Chapter 1, your strategy must be to align all your efforts and drive success across every channel you serve. Being able to make comparisons among those channels and your departments is one of the keys to success.

We recently worked with a shoe company that has incredible products and eager customers. Their business has been growing rapidly over the past few years, and they recently signed a big-time celebrity personality to an endorsement contract. In short, their business is growing and has huge growth potential.

Every six weeks, they do an integrated online and offline campaign that encompasses their entire online strategy, including their site, landing pages, pay-per-click, e-mail, third-party co-sponsored sites, viral campaigns, and community. With the signing of this celebrity, the marketing team at the client wanted to put her picture on the home page with the dominant share of screen real estate dedicated to the promotion. There were secondary promotions of product pictures that ran horizontally across the bottom of the home page, with approximately 10 percent of the total real estate supporting three separate promotions. If you do the quick math, each secondary promotion received approximately 3 percent of the screen real estate. Interestingly, people clicked the secondary promotions four to eight times more frequently than the primary promotion of the female celebrity. This was a strange take on the 80/20 rule but certainly not what the site designers intended.

We've since changed campaigns multiple times with a diverse mix of promotions. No matter how compelling the celebrity endorsement, promotional incentive, or product promotion, each and every time, people click the shoes. The good news is that the product is king; the bad news is that marketing of other brand drivers is secondary. We never would have known this if we hadn't historically benchmarked and relatively scored the performance of campaigns and promotions over time. Now we have a clear indication from the consumer of what they care about, and we can have a much more objective conversation among the e-commerce merchandisers, the brand managers, and everyone in between. In the past, this would have been a classic argument of wills between these roles in the organization.

Data depends on the current baseline benchmark, comparing that benchmark to other benchmarks (internal and external), rationalizing your goal, measuring against that goal, and understanding the drivers to the variance (whether positive or negative).

Whenever you create a report, always create a historical baseline to understand where you are today. When you're creating the baseline, keep in mind that visitor behavior varies dramatically depending on many factors such as time/day of the week; day of the year; seasonality, such as holiday and back-to-school shopping; external factors, such as broadcast/PR/direct mail activities; and so on.

What Is a Relative Index?

A *relative index* is a comparison of one online behavior to others in order to get a relative comparison. It may sound simple, but multiple steps are necessary before you can get to the point of having these indices. Most of this book describes the things you must do to first get the data for computing your indices. Once you've made the investments necessary to get that far, you can begin to make comparisons.

If you think that having the data is good enough, then you should consider the strategic questions you're trying to answer. It's never just about the data; it's about the meaning of the data and the activities that drive marketing success. Relative comparisons help you decide where to invest your marketing budget.

Examples of Relative Indices

The specific relative indices that are important to you are closely aligned with your business and your marketing programs. The things you compare may have little or no meaning to another business (or even another department in your own company). Some common indices that arise in much of our work can serve as examples for your own evaluations:

Overall business performance indices:

- ZAAZ performance index

Commerce indices:

- Visit to purchase index
- Average order value index

Demand-generation indices:

- Pay-per-click index
- Cost per conversion index
- Cost per acquisition index

Brand affinity indices:

- Click-depth index
- Recency index
- Duration index
- Brand index

- Blog index
- Conversion index—in this case, session- or order-based conversion
- Opt-in index

Site behavior indices:

- Visit to purchase index
- E-mail opt-in

These indices don't just appear on the reports you get from your analytics software. You have to work closely with your analytics team to define them and ensure that they're calculated correctly and consistently.

Before we dive into the nuts and bolts of relative indices, we want to talk a little about what you should try to achieve through the comparisons: better customer engagement.

Customer Engagement

Have you visited a website recently and found yourself drifting from page to page without paying attention? Perhaps you find a site that is interesting the first time you visit but becomes less appealing every time you return. If you're like us, you find yourself so deeply engaged in some sites that your boss has to come tap you on the shoulder to remind you of the meeting that started 15 minutes ago.

Remember, analytics drives your strategy, and your strategy is all about getting your customers engaged. We know this, and we work closely with our clients every day to make it a reality. Much of the dialog in the larger web-analytics community revolves around this same issue, and one of the leading voices is Eric Peterson. Eric has created a simple list of criteria for well-engaged visitors to his site. Well-engaged visitors will do the following:

- View a relatively large number of pages in a given session
- Have visited the site in the last four weeks
- Have relatively long sessions
- Come directly to his site or come from an *Eric Peterson* branded search
- Read his weblog in addition to non-blog content
- Buy one or more of his books through his website

Given these factors, Eric's visitor-engagement metric is composed of six submetrics, each of which can be examined individually to provide context to the larger calculation. The six submetrics are as follows:

Click-depth index Percentage of visitor sessions of n or more pages

Recency index Percentage of visitor sessions occurring in the last small n weeks

Duration index Percentage of visitor sessions of n or more minutes

Brand index Percentage of visitor sessions originating directly or originating from search-engine searches for terms like *eric t. peterson, web analytics demystified*, and so on

Blog index Ratio of blog-reading sessions to all sessions

Conversion index In this case, session- or order-based conversion

Keep in mind that engagement is a visitor-based calculation, one designed to look at the lifetime of visitor sessions to the website. This yields a simple rule: *The engagement of any visitor is a function of their lifetime of visits.*

Methodology: Leveraging Indices across Your Organization

Our methodology incorporates the following nine steps:

1. Define the key index.
2. Determine the frequency of reporting.
3. Cultivate a culture of analysis.
4. Make budget allocations.
5. Benchmark marketing initiatives.
6. Benchmark site-behavior types.
7. Prioritize resources.
8. Learn.

Step 1: Define the Key Index

Understand the language your executives already speak. Be aware of the data points that are already in their vocabulary. Getting the executive team to understand the importance of a benchmark is critical to success. When done well, benchmarking can become a fundamental tool in your organization.

Look for a key metric that they already track, which you can augment with a behavioral index. Nothing gets the attention of executives more than converting the conversation to how a change will generate more revenue or save on costs. A few common examples are::

Revenue indices: ROI, gross margin ROI

Cost-saving indices: cost per acquisition = the average cost per acquisition (total demand generation costs / number of conversions = CPA)

Whether you're a large, complex enterprise or a small organization, it makes sense to start with the basics and enhance the sophistication of these indices over time as you gain successes, confidence, and cultural support.

Step 2: Determine the Frequency of Reporting

To determine the right frequency of reporting, follow the lead of other management reports. This shouldn't be a separate report; rather, it should be a simple add-on to existing reports. Most executive management teams operate based on five or fewer key reports. These reports are core to the business and are reviewed weekly.

Step 3: Cultivate a Culture of Analysis

One of the key dependencies to building benchmarks and indices in your organization is to get executive buy-in and sponsorship. In Chapter 1, we reviewed many of the changes taking place in the marketplace that will force organizations to adopt a culture of analysis.

Step 4: Make Budget Allocations

Sophisticated marketers use these tools to understand which marketing investments work best. Each year when budget time comes around, there is often the tendency to invest either in more of the same or in something completely new. Sometimes the data supports these investments, and sometimes the marketer goes with their gut. In either case, having a set of relative indices makes the decision better and means that next year, you can know what worked and what didn't. We think that is one of the most powerful outcomes of relative indices: spending money wisely.

Step 5: Benchmark Marketing Initiatives

You should test the value of every type of marketing you do:

- E-mail
- Banners
- PPC
- Direct mail
- Call center inquiries
- Online help

Step 6: Benchmark Site-Behavior Types

You should test the value of every type of marketing you do:

- Lead generation
- Online sales
- Product consideration
- Brand loyalty
- E-mail opt-in

Step 7: Prioritize Resources

Perform dynamic prioritization based on ROI. See Chapter 10 for more explanation and examples of this task.

Step 8: Learn

You should plan a lessons-learned step after every marketing effort:

- Learn from your failures.
- Failures are as important as successes.
- Learn from your successes.
- Prioritize initiatives.
- Perform employee reviews. It's powerful to have a relative score (such as ROI) that can be tracked to a specific employees' impact on the business success. At one level, this can be interpreted as a potential negative situation for a rank-and-file employee. Our experience is the opposite. Employees who know what's expected of them are more apt to strive to achieve those expectations. The ability to objectively measure their impacts is critical. One of the fundamental differences between working in a small company versus a large enterprise organization is the impact employees feel they have on the success of the organization. Small organizations live and die by the performance of each individual. In larger organizations, the connection between an individual's success and the overall success of the business is often tenuous. If you establish a connection through individual rewards and business performance, you're highly like to develop a more empowered team.
- Leverage indices across multiple business units or product lines. In larger organizations, comparing the success of initiatives can be powerful. It helps you predict the potential impact of a marketing initiative on the various parts of your business. For example, if an e-mail campaign to existing customers typically generates a 5 percent conversion, you can quickly estimate how many customers you need to target in your database segmentation. And your IT staff will be able to predict the server-load forecasts for customers opening and clicking through to your website.

Case Study: Leveraging Different Data Types to Improve Site Performance

To help illustrate how this process works, we'll share a story from a recent client of ours. To protect the client's confidentiality, we'll say it was a wireless phone company, although this isn't accurate.

Through analysis of behavioral web-analytics data, we found that the product pages for mobile devices weren't prompting people to put them into their shopping carts at a good rate. In other words, visitors were looking at product information but not buying products often. Based on past experience in the industry, we felt they should be doing better. We knew that if we could get more people to add phones to their carts *and* hold the conversion rate steady through the rest of the funnel, we could make a significant impact to online revenue.

To find out why people weren't putting phones in their carts, we looked into several other types of data:

Attitudinal We placed a survey on the device product pages to better understand what people were looking for. In addition, we presented separate surveys to two groups: people who did add a product to their cart and those who didn't. This helped us better understand what people were looking for, what their intentions were, and some of the reasons they did or didn't add a device to their cart. We discovered a few things we could address and a few, such as product attractiveness, that we couldn't.

Competitive analysis (round one) Competitive analysis allowed us to analyze how the other wireless providers were performing with regard to getting people to add devices to carts from product-detail pages. With this information, we could determine whether there was significant upside potential in optimizing the pages. In this case, we found that the answer was yes: Our client was in the bottom half of product-page performance.

Heuristic and expert review We conducted expert reviews of the product-page template on our client's site as well as on competitors' sites to identify potential areas of weakness. This analysis pointed out several things that were likely contributing to the problems on the page. It eventually helped us devise test ideas. In doing this review, we were also able to leverage some of the results from the survey.

Segmentation analysis By understanding how different segments were accessing the site, we found that the product-detail page was performing quite a bit better for certain groups of people and poorly for other groups. This let us know that there most likely was no perfect page for the entire audience; rather, we needed to explore presenting different versions based on different audiences to see if doing so would continue to have a significant impact.

Competitive analysis (round two) At this point, we created a series of hypotheses to test. But before going too far, we dug back into a second round of competitive analysis. This time, we looked at sites with similar target audiences, based on demographics, to determine which ones had the best-performing product pages. Along with our other insights, we wanted to look for ideas we could test to see if they made sense for our audience.

Testing We were then ready to formalize our test strategy and begin conducting multivariate tests. As expected, we saw significant differences in how each variant performed with different audience segments. So, we eventually launched several different designs that were triggered based on the audience segment to which a user belonged. These changes ended up delivering a significant lift in overall conversion rates and ultimately resulted in a seven-figure increase in online revenue. And that's just by improving one page.

Next steps We looked back at the competitive data to see where we stood. We didn't take first place, but we did rise from the bottom half to the second-best performing product page in the industry. We also conducted surveys that revealed that we had increased customer satisfaction.

The most interesting part of the story occurred a few months after we jumped into second place. The company that had the best-performing product page rolled out a rebranded design of its website. They ended up changing their product page and reducing its overall effectiveness as well as its overall online conversion rate. This put our client in the top spot in terms of performance. We're willing to bet that the other company had no idea that it had the best performing page and killed it when they rolled out their new look. It was clearly a case of a company that was more concerned about a redesign than providing the best site experience and performance.

Recap

Prior to this chapter, we've mainly discussed the use of behavioral or standard web-analytics data. In this chapter, we showed that using this type of data alone merely tells you what's happening on your site. Thanks to other data, you can learn why it's happening and what you can do to improve.

We started by looking at attitudinal data, such as surveys, and how it can tell you why users are behaving the way they are. Then we discussed the different kinds of competitive data that are available. These data types allow you to understand whether the metrics you're seeing on your site are good or bad; they can also give you testing ideas for improving your site.

Finally, we looked at a broad category of other data types that includes everything from third-party reports to usability benchmark tests and heuristic analysis. All of these can play a significant role in rounding out the picture of your web performance and suggesting possibilities for improvement. In addition, we examined relative indices and the need to compare performance across many dimensions.

In the end, we walked through a case study that showed how we used different types of data to improve the performance of a company's product pages. Thanks to a lot of detailed testing, we were eventually able to segment the site's visitors and see a seven-figure increase in revenue. Such results aren't outside the realm of possibility if you leverage all the data your company collects to give you a rounded, insightful picture of what's happening on your site.

Analyzing Site Performance

After covering many of the fundamentals of web analytics in earlier chapters, we'll now turn to some of the mechanics of analyzing the site itself. An important distinction we'll make is between reporting and analyzing behavior. The focus of this chapter will be getting into the details and seeing what they can tell you about a site.

9

Chapter Contents

Analysis vs. Reporting

There's a good reason we call it web analytics, and not web reporting. As we've noted before, companies traditionally view data as a previous month's scorecard. They use it to gauge how a site is doing according to large but often misleading metrics such as page views and average length of visit.

When using the analytics methodology that we outlined in Chapter 5, we begin by defining overall business and site goals and creating agreed-upon KPIs and supporting metrics. We also conduct an audit to ensure that we're looking at accurate data and configure our web-analytics tracking tool to give us the information we need.

At this stage in the game, the third step in the ZAAZ analytics methodology, we should collect a reasonable amount of data before moving forward—it's good to start with at least a month's worth. Then it's time to try to make sense of visitor behavior and identify opportunities that can help us improve site performance. This isn't the same as merely creating a report. If you're not sure of the difference, the following lists should make it clear:

Web reporting

- Compiling data to share throughout the organization
- Sending reports to people in the organization
- Finding a way to get as much data as possible in an easy-to-view format

Web analysis

- Leveraging different data sources to understand visitors based on your key business goals and to make recommendations for improvement
- Using past visitor behaviors to identify opportunities to improve the site
- Distributing data with a story detailing specific findings and recommendations based on what has happened in the past

The biggest problem with pure reporting is that it produces *rear-view mirror syndrome*: Companies end up looking at the past to see what has happened on their sites, rather than looking toward the future at what might happen if changes were made to improve performance. In a way, rear-view mirror syndrome is partially the fault of the power of the top-tier analytics tools. They can generate millions of possible reports, and when you log in to them, they make it easy to find generic information. Unfortunately, most of the data that can truly help you understand how to drive your business lies deeper within the tool and requires an additional level of configuration.

When you're starting analysis, it's all too easy to be overwhelmed by the amount of data. Instead, you should focus on what really matters and on specific behavior you're trying to understand. If you're an e-commerce company, you may want to understand your shopping-cart conversion or how your product pages drive successful checkouts. For a lead-generation site, you may want to know what drives people to request more information or start a dialogue with your company. If you're just starting with analytics, you should always begin with your single most important behavior and ignore all the other data.

Don't Blame Your Tools

Many companies invest in powerful analytics tools and only use them to look at top-level metrics. They never reach the point where they leverage the information gathered with the tool to identify problems, test solutions, and improve site performance.

Perhaps it's a human reaction, but when companies like these fail with analytics, they most often blame their tool for this lack of success. Many times, we hear the complaint, "If only we had a better tool, we could get that analytics data we need." In some cases, that may be true; but as the old adage goes, a good carpenter doesn't blame his tools.

We work with many powerful analytics tools to help companies better use web-analytics data. Even when our clients believe that their current tool is failing them, we usually find that it's capable of providing them with the insight they need to optimize site performance.

This is almost always the case if the company is using one of the higher-end solutions such as WebTrends, Omniture, HBX, Visual Sciences, or Coremetrics. These vendors don't like to admit it, but 95 percent or more of the data they provide is extremely similar. Their tools all have unique offerings that differentiate them a bit, but when you get down to it, they can all—if used properly—lead to tremendous success.

However, as of now, none of the tool providers offer something that you implement out of the box and that automatically shows your site performance; it's just not possible. Selecting and configuring the tool is only the start. Once you've done that, the real analytics work begins. Unless you commit to doing that work, you'll never begin to see the ROI that these tools can offer.

Where Did We Go Wrong?

Your analytics tool is probably not the reason you aren't successful with analytics. More likely suspects follow:

Lack of methodology to use the data Top-tier tools can provide over five million different views of your website data. You need a methodology in place to analyze the data based on your overall site goals. And you must have a process and team in place to move your efforts forward.

Not focusing on the right metrics Unless metrics are clearly defined and prioritized, companies often focus on less useful, high-level metrics.

Poor tool implementation and configuration If the tool hasn't been properly set up to provide data on key metrics, companies often blame it for not being able to do the job.

Accuracy issues If the data isn't accurate, you won't want to act on it. All too often, we find that clients blame their tools for inaccuracies. In most cases, they have incorrectly configured it or don't understand the data it's producing.

Poor communication of site goals If the people who manage the tool aren't communicating with the people who are responsible for the site, it will be difficult to be successful.

Lack of training on the tool Each of the tools presents data in a unique way. Almost all of them can provide the data you need, as long as you know where to look.

Too much data Some companies collect too much top-line data instead of focusing on the important metrics.

Sometimes there are reasons to switch tools, especially if you aren't using one of the better ones. But remember, you should also solve the non-tool issues that are normally at the root of the lack of analytics success. It's far more worthwhile to spend time and money improving your internal processes around how you're going to use web analytics rather than on selecting and implementing a new tool.

Examples of Analysis

Because it's difficult to talk about analysis conceptually, in the following pages we'll look at it in the context of several real-world examples. Our intention isn't to suggest guidelines for analyzing your site, or even to teach you how to analyze data. Rather, we'll explain what analysis is and how you can use it to start thinking differently about your business instead of focusing on top-line reporting metrics.

The examples we'll look at include how to do the following:

- Analyze purchasing processes to find opportunities
- Analyze lead processes to find opportunities
- Understand what onsite search is telling you
- Evaluate the effectiveness of your home page
- Evaluate the effectiveness of branding content
- Evaluate the effectiveness of campaign landing pages

Analyzing Purchasing Processes to Find Opportunities

One of the most important processes for any e-commerce site is its conversion funnel and checkout process. Whether you sell shoes or airline tickets, a breakdown in such a process can be catastrophic to your site. On the other hand, making small improvements in this area can sometimes lead to significant gains in revenue.

When you're analyzing a sales funnel, it's important to understand that the overall conversion is made up of a series of microconversions. The process presents users with a series of steps, and in each case, the user can make one of three decisions:

Continue to the next step in the funnel This is the desired behavior.

Leave the funnel, and go to other content on the site In many cases, people leave the checkout process to seek more information, usually to support their purchasing decision.

Exit the site altogether Obviously, in this case, the site loses its chance to convert or cross-sell its users. In addition, if users leave the site, the site can't get them to convert on secondary goals or other desired behaviors outside the primary funnel.

Depending on the tools you use, you can see this data by analyzing funnel paths, page-pathing data, exit reports, or other means. Be creative with how you use your analytics tool to understand these behaviors.

Handholding

It's important to make sure that at every step in the process, users make the right decisions. The first step to improving the performance of a funnel is to break it down into discrete steps and find out where the opportunities are and where people are abandoning the process. For example, in an eight-part conversion process, a user performs the following steps:

1. Visits the site.
2. Views a product detail page.
3. Adds product(s) to their cart.
4. Clicks to start the checkout process.
5. Enters shipping and billing addresses.
6. Enters payment information.
7. Reviews the order confirmation/review page.
8. Clicks to place the order, and sees the order-complete/thank-you page.

This represents a generic and particularly ideal process. Of course, just because we can divide up a sales funnel doesn't mean that visitors will move through it in a linear fashion. No one navigates the Web that way. Visitors may review multiple products, add a few to their cart, leave to do research on another site, come back and add another product to their cart, look at shipping information, have lunch, take a nap, and finally finish the checkout process. Needless to say, for analysis, we need to be cognizant of these things.

Data for all these steps is readily available in nearly all analytics tools, from basic to advanced. Again, it isn't typically a question of *whether* the data is available, but *how* you look at the issue as a business problem and then use the data in the right way to identify opportunities.

Commitment and Acceleration

Most top analytics tools have ready-made functionality to analyze processes like these. Each tool is different, and some perform better than others. But all of them can gather data on every step we've explained.

Once you've gathered your data, it's time to analyze the different behaviors you see throughout the process. At each step, you should consider what the visitor did to reach that point as well as how they may view the site visit. Merely because someone comes to your site doesn't mean they intend to purchase. The same can be said about someone going to a product-detail page or adding an item to the cart. A certain percentage of visitors come to browse; others add products to shopping carts as a way of keeping track of them. Buying may not be on their mind.

When people start the purchasing process, you begin to see a process of increasing commitment to purchase. It starts at zero when they arrive at the site, and it builds slowly as a product is added to the cart. Then, it accelerates greatly when the customer begins the checkout process. It continues to increase as they enter personal information and move through order confirmation. Finally, it reaches a fever pitch at the money stage—this is where you don't want to lose them. But it doesn't stop there: Your site should continue to sell the decision to the customer, even on the order-completion and thank-you pages. After all, a buyer can always cancel an order or return the product.

Because the commitment level grows throughout the key steps, you should see the abandon rate drop as customers move through them. In the previous example, it would be worrisome to see a high abandon rate from order-confirmation or order-complete pages. At that point, visitors have already gone through the entire process, down to entering personal and payment information. They're so close! If you have problems there, it's an obvious area to focus your attention.

Helping the Decision

As you analyze your conversion funnel, you first need to determine at each step which of the three choices visitors have made (continue, visit other site content, or exit the site). You also want to know why they've made that choice.

There are several ways to find out why people are abandoning your funnel. One of the best approaches is to look at where they go next. If they head to other parts of your site, perhaps you're cross-selling too much in the wrong place. If they head back to the original product page or to a competitor's site, they may be questioning their decision and seeking more information.

Another important behavior to look at involves visitors who leave the funnel and then return. What content did they look at in the interim? If you can find out what additional information they're seeking, you can provide it to them in your funnel to keep them there.

Fine-Tuning for Your Audience

Every conversion funnel is different, and visitor behavior within each process is different. But by approaching conversion funnels in the manner we've described, you can identify how to improve your overall conversion rate as well as microconversion or step-conversion rates.

This section has outlined ways to start analyzing your checkout process; you can look at many more things once you get the basics down. Some of these include understanding behaviors based on different product lines, campaigns, or audience segments. By exploring different behaviors based on new versus returning visitors, repeat buyers, traffic from different campaign sources, or weekday versus weekend visitors, you can further fine-tune your site and significantly increase conversion.

Analyzing Lead Processes to Find Opportunities

In many ways, conversion processes on lead-generation sites function similarly to e-commerce sales funnels. To analyze one, you can use many of the same principles outlined in the previous section. What decisions are your users making on product pages? At request forms? What is causing them to abandon the process?

However, there is one substantial difference with e-commerce sites: lead-generation sites often have more than one way that they drive users to make contact with a sales representative. These can include the following:

- Request-more-information forms
- Webcast/webinar sign-ups
- White-paper downloads
- Account opening
- Quote requests
- Contact Us buttons (the worst call to action ever)

Each of these calls to action performs individually and elicits different responses and conversion rates. Depending on what people respond to, the lead types have different values as well. For example, perhaps only 2 percent of leads that come through a "request more information" result in sales in a six-month period, whereas 22 percent of leads that originate from downloading a white paper close during that same period. Understanding how each call to action performs is critical in determining which contact method you want to push. At the same time, you should always leave options that speak to different customers in different phases of the consideration and decision-making process.

The first step in analyzing lead conversion should be to learn which offers drive the most value. From there, you can test out wordings and calls to action. Typically, calls to action work in different ways depending on where they are on the site. For example, certain wording and creative concepts may perform well on the home page but poorly on a deeper product page. You should fully understand which calls to action to which method of contact perform the best on all different levels of your site. Although this may sound like a lot of work, leveraging basic testing solutions can make it fairly easy and will almost surely increase your lead-conversion rates.

Understanding What Onsite Search Is Telling You

Do you have a search engine on your site? If so, do you know how it performs? If you look beyond the basics, such as the number of pages indexed, you can collect a great deal of valuable information that can help measure your site's overall effectiveness.

Search is one of the most important features of a site, and it's often a default behavior (the first thing people do when they arrive). In many cases, visitors don't explore the navigation but go straight to the search box. No matter what percentage of visitors rely on search as a first or second option, maximizing the effectiveness and value of your on-site search should be imperative for any site.

Over the years, we've worked with several on-site search tools, each with different levels of sophistication and reporting capabilities. Along the way, we've come up with some metrics to help you understand the effectiveness of your on-site search tools. The most important are as follows:

Percentage of visitors using search Do people automatically start their visit with search, or do they move through the site and rely on search when they can't find what they want?

Searches per search visit This is a measure of the number of searches a visitor conducts. The ideal is one search per search visit, which means that whenever people search, they find what they want. Unfortunately, most sites record three or more searches per search visit.

Percentage of exits from the search return page One indication of a failed search is visitors who exit the site from the search return page. Ineffective searches can be frustrating if visitors follow several links and still don't find what they want. If visitors find what they want, they link off the results page and continue the visit on the site.

Conversion of search visits to sales It's important to understand how your search users convert on key metrics, such as sales and lead generation, compared to nonsearch users. Depending on the difference, you may want to point more or fewer people to your on-site search. If search visits convert at a higher rate, it may be worth analyzing the content visitors see when coming through search pages. By making it more prominent or easier to find, you may also increase sales.

Average items per order for search visits vs. nonsearch visits As with the basic conversion, you may see a difference in average items per order or average order value.

Percentage of searches with no results What percentage of visitors use on-site search and get no results? What are they looking for? What do they do when they don't get any results on the search return page?

Top 10 searches What do people search for? Understanding the most common search terms can help you determine why visitors come to your site. With this information, you can improve navigation or call-outs so people don't need to rely so heavily on search.

This is another example of how to use web analytics to understand site performance. These metrics aren't necessarily generic or prepackaged reports you'll find in WebTrends, Omniture, HBX, or the other tools, but they can provide valuable data points for understanding performance. Think about the issues you want to solve rather than focusing on standard, prepackaged reports.

Once you understand these behaviors, you can fine-tune your search or site navigation. On-site search behavior is often reviewed only at a high level, but the information that can be gleaned from it can help greatly improve the user experience and, often, boost your key conversion metrics.

Understanding the Terms Visitors Search For

What should you look at when you study searches? People search several different ways, and you may find the following categories useful in determining your visitors' intent:

Aggregate search terms Looking at aggregate search terms can help you understand what people are looking for the most. To do this, take a data sample at least a month in length. Then, create a list of the most common search terms and group them into categories. Look for common patterns or large percentages of people searching for the same thing or the same types of things. That way, you can know what items you might want to call attention to on your site. You can also identify trends, such as what content is the most popular, or what concerns your visitors have.

Search terms by site section or page Once you've viewed search terms for the overall site, you should try to understand the terms by site area. In this type of analysis, you look at the most common search terms based on where people search from (site section or even individual pages). This allows you to understand specific problems or concerns people are having on those specific pages compared to other sections or pages throughout the site.

Segmentation based on visitor type Another way of understanding what visitors are looking for and thinking about is to analyze search terms based on visitor segments. It's an easy task to compare the search terms used by first-time visitors against those used by returning visitors and previous buyers. By understanding the different terms they're searching for, you can better understand what questions they need answered and what their key interests are.

Micro–Case Study: An Apparel Store

We once analyzed search data for a company that sells apparel and related products online. It allowed us to identify a few interesting trends.

The first was that most visitors were searching within specific lines of products by color, not by style. This helped drive a change in the way products were displayed and sorted. It also helped us adjust the colors that came up based on different terms. If a specific product color was officially "pumpkin," for example, we made sure that when someone searched "orange," the pumpkin-colored product returned.

We also found a lot of searches regarding order tracking. Even though it was listed as a key option in the top navigation, people just didn't see it. By enhancing the design treatment of the button, we were able to reduce confusion and the need for people to search.

We're not saying that you'll find the same issues on other apparel sites, but you should look at your search terms and see what you discover.

Evaluating the Effectiveness of Your Home Page

In many cases, your site's home page is the first impression visitors get of your online business. The purpose of the home page is to position the company to site visitors and help them find what they need.

Some companies react by putting a lot of content on their home pages or providing links to everything anyone could ever want. Unfortunately, behavioral and attitudinal data, as well as usability best practices, have proved that within reason, less is more when it comes to giving your visitors choices on the home page.

To help understand home-page effectiveness, consider this simple observation: When people can't find what they're looking for on a page, some percentage of them (can often be high) invariably leave the site. A small percentage of people will continue to dig through the site looking for what they need, but you don't want to count on them needing to explore aimlessly. We need to make it easier on them. You can use this measure to gauge dissatisfaction by looking at something we call the ZAAZ Exit Ratio™. It measures the percentage of site visits that exit from the home page:

ZAAZ Exit Ratio: Site exits from a page / page visits to that page

Do you have any idea what the ZAAZ Exit Ratio is for your site? Would you be surprised to find it at 20 percent (meaning one in five visitors leaves from the home page)? If you haven't looked at it before, consider yourself lucky if it's only 20 percent and not closer to the 30–50 percent range.

It's also important to understand where people are going from the home page and what they're searching for, assuming you have an on-site search. Looking at this information with an attitudinal survey can be helpful in determining what you need to do to improve the performance of your home page and drive more of your site visitors deeper into the content. Remember, if they leave, there's no way you can entice them into desired behaviors and increase their overall satisfaction.

Evaluating the Effectiveness of Branding Content: Branding Metrics

Do you consider branding a key goal for your site? You aren't alone if you're spending money to drive online branding. According to Forrester Research, 66 percent of marketing executives said the Web is an effective or more effective branding medium relative to traditional channels. And according to PointRoll, branding is now the leading online advertising goal. But how do you measure brand online? What are the KPIs to track branding effectiveness? Are they hidden in your web-analytics tools, and you don't know it?

The first step in analyzing branding is to be sure it isn't a convenient excuse for you to avoid defining other site-performance metrics. For most sites, branding is only one part of the site KPIs. Relying on branding can lead you to ignore commerce, lead generation, customer service, and other areas.

Branding metrics are often difficult to identify and measure. But like everything else you do online, you must start by defining your overall business goals and then determine which ones can be influenced by increased branding. This is never easy, and it's an idiosyncratic process for every company. No two companies have the same relationship to their brands, and the drivers can vary greatly.

Even so, over the years, we've developed a list of metrics that can measure a site's effect on overall branding. Some may or may not make sense for your business. And it's important to remember that we're looking at on-site branding drivers, not off-site banners or online advertising:

Direct visitor traffic This is the percentage of traffic that comes directly to the site. This number doesn't include those who come from search, links from other sites, or other campaigns. It isolates the number of people who came directly to your site by typing in the URL or using a bookmark. This is a strong indication that they know exactly who you are.

Perception studies By conducting surveys of visitors' entry to and exit from the site (analyzing different users in each set), you can measure the lift (or lack thereof) in perception. You can also quantify the effect and see if it's different depending on the behaviors of users while on your site.

Depth of exploration This metric looks at how deep into the site your visitors explore. You can quantify this by noting the number of site visitors who view X or more pages on the site. Overall, this is a much more telling measure than the traditional "time spent on site."

Repeat buyers What percentage of buyers return to make purchases online?

Customer-satisfaction studies By using products like ForeSee Results, you can understand how your site is impacting your visitors' overall satisfaction. You can also learn how you compare with others in your industry. In addition, you can understand how different sections or pages of your site affect customer satisfaction, whether positively or negatively.

Branded searches By understanding the number of times branded search terms are searched on the Web and changes in those searches, you can get an idea of your brand strength and how it's changing over time. One note: This measure can easily cause confusion. You aren't looking at the number of times someone searches for a term and comes to your site; you're looking at the total number of times the term is searched on the Web, whether or not the user clicks through and visits your site. Tools are available that can provide this data. We've worked with companies that boast 90 percent of search traffic referred to their site is from branded search terms. Because of this, they believe their "brand is strong." In most cases, this is a result of poor search-engine optimization—people find the site only if they search on the exact branded term, and the site is missing people who are looking for similar products or services.

Survey of offline purchasers Another way to evaluate the impact of the website offline is to survey people when they buy offline to determine what percentage interacted with the brand on the Web. Looking at how this number changes over time can help you understand the effect the site is having on the brand.

Referral actions by visitors This metric looks at the performance of "refer a friend" actions on your site. There are two interesting measures here: the number of "refer a friend" actions that your customers initiate, and how often the friend responds.

Offline campaign offers and coupons By setting up special landing pages or offers promoted in the offline space, you can get a better view into how people interact between different media.

Blog buzz This is a new measure. Blogs can have a powerful impact on a brand, both positively and negatively. Blogs can respond quickly to news and experiences and be easily influenced by unhappy customers as well as by competitors. For that matter, companies can plant seeds in blogs for new releases, and so on. Tools are emerging to report on every mention of companies or products in the blogging world. This can be a great measure of buzz.

Notice that we've deliberately excluded things like purchases, registration, lead generation, and e-mail sign-ups, because we often look at the overall impact of those factors outside of branding. Nevertheless, positive experiences with those things can also impact your brand in a positive fashion.

Evaluating the Effectiveness of Campaign Landing Pages

Landing pages are created when you have a specific marketing campaign that drives users to your site. It serves as a transition between an offsite experience and your website. All of the following initiatives can warrant a landing page:

- Online banner ads
- E-mail campaigns
- Links from partner sites
- Offline campaigns
- Search engine marketing (SEM)
- Community-based promotions (for example, a special page for visitors from MySpace or YouTube)

These pages should reflect the experience that visitors had which drove them to click in the first place. In the past (and, unfortunately, sometimes today), companies asked campaigns to drop people off at their home page. This can be a jarring and disorienting experience—something you want to avoid. Analyzing what landing-page message will perform best based on your different audiences can be invaluable in optimizing your campaigns.

Not surprisingly, a good landing page can make or break any campaign. It can take a so-so ad that drives only a small amount of traffic and make the most out of it, or it can turn a traffic-driving dynamo into a flop.

Analyzing landing pages allows you not only to fine-tune the message of your campaign, but also to experiment so that you can determine what converts different visitor types once they arrive.

Let's look at an example. Suppose we have three campaigns running for a new wireless device:

- A campaign targeting myspace.com users, introducing a new feature that allows them to access MySpace from their device

- An online and offline campaign targeting potential business customers, to get them to switch to the new device

- An e-mail campaign targeting current business customers who have other devices, encouraging them to upgrade to the new device

It's easy to see that these audiences have different needs. We hope the three campaigns aren't dropping everyone off on the home page of the device-maker's site. It would better to drop them off at the device product page. That's more relevant than the home page, but it still doesn't account for the differences between these three groups. Instead, we can dig deeper into the three campaigns and understand what works well for each audience. By analyzing how each landing page performs based on the marketing campaign, we can begin to tune it to make it more effective for each campaign.

You should analyze what the audiences from different marketing campaigns respond to. You may find that they're interested in different information and have different triggers that drive to conversion.

Once you understand this, you can create different versions of the landing page that speak directly to what matters to them. In the MySpace case, the features we'd promote and the tone of the promotion would differ significantly from the features and messaging needed to entice the new business customer.

Another common example that many companies are having success with is related to search-engine marketing (or pay-per-click terms). If you use the term that people initially searched for heavily on the landing page, the conversion generally increases significantly.

If you step back, it all makes sense. It's typically well worth the reward to put together a landing-page strategy rather than dropping everyone into a generic landing page or on the home page. Experiment, and see what such an approach can do for you.

We'll dig into other forms of segmentation next.

Segmenting Traffic to Identify Behavioral Differences

Knowing what your audience is doing on your website is good. Knowing a thing or two about your visitors so that you can classify them into segments is much better. And reaching different segments with specialized messaging is best of all.

Getting to that last step requires audience segmentation analysis. In simple terms, it optimizes site performance by customizing the experience for different parts of your audience. To do this, you needn't go to one-to-one extremes like Amazon.com. A little segmentation goes a long way.

What exactly are we talking about? When traditional advertisers talk about segmentation, they're usually thinking in terms of age or demographics. They want to market Cheerios to children and heart medication to people in their fifties. On the Web, you're not always going to do that.

What segments can you go after? It's easy to understand that you may want to provide different information to someone who has purchased from your site six times over the past year and visits the site weekly, as opposed to a first-time visitor. If you offer only one version of the page, typically you'll end up under-serving both groups. Let's take this example much further and look at other segments and understand what is important to them.

Segmenting Your Audience

Analyzing and understanding how certain aspects of your site are performing should be viewed as a requirement by now. And looking at that information in an aggregate view is a great starting point. You should understand how the site is performing for different segments and, again, always be thinking of ways you can improve the site for all your audience segments. You can create some easy segments using current web technology. Some of the more useful ones (and there are many more) include the following:

- First-time visitors
- Repeat visitors, or people who pass a certain visit-count threshold
- Returning customers
- Registered visitors
- Visitors from certain marketing campaigns

- Repeat buyers
- Visitors who reach you directly from partner sites
- Visitors who responded to a particular call to action or promotion on your site
- Visitors who exhibited certain behavior in a previous site (such as adding a product to the shopping cart or looking at a specific product line)

When you're defining user segments, you should always keep an eye on site business goals (and overall enterprise goals). If your visitors aren't proactively segmenting themselves (by registering or other means), you should use cookies or landing pages to track who's who. You may find that some segments favor certain types of content and ignore others; or some calls to action work well for some groups but poorly with others. It's important to realize that a particular segment's behavior can differ greatly from the behavior of the majority of people on your site.

As with any analytics process, your next step is to define desired behaviors for each audience segment. Segments typically bring slightly different agendas to the website. Most likely, you'll want them to do different things, too.

Finally, customize content on a per-segment basis. A simple way of doing this is to designate a *hot box* on each page—a dynamic zone where content is determined by each visitor's segment identity.

Case Study: Segmenting for a Financial Services Provider

Segmentation is a less daunting task than you may think. A while ago, we implemented a basic segmentation strategy for a big financial services provider. We started out small (remember that tip?) by defining three basic segments: noncustomers and infrequent visitors, customers who'd registered for online banking; and customers (or regular visitors) who hadn't registered for online banking.

For online banking organizations, sign-ups are a big priority; but you don't want to badger the converted with sign-up propositions. As a result, we set up a hot box on prominent pages and used it to promote three different calls to action. Depending on the user segment a person was in, they saw a different promotion:

- Noncustomers were invited to sign up for a new account.
- Online bankers were cross-sold additional financial services.
- Customers without online banking were encouraged to sign up.

The payoff was that conversion rates went up in all three segments.

Obviously, you can take segmentation and personalized messaging to extremes. But even modest initiatives work; you don't have to be Amazon to impress visitors and score business gains. When you see different audience segments using your website in different ways, the benefits of treating people differently quickly become apparent.

Analyzing Drivers to Offline Conversion

Unless you're an e-tailer, your site won't let you close a deal or complete a sale online. Even if you rely on partners and resellers to complete transactions, you should track the value your site adds to the bottom line. In such cases, it's imperative to understand handoffs and measure their success.

Tracking Online Partner Handoffs and Brick-And-Mortar Referrals

We work with a fairly large consumer brand that features many different products on its site. When visitors want to buy, they're given two options: find a brick-and-mortar store, or buy through an online reseller partner.

For this group, we like to track the following metrics:

- Percentage of visitors exploring product-detail pages
- Number of product-detail pages the average visitor views
- Percentage of product-detail page visits that result in a store locator search or a handoff to an online reseller partner
- The likelihood of purchasing, which is measured through surveys conducted upon entry to the site for some people and exits from the site for others

Although tracking these metrics is important, you won't get the full picture unless you track improvement all the way to the final transaction. For example, if a company drives three times more traffic to its reseller sites, but the conversion rates there drop by 75 percent, traffic drivers alone will inaccurately reflect a successful handoff. What are they not seeing? What can we (or our partners) do to increase the conversion rates?

The client we were discussing earlier works with their largest online resellers to track conversions from referral to final sale. As the company makes changes to their site, they continually look at the effect of those changes on the number of referrals to the partner sites, the percentage that close, the number of items sold, and the average order value. This way, they can assign a more definitive value to the effect of site changes.

Tracking Offline Handoffs to Sales Reps

Working with online partners may seem straightforward, but closing the loop with offline resellers can be more complex. We've helped various companies solve this problem, including a large community development firm with multiple locations throughout the country.

This company sells homes and condos ranging from $150,000 to over $10 million. Their website is a great tool to educate interested parties about different communities and offerings, but it isn't the appropriate channel to complete a home-purchase transaction. The primary call to action for site visitors is to request more information about a community or to arrange a time to visit one.

The form people use to request more information has a box for them to explain which campaign drove them to the site. This information is fed into the client's sales-tracking system, where it becomes the main record for the lead throughout the sales process. The client can then track the percentage of site leads that convert to sales. They compare this to their other lead sources to evaluate conversion rates, average value of the closed sale, and time to close.

Even if your site's elements don't at first appear readily measurable, it's worth the trouble to find a way. And make sure that changes you make don't affect just a partial conversion, but the ultimate conversion—the one that drives the bottom line.

Tracking Visitors to a Call Center

As we've mentioned in previous chapters, you can put unique toll-free numbers on your site to track calls to a call center. By analyzing these calls, you can often make significant improvements to your site.

An example will help explain what we mean. Last year, we added unique numbers to a client's site and segmented them according the location where they were found. The support section had its own unique number; a section of the site that featured high-end, expensive products had a different one; and there was yet another number for users who had progressed to the shopping cart.

First, the company was surprised to find how many calls originated from its website. But more important, we were able to use the information to make improvements. By looking at the content of the calls from the support section, the company began to understand what questions weren't being answered sufficiently online. Using this information, they changed the content and FAQs on the main support page and were able to address more of the issues online.

They found that people who called in from the site had a higher close rate; those people also closed in less time (saving call-center costs) and for a higher dollar value. At first blush, you might think the company should have moved as many of those calls as possible to the online channel, but that turned out not to be the case. They learned that the additional revenue generated through upselling at the call center made up for nearly all the additional call-center costs.

In the case of the site section with high-end, more expensive products, customers needed more hand holding and much greater product expertise. By ensuring that those calls got to the most experienced people in the call center, the company was able to significantly increase revenue.

The key to all these improvements is to understand the online and offline interaction between the web and call-center channels. Remember that you must consider the impact of the web channel on other channels. The Web can't be seen as a siloed enterprise: Visitors don't think of your company that way, and they don't make decisions based on your website without considering other factors.

Delayed Conversion

Many businesses have conversions that start online but ultimately occur offline at a later date. We refer to this as a *delayed conversion*, and it's a significant area of focus for many organizations. More than likely, your site includes some form of delayed conversion, although you may not think of it that way.

For example, financial service websites are filled with delayed conversions. Think of the last time you or a friend got a mortgage. You may have visited sites, talked to a few people, and checked out rates. Before house hunting, you may have been prequalified or preapproved online. From a web-analytics standpoint, this appeared to be a successful conversion through the application process, but the company hadn't yet made money on the transaction.

Let's assume you continued to the next step of finding a home. It may have taken another 60 days to find a house and have an offer accepted. At this point, the bank still hadn't made a cent on the preapproval conversion that occurred on its website. The sellers then scheduled to close on the house in 45 days. During the process, perhaps you found financing through another lender.

The key is the bank doesn't start making money until the sale closes. In this case, 105 days passed between approval on the website and the time when the bank knew it would make money on the application. That's why it's important to track the conversion all the way from online initiation to offline close.

There are many other examples in the web world, including two that we've discussed before: real estate development and lead-generation sites. Delayed conversions can create challenges when you're optimizing sites through testing. You may test a new call to action or offer to get someone to complete the online portion of the conversion. In these examples, that would involve filling out a request for more information or submitting an application. But that online conversion to a lead may or may not continue to the much more important delayed conversion.

You may find that you can greatly increase online conversions by offering an incentive. According to your analytics data, this may look like a success. But when you examine the moneymaking conversion—the delayed conversion—you may find that the numbers are down or that they convert on sales with lower dollar values.

To evaluate the true value of your site-optimization work, you must follow analysis through to the delayed conversion.

Tracking Delayed Conversion

In the previous cases, understanding the initial conversion is important, but understanding the delayed conversion is often more valuable. If you can't measure all the way through to the delayed conversion, it will be difficult to understand the web channel's value and how effectively your site helps you reach your business goals.

Tracking delayed conversions can be tricky and cause difficulties in reporting and sharing data in a timely manner. But there are several ways to do it, depending on the tools you use and the type of delayed conversions you want to measure. Here are a few examples:

Origination/promo codes You can assign a code to the initial conversions or leads that come through the site. Then, you can track how many of those close over a specific period of time. For smaller sites, this can be a manual process, although it can quickly become unmanageable as the number of leads grows.

CRM systems If you're using a Customer Relationship Management (CRM) tool, you can flag the opportunity as originating from the site and credit it back when the sale closes. Many analytics tools are beginning to work with systems such as salesforce.com. They allow you to run reports that show conversion of opportunities, dollar value, and other metrics.

Once you can track the delayed conversions from the site, you can compare the quality of these leads or opportunities to ones you generate through a call center or other means. You may find that the leads from the site close at a higher or lower rate than other opportunities. Often, we see not only different close rates but also time-to-close differences. By understanding how your site leads differ from other means, you can tune your overall strategy to generate opportunities.

Reporting in a Timely Manner

Delayed conversions can take months, and you won't want to hold up January's reporting until June or July to learn the full story. One way to get around this is to set a baseline for what percentage of these leads (or initial conversions) typically close during a given period. You can use that as an estimate on a scorecard or report. This approach lets you provide reporting with a reasonable turnaround, and you can update the report as time passes and more conversions are in place. Over time, estimates can be tuned and tightened up to reflect changing conversion patterns.

When you want to improve site performance through optimization efforts such as A/B or multivariate testing, measure both the initial conversion and the impact on your delayed conversion rates. This way, you can ensure that you're driving not just more opportunities but more high-quality opportunities that ultimately convert into sales.

Recap

In this chapter, we've looked at how you can analyze data to make better decisions. We began by drawing a careful distinction between reporting and analysis. Web reporting is the collection and presentation of data—and it can give you an interesting overall perspective on how your website has been doing recently. Analysis, on the other hand, is the process by which you sift through that data and identify opportunities for improving your website.

Because the practice of analysis is easier to understand through examples, we walked through five scenarios and how to resolve them through the use of analytics. We started with a purchase funnel and looked at the different ways people buy online. As part of that discussion, you learned about commitment and how companies need to make sure customer interest stays firm throughout the buying process.

From there, we took up lead generation. Although it's similar in many ways to purchasing funnels, it differs in that users have varying ways to convert. We also examined how search processes can inform you about your business. And we looked at home pages, branded content, and how to evaluate the success (or failure) of campaign landing pages.

Finally, we discussed segmentation analysis and the principle of delayed conversion. The first of these shows how you can increase ROI by giving different users different experiences; the latter looks at your website in terms of the entire ecosystem of your business. You saw that you should not only track what users do on your own site, but also create ways to follow their behavior when they move to other sites or into offline purchasing channels.

Analysis is a crucial process for getting actionable intelligence on your site. If you simply report, and fail to analyze, you'll never see the returns you're seeking.

Prioritizing

If one chapter in this book may have immediate impact on your business, it's this one. By following the tenets of Dynamic Prioritization™, your organization will spend more wisely and keep focused on the initiatives with the greatest upside for your business. This is a chapter you'll refer to again and again.

How We Prioritize

If you talk to any web group in any Fortune 1000 company today and ask them what initiatives and projects they hope to tackle in the next two years, you'd better get comfortable; it's going to be a long list. They'll probably mention everything from adding new products or services to their site and improving campaign strategy and traffic drivers, to a comprehensive redesign scheduled to launch in about 12 months. There will also be many technologies they're considering leveraging, such as blogs, better on-site search, attitudinal surveys, personalization initiatives, improved content-management systems, and enhanced analytics tracking. And that's all in addition to the general maintenance and updates that keep most groups busy on a daily basis.

Any organization facing this overwhelming number of initiations must somehow prioritize them. But how? In most companies today, a web project's priority depends on two things:

- The time at which it entered the project queue (first in first out)
- The seniority of the person who requested it

This approach is human, but it's hardly scientific. Priority projects are accepted or rejected on purely subjective grounds. Not surprisingly, the ranking of initiatives is a key failure point in many web organizations. Projects with limited impact on the business are addressed, whereas other projects that could have a much more significant effect are delayed or rejected.

To get around this issue, we'll introduce a concept called *Dynamic Prioritization*. It can help your company focus on the correct initiatives by providing a framework for making decisions and the flexibility to ensure that you're concentrating on the right things.

The Principles of Dynamic Prioritization

We first used Dynamic Prioritization several years ago. We were working with a client when the following situation arose. During our monetization exercise, we found that the revenue impact of a specific opportunity was nearly $2 million for the following three months. If we delayed six months, it would cost the company $4 million in revenue.

We presented this information to the company, but to our surprise, the managers wanted to delay the project. To complete it, they told us, they would need to leverage internal expertise. Unfortunately, no one with the expertise necessary would be available to spend any time on it for the next six months—they were all buried on another project.

And so, we worked with the client to evaluate the other projects the experts were scheduled to work on. We found that many of those projects didn't have a clear tie to overall business goals or the ability to move important metrics. From there, we helped management to re-sort its projects based on their impact on the bottom line. As you can imagine, it wasn't easy to push some things off. But with support from key executives, we were eventually able to redistribute the resources much more effectively.

Of course, we didn't completely reorder them—some projects that didn't have much potential value were left in process. But the prioritization exercise helped refocus the company and allowed them to take advantage of some big opportunities.

We went through this exercise several times more, and it finally changed the way the client's web group evaluated new opportunities for the queue. Instead of putting them all on a list, they began assigning them potential impact values first. Needless to say, the initial $2 million opportunity we identified got the resources it needed.

Over the past two years, we've used the same process to help many companies focus on opportunities that drive success. It's not always easy. Some people in every organization push back, and the change almost never happens overnight. But eventually, nearly everyone can change the way many opportunities are prioritized.

How do you handle the prioritization of opportunities? Can Dynamic Prioritization work for you? Let's look the tactics you can use to focus on the opportunities that drive your business.

Traditional Resource Prioritization

The best way to explain Dynamic Prioritization is to compare it to the traditional way web organizations work. They usually plan their long-term, strategic initiatives by using a *project queue*—a list of projects that are usually done in the order they're received. Whenever a new project comes in, it's placed at the back of the line to wait its turn. Resources, such as designers, developers, information architects, and so on, work continually on this list. A senior manager can intervene in the process and prioritize one initiative over another, but that is often done in a haphazard way.

Some of the features of traditional planning include the following:

- The project queue for potential projects is long, often stretching out 4–6 months.

- The impact a project may have isn't analyzed or compared to other monetized initiatives to see which ones best support overall company goals.

- Site releases are scheduled far in advance and may happen only on a monthly or quarterly basis.

- When new content is added to the site, it includes designs and copy perceived internally as the best option.

- When a new project launches, the company doesn't measure its business impact or identify follow-up opportunities.

- The website contains a single page or solution for all site visitors.

- The success of a completed project is the launch itself. The organization considers it successful if it hits the target timeline and budget constraints.

- After the completion of a project, the team shifts to the next one, which has probably been sitting on the list for a number of months.

Sounds familiar? It should. This is the way most companies (including many Fortune 1000 companies) run their web channels. Many large agencies exacerbate this problem by making plans in a similar way and constructing rigid processes and timelines.

Web Steering Committees

A variation on this theme is provided by web steering committees. These are governing bodies, usually composed of managers and experts in the field, who approve and reject web initiatives. Although they offer a much better method than allowing everyone in an organization to launch projects, they also raise a few key problems:

- Steering committees often make decisions based on gut feelings and rarely quantify their impact on the business.
- They're often more insistent that web groups tackle projects using a queue system.
- They slow the entire process.

It's sometimes useful to have experts help out with the process, but there is an even better way of doing things.

Dynamic Prioritization

Considering how popular they are, the methodologies we just described ought to be effective. In fairness, they're not a bad approach. Publications such as newspapers and magazines have traditionally worked this way. But the Web offers opportunities that good businesses can't afford to ignore. Because you can measure the performance of your sites so precisely and change them so easily, you can say goodbye to the traditional way of planning projects.

Whereas traditional companies make plans according to arbitrary notions of time and resources, Dynamic Prioritization allows organizations to schedule projects according to what will help their business the most. The following sections examine some features of this approach.

Prioritization Based on Business Impact

With Dynamic Prioritization, organizations assess the impact of all initiatives based on monetization models. It doesn't matter whether the initiative involves branding revenue generation, lead generation, cost savings, or a simple enhancement in site efficiency. All these things can be assigned a dollar value and prioritized according to their potential impact.

This may sound easier than it is. Within your organization, you'll encounter significant resistance when you try to delay initiatives. Although the marketing manager for a top priority may be happy, there are always people whose careers are tied to projects whose priorities are low. Strict prioritization may turn out to be so disruptive that you won't be able to implement it without mass resignations.

Take it slow. Start by conducting monetization exercises and using them to inform your priorities. Make sure you focus on initiatives that will have the highest impact, and try to deemphasize those that merely cost money. Above all, don't try to implement a draconian ranking process for every project at once. As time goes on, these exercises may change the way your organization evaluates potential projects. Your team may begin looking at assigning potential impact values to all items before they decide to put them on the schedule. In the meantime, be patient. Any prioritization you do will have a positive effect, so even small changes in your project queue can be considered big wins.

Optimized Resource Planning

Along with prioritizing projects, you need to organize your resources to cope with them. Organizations using Dynamic Prioritization typically have staffs whose workload isn't dictated by a long-term project schedule. They can flexibly leave projects and form teams to take advantage of new opportunities or optimize existing initiatives as needed.

You should build flexibility in your team. In traditional workflows, designers, developers, and information architects have their time booked long in advance. When they adopt Dynamic Prioritization, organizations typically set aside some of these peoples' schedules so they're always available to jump on opportunities when they arise.

Accelerating the Release Cycle

Does your business work on a quarterly or monthly basis? Outside of financial reporting, companies should be able to move and react flexibly. If you're truly a data-driven organization, you shouldn't have to hold yourself to arbitrary release cycles. Instead, your site releases should be small but common. You should continually be looking for opportunities using analysis and be prepared to make releases weekly, if not more often.

How do you know when to schedule a new release? Under Dynamic Prioritization, whenever you launch a page or other initiative, you should test a number of options using A/B and multivariate testing. These tests should allow you to quickly identify opportunities and optimize your site to get the best results.

Holding Initiatives Financially Accountable

Whenever you launch an initiative, you should have already put together a forecast of its potential impact on the business and the bottom line. When these projects are complete, you also want to know how the outcome of the project compares to your earlier estimates. For this, you need to include full post-launch analysis in your process. You should not only focus on the outcome, but also use the opportunity to look at the forecasting process itself. Are you making accurate predictions? Does something need to change?

At the same time, the exercise will help you identify potential places for improvement. Depending on the value and effort required, you may want to optimize the initiative or perhaps feed it back into a queue where it's ranked on its potential value.

Dynamic Prioritization Scorecard

Are you prioritizing your projects dynamically? You may want to review the following list and see where you stack up:

- Do you prioritize projects and allocate resources based on their potential to have an impact on the business?

- Do you asses impact to the overall business for all opportunities based on monetization exercises that are used to calculate the expected impact of the change?

- Do you refresh your site often? Releases should occur weekly instead of monthly or quarterly.

- Do you try out a number of options using A/B and multivariate tests?

- Do you use insight from behavioral analysis, attitudinal studies, and competitive intelligence to determine the best possible options and hypotheses to test?

- Do you do a post-launch analysis for all initiatives to determine their impact to the business compared to the original forecast?

- Do you identify segmentation opportunities to determine the best possible solution for different audience segments?

- Do you document and share best practices to help inform future efforts and initiatives?

Dynamic Prioritization is a framework for making smarter business decisions. It helps overcome the political agendas in large organizations and holds people accountable for forecasts and results. The action of having people put targets on the table and understand what metrics they're striving to move can change the way your organization approaches and leads projects.

Dynamic Prioritization in Action

Interested in knowing how this works in practice? In the following sections, you'll learn about three common opportunities for improvement and ideas on how to prioritize their value.

Lead Generation

If you have a lead-generation site, you should consider improving your calls to action, and then assess how much you think you can affect them. If the lead generation's conversion rate is 20 percent, can you drive it to 22, 25, or 50 percent?

If you can, ask questions such as:

- How will increasing the conversion rate affect the number and quality of leads?

- Will we generate more leads of significantly lower quality, or can we keep the lead quality good while increasing the number of leads?

- What's the lead's value?

Once you determine a lead's value and the results you believe you can gain with optimization, you can calculate the upside of the proposed changes. At the same time, you should calculate how quickly the improved site can pay for the optimization.

Online Commerce

The same principles apply to online commerce. To start moving to Dynamic Prioritization, you should assess the outcome of improving the conversion rate of a single step in the purchase path and tie it to your overall conversion rate and bottom line.

In doing this, remember to look at both revenue and profit. You probably don't want to spend $50,000 optimizing something to increase sales by $200,000 for the year if your profit margin is only 10 percent. And remember, these kinds of calculations can be tricky. In some cases, the initial improvement may not make sense, but you may find a different story if you take into account the lifetime value of new customers.

Again, consider how you can affect the bottom line by tuning the purchase path. Don't focus on one specific number; look at a range you think you can achieve.

If these changes pay off, and there is still upside potential for improvement, you may go through three, four, or more rounds of optimization to continue driving that metric higher. As long as the return outweighs the costs (money, resources, and opportunity cost), it makes sense to keep tuning.

Customer Service

Although customer service isn't the same as lead generation and e-commerce, you can use Dynamic Prioritization to compare the potential for changes with the other options you have for improving a site.

For example, you can see if it's possible to improve customer service on the site to reduce the number of inbound calls and e-mail messages. If you can deflect 1 percent of all call-center calls per month, you may save hundreds of thousands of dollars or more each month. Evaluate the cost of servicing someone on the Web versus through the call center. Look at ways to swing the numbers more to the Web, and see the results that even a small percentage can return.

Forecasting Potential Impact

Part of prioritizing opportunities is forecasting how much you can improve a certain metric. We're often asked, "How can I determine potential lift so I can prioritize opportunities based on the greatest impact to my business?"

Before you can forecast the lift, however, you must assign a value to the desired site behavior. Several examples we've used before include the following:

- The value of a lead for a lead-generation site
- The value of an additional sale on a commerce site (you may want to look at this from a profit standpoint, not just a revenue standpoint)

- The value of deflecting calls from the call center
- The value of visitors locating a retail location
- The value of a newsletter sign-up or other registration
- The value of a page view, mainly for sites that primarily generate ad revenue

There are plenty of other behaviors you may want to affect. Once you've identified the desired behaviors and assigned a value to each, you can forecast the potential impact of a change. Unfortunately, there's no specific equation to determine how much you can realistically lift a specific KPI. But there is a general method for doing so.

The first step is to learn everything you can about the desired behavior you're trying to affect. You can break this research into three categories:

Behavioral Through web analytics, you can understand where people are going, where they came from, where they drop out, and what might help them convert.

Attitudinal Through surveys, attitudinal studies, or usability groups, you can begin to understand the underlying reasons behind the behaviors you see.

Competitive Using competitive data from the likes of comScore, Hitwise, and Nielsen//NetRatings, you can see how your conversion or flow compares to that of similar sites.

When you look at this data, it's also helpful to look at visitor segments. You may find that what works for some users won't work for others; and you don't want to change something that's already working well for one group. By using these three types of data, you should begin to understand the problem behind the behavior you're trying to improve.

For example, suppose your site focuses on generating leads and currently has a visit-to-lead conversion rate of 3 percent. You research the problem and find a few potential issues. No matter how great you may think the potential is, you shouldn't forecast the impact of changes for something as large as 5 percent. Instead, select a range based on what you see in the research, and then tune that over time as you run tests. You may put together a range, such as 3.25 percent to 3.75 percent in 0.1 percent increments, to understand the value. Again, you can tune this over time, but from a prioritization standpoint, you want to be conservative and look at a range you think you can realistically hit through one or two tests.

As you do more forecasts, you'll get better at determining the potential lift, and you'll be able to tighten your range of estimates. The key is to start prioritizing opportunities based on monetized values and quickly move into testing different ideas through either A/B or more advanced multivariate tests using tools like Offermatica. Make predictions based on what you think you can realize from the different opportunities, and be prepared to be wrong. You'll nail some forecasts and miss others, and that's OK. Remember, you're creating forecasts to help prioritize your opportunities based on the greatest impact, as well as to help your organization realize the potential in opportunities.

Comparing Opportunities

Now that you've monetized all your initiatives based on their potential impact to the business, it's time to start comparing them against one another. This isn't entirely the same thing as looking at the monetization charts you saw in Chapter 7. There, you were forecasting the possible impact a change might have on a business. For example, you might find that improving a certain process has the potential to add X dollars in revenue. But to prioritize that against other projects, you have to look at a number of other factors as well:

Cost of the initiative (internal and external costs) What will you need to invest to take advantage of the opportunity?

Likelihood of attaining the target range Do the forecasted changes seem reasonable? How confident are you that you can hit the range?

Profit potential of opportunity Revenue and profit are separate things. Two opportunities that have the same impact on revenue rarely offer the same potential profit.

Potential offline impact Will the change to your site impact your offline revenue positively, negatively, or not at all?

Timeline How long will an initiative take to address? Some initiatives may have a great potential impact, but if their rollout takes too long, you may want to consider quicker initiatives that will start paying off immediately.

Payback period How quickly will the investment pay for itself? Is there a chance that it will cease to be as valuable in a few years and thus not pay for itself?

Total impact on site experience What effect will these changes have on your overall site visitor, customer, and prospect satisfaction? Will the opportunity significantly impact your overall brand? This consideration can be overused, but you should think about it.

Depending on your business, target audience, and industry, you may look at other ways to help prioritize opportunities. The key is to build a framework for prioritization that will help remove most of the subjectivity, and then use that to make your decisions.

Above all, remain flexible. You may have five opportunities one month, the best of which is A. The next month, you may be comparing opportunities and find that you made such significant progress on A that it no longer has the same potential for impact. Instead, you may want to consider focusing on another project.

Moving Your Company Toward Dynamic Prioritization

Like many of the changes we've discussed, getting your organization to adopt Dynamic Prioritization is much easier said than done. This process will involve a significant change in the way you work and will mean saying goodbye to the egos, pet projects, and in-house politics that are endemic to the way many organizations prioritize web projects.

Because it's such a new thing, where do you begin? For starters, make sure you don't set expectations too high. Forecasting isn't an exact science. It relies on an assessment of behavioral, attitudinal, and other data—as well as a healthy amount of intelligent guesswork. You don't want to lead off by giving predictions that may turn out to be false. Someone in your organization will certainly point out the shortfall.

In addition, you should start small. If you've already begun to define the value of different site behaviors and leverage some of the monetization models, you can look back at past initiatives and try to determine what impact they had on the business. Did your latest major redesign change behaviors and help improve the business, or was it an expensive exercise with no real benefit?

From there, try to generate executive support for the initiative. If you're an executive, this is, needless to say, much easier. Otherwise, you'll have some convincing to do. Showing past success is a good way to do this. And even if you do have the good fortune to be at a high enough level to drive the change, you should still show results to get buy-in from the rest of the organization. After all, you'll be asking them to fundamentally change the way they perform their day-to-day roles. You'll run into problems, people will get frustrated, and they won't understand why they have to do their jobs differently (perhaps they've been working the same way for years, and "site traffic keeps going up").

Once you've obtained executive support, try to get a few wins with the process. In doing this, you should look to delay pet projects that won't affect the business and concentrate on well-thought-out and well-researched initiatives that will have a significant impact.

Overcoming Common Excuses

In trying to implement this process, you'll hear many excuses why this process won't work in your organization. Some of them are legitimate. Usually, however, people are resistant to change and scared of something new, especially when they don't understand a new approach.

Some of the common excuses you should be prepared to hear are as follows:

Our site isn't set up for incremental change You'll often hear that because of the way your site is coded, you can't conduct testing of different content or concepts. Nine times out of 10 this isn't the case, but if you're that 1 in 10, you need to start working with your executive sponsor to implement changes that will allow your site to conduct ongoing testing. The upside potential is too great to ignore.

We only roll out changes to the site every two months, with a two-month lead time for testing This will need to change. Six updates a year aren't enough to take advantage of opportunities to drive your business. Executive support will be required to change the current process.

We have to lock down projects at the beginning of every quarter so we can line up the needed resources This is another situation that needs to change. You'll always have some initiatives that span a long period of time. To start doing projects more quickly, you may want to create a SWAT team or have your agency allocate a group of people who can help address these opportunities. We'll go into this in greater detail in Chapter 11.

We have to lock in budgets and all projects by mid-October for the next calendar year This is possibly the scariest excuse of all. How can you possibly take advantage of the best opportunities if you plan all your projects 12+ months ahead of time? The simple answer is that you can't. To change this situation, you'll need support from others in the organization. You may start to create a "project" with an assigned budget that is tied to Dynamic Prioritization and commit to reporting back on detailed progress on a quarterly basis. At first, this will be a big change, but you'll find that the people holding the purse strings prefer to know their money is being spent wisely. They also love to see results.

Jim has spent three months getting ready to do this project; it's too late to stop That may be the case if it's launching next week. But if someone has been planning for three months and the project will take six months more, it's better to pull the plug now and focus on something more valuable.

What was wrong with the old way we did it? This is often asked out of frustration, when someone is trying to push through a project that doesn't stand up and have a solid business case. These comments too will pass.

Conclusion

You'll hear many more issues as you evolve your organization. But eventually, you'll start to hear comments like these:

- "How did we ever get anything worthwhile done before we started this process?"
- "That project returned the highest ROI of any project this year."
- "Before we go much further on this idea, let's determine the impact it will have on the business."
- "This is a huge opportunity that will impact the bottom line. Let's monetize it and forecast the value and see if we can get it in the queue for the week after next."

It will be a while before the transition is complete; some people will embrace the concept faster, and others will lag behind. But remember, you're changing the way your entire organization views the web channel. It takes time.

Recap

In this chapter, we've looked at how companies can transform their decision-making processes through a concept called Dynamic Prioritization. Traditionally, web organizations have relied on a structure that features regularly scheduled updates and a project queue that doesn't use monetization models to determine the value of initiatives. With Dynamic Prioritization, all projects are assessed according to their possible impact on the bottom line of a business. These assessments provide the basis for deciding which opportunities the company should pursue and which ones it should push off to another date.

From there, we discussed how you can forecast opportunities and then compare them to one another to come up with a prioritized list of initiatives. Dynamic Prioritization is a new process, and doing this will probably ruffle a few feathers. That's why we recommend starting small and making sure there is plenty of executive support for what you do. The only way you'll make Dynamic Prioritization a success is if you get everyone on board.

Moving from Analysis to Site Optimization

11

By this point, you've gone through the difficulty of setting up your analytics tool and collecting and analyzing data. You've managed to identify some opportunities, and you've prioritized them according to their potential impact on your company's bottom line.

Testing and site optimization are where the rubber meets the road in web analytics. Throughout this chapter, we'll describe the different ways you can act on data to improve your site performance. We'll also explain how to create an effective test, how to evaluate the results, and how to build the right team.

Chapter Contents

Testing Methodologies and Tools

Above all, optimization is the process by which you refine your website to drive performance. As a result, the process requires participation from your entire online organization, including creative design, copy writing, development, information architecture, analytics, and every other element on your pages.

A/B Testing

A/B tests are not only easy to understand, they're also effective and relatively uncomplicated. In such a test, you put up two versions of a page and test them against one another to see which performs better against a set of predetermined metrics. One of the versions is typically called the *test* version, and the other is the *control*.

Ideally, the test and control versions have only one element changed. Let's say you run a site that sells widgets, and you have a call to action on a page that reads, "We have the best widgets in the world; check it out." You may want to find out what happens to your visitors if you change that headline to "Nobody beats our widgets…ever. Check them out!" And so, you create the two options and divide traffic between them to see how click-through rates are affected.

This method of testing has one big drawback: It can be time consuming. Even so, it delivers results with a high level of statistical certainty.

A/B/n Testing

A/B/n testing is similar to A/B, except that you test three, four, or more versions at the same time. In each version, the same element changes. To flog our widget example a little longer, you can build two additional versions with the headlines "The best-selling widgets in the world" and "Can't nobody beat these widgets." Let the best one win.

A/B/n testing delivers the same statistical certainty of an A/B test, but it allows you to explore more options. The methodology's drawback is that it can also consume a lot of time.

Multivariate Tests

Multivariate tests allow you to look at a number of site or page elements at the same time. Why would you want to do this? Let's say you want to assess the effectiveness of three elements on a page—the headline, the main image, and the body copy—and how they work together. Ideally, you want to see how each different combination performs. If you have two versions of each element, for example, you have eight variations (two headlines × two images × two types of body copy = eight possibilities). An A/B test would take a long time to test all the combinations. If you added a third version for each element, you would have 27 variations; A/B testing at this scale would be impractical. With multivariate tests, you can test all elements simultaneously, albeit with much smaller sample sizes per variation.

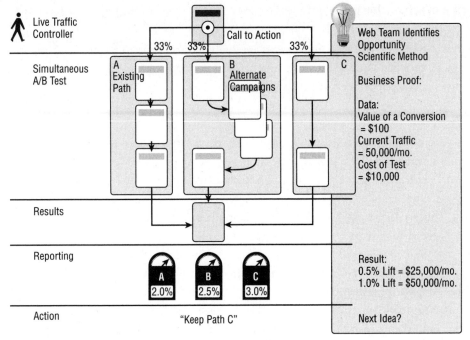

Live Traffic Controller

Call to Action

33% 33% 33%

Simultaneous A/B Test

A
Existing Path

B
Alternate Campaigns

C

Results

Reporting

A
2.0%

B
2.5%

C
3.0%

Action

"Keep Path C"

Web Team Identifies Opportunity
Scientific Method

Business Proof:

Data:
Value of a Conversion
= $100
Current Traffic
= 50,000/mo.
Cost of Test
= $10,000

Result:
0.5% Lift = $25,000/mo.
1.0% Lift = $50,000/mo.

Next Idea?

Figure 11.1 A typical A/B/n test

You may be asking yourself whether you have to put together 27 different versions of a page to do multivariate testing, and the answer is no. There are testing tools that automatically produce the scenarios and serve them all out equally to site visitors. This significantly reduces the amount of time needed to test all possible variations, which can be critical when if you're testing something with a finite lifespan, such as a promotion.

This may seem like a fantastic revolution in site testing, and it is. However, you should be aware of a few things. First, the sample size required to reach statistical certainty can be large. Second, if you run several multivariate tests across the site at one time, you exponentially increase the number of variations and the sample size needed for statistical accuracy. For example, if you have one multivariate test running on a landing page and another on a sign-up page, you can have hundreds of possibilities. As a result, this type of testing can yield uncertain results.

How to Choose a Test Type

Here's a handy list of when to use each type of testing:

A/B testing Use this type of test when you want absolute statistical certainty of a single element with two possible variations.

A/B/n testing Use this when you want to test a single element, but you have a number of versions. Statistical certainly is also important to you.

Multivariate testing Use this approach when you want to test multiple elements on the same page, or when you have a short time span to conduct multiple tests. Statistical certainty isn't as important as an indication of trends.

Testing Tools

When you're conducting tests, you'll most likely be working with a testing tool. The good news is that you have plenty of possibilities. Many of the leading analytics tools also work with existing analytics providers such as Omniture, WebTrends, and Web-SideStory. They include such companies as Kefta, SiteSpect, Verster, Optimost, Offermatica, Touch Clarity, and Google Website Optimizer.

These vendors vary by price, target market, and functionality. Most of them claim that their product works in all possible scenarios, and although there is some truth to this, not every tool is right for every customer. Before you undertake any testing program, we recommend that you look at least three vendors. And fair warning: Some of these tools are expensive and require a considerable commitment. You should examine both their capabilities and your own testing program. Remember that the tool's cost is just one part of the process. You also need to take design, website development, project management, data analysis, and program management into account. If you don't consider all these costs, you may have an expensive tool but no budget left for the tests. We've seen it happen.

What to Test

When it comes to testing, the sky is open. You can theoretically test anything you like on your site. There are academic researchers who use these methods to try to better understand online behavior; obviously, you shouldn't spend your company's money to do that. Your testing should be based on your company goals, site architecture, technical capabilities, and industry.

From a general standpoint: most tests fall into one of six categories:

Pricing Price testing gives you the opportunity to find that ideal point at which you can maximize revenue and profit for a particular item. At a more sophisticated level, price testing can also give you deep insight into price elasticity. It can even help determine at what price substitute products start to play into the consumer mindset. As a result, this kind of testing can be a powerful tool for those who manage e-commerce sites.

Promotion Promotional testing involves looking at the factors that can drive a consumer to accept an offer. For example, you may study whether it's better to give your consumers a percentage off a price or to list the discount in hard currency. You can test whether free shipping is more attractive than a free product upgrade. Such questions are hard to know ahead of time, but they can quickly be established by a test.

Page layout Page layout is a crucial and sometimes counterintuitive part of web design. Studies show that most consumers don't read websites left to right or line by line, as they do traditional printed pages. They can read quite idiosyncratically. With layout tests, you can break down the areas of the page and determine where you should put your most important promotions.

Message Until not long ago, it was conventional wisdom that no one read on the Web. Message testing has proved otherwise. The copy you place on a page can have a significant impact on the effectiveness of a promotion. With message testing, you can determine what headlines and copy resonate best with a customer.

Message testing is particularly powerful on promotional landing pages. Chances are, you've spent a lot of marketing money to drive customers to your site, and you need to make sure they find the content they expect. Too often, landing pages have leakage rates of 30–90 percent, which is ineffective. Landing-page testing can provide some of the greatest bang for the buck in online spending.

New functionality Whenever you plan to roll out new functionality, you should always test it live before a full launch. This can be a complicated process, especially if the new functionality appears sitewide. An example is a sign-in bar on the side of a page, or a shortened checkout process. Luckily, customers typically respond positively to change, as long as it's good for them. However, if you change something and it degrades their experience, you could be facing a disaster. New-functionality testing helps eliminate the guesswork.

Site navigation Site navigation is a challenging area to test. Nowadays, most site navigation is designed by information architects who use techniques like thought mapping and focus groups to determine what should go where. Even so, in many cases, companies end up with a navigation that reflects their organizational structure rather than the needs of their users. For example, a widget company may like to divide its site according to widget model—a situation that is typically incomprehensible to the average widget consumer (who wants widgets displayed by color), although it makes perfect sense to people inside the organization. If you're wondering if you face a similar problem, you may want to consider testing your navigation.

Unfortunately, navigation testing is often complicated and expensive. Because there are so many paths and combinations, you can only look at high-level metrics. Even so, there are simple and effective navigation tests you can conduct. You might look at whether your sign-up process should include one step or six steps. Should you put more content in the purchase path of a product, or not? Such questions can be answered easily and often lead to valuable results.

Prioritizing Tests

Once you understand that just about anything can be tested online, you'll want to know what you should test. The short and obvious answer is that you should test according to your site goals, but that leaves a broad field of possibilities. As you saw earlier, A/B tests are relatively finite and time-consuming, whereas multivariate tests can quickly become so vast that statistical accuracy is degraded. No company has the time or resources to test everything all the time: You have to prioritize your tests.

The first step in doing this is to identify all the possible tests you could do. You can do this in a number of ways. The four most common are as follows:

- Do a deep analytics dive into the current situation on your site. Find out what pages are the stickiest, which ones have the highest leakage, and which ones are visited most often. This should give you a good idea of where your site is working and where it's not.

- Ask the customer. Through focus groups, surveys, and user testing, you can get a good idea of what customers think of your site and where they want to see improvement.

- Do competitive research. See what your competitors are doing and how they rank in industry rankings such as Hitwise, comScore, and Keynote. Try to get an idea of what they're doing better than you and what the best practices in the industry are.

- Ask your managers what they think are the pain points and areas of excellence on the site. What have they seen work, and what have they seen fail? What would they like to see tested?

After you identify all the possible tests, it's time to prioritize. To do this, you should ask yourself a series of questions, including these:

- What is the potential upside of this test? Leveraging the monetization model to compare the potential upside in real dollar terms can be helpful at this stage. (See Chapter 7.)

- What is the ease of technical implementation?

- How easy will it be to measure the results?

- How much human-resource time will it take to execute the test?

From there, you should be able to assess the relative value of each test to your bottom line. Make sure you balance the potential upside of a particular test against its complication, time horizon, and resource requirements.

To get the most out of any testing program, you should also implement and support it systematically. Many site managers typically want to execute one or two tests according to their own opinion of what should be happening on the site. Throughout this book, we've emphasized that you should step back and institute a formalized process for web analytics that tries to avoid the kinds of personal interference so common on the Internet today.

Creating a Successful Test

Once you've identified and prioritized your tests, it's time to create a specific test plan. In this section, we'll detail a real-life example that shows the steps required to conduct a successful test.

A while ago, we presented some analytical findings to a new client that sells consumer-oriented monthly services. The company was using one of the top analytics tools available but had only been looking at high-level visitor information, such as site visits, page views, and page data. They had yet to formulate a complete picture of their overall site performance. We worked with the company to identify key products and analyze the purchase path for these products:

Step 1: Identify opportunities The first step of any testing process is to identify an opportunity. With this client, we isolated which steps in the purchase funnel weren't converting enough visitors to the next step in the process. We flagged those as key opportunities and then prioritized them based on the company's focus and potential consequences of changes.

Step 2: Develop a hypothesis Obviously, to make a test, you need a basis for it. You have to construct hypotheses as to why people are behaving the way they are. In this case, we made two. Our first hypothesis was that the message had to be simplified. The second was that people needed more information about the company's product offerings. These involved two different approaches.

Step 4: Determine the test methodology We needed to decide which of the different methodologies was most likely to give the results we wanted. Because we were focusing on a purchase funnel, where we were trying to influence conversion rates by small amounts, we wanted our tests to be statistically significant. So, we decided to conduct an A/B test on a key page in one of the purchase funnels. Our next steps were to determine the start and end date of the test and to calculate the sample size required to capture meaningful results.

Step 5: Define success metrics Whenever you do a test, you should be sure in advance exactly what metrics you want to influence. The top metric in our case was the conversion rate of visits to the main product page to a successful checkout.

Step 6: Design your options Next, you create the different versions of the page. In our case, we developed five options.

Step 7: Launch your Test & Analyze your results We were ready to conduct the test, gather data, and look at the result. Happily for us, all five options outperformed the existing page. But two designs clearly outperformed the others and improved the conversion rate by approximately 0.5 percentage point. Although that doesn't sound significant, the initial conversion rate was 3–5 percent. That 0.5 percentage change sounds small, but its cumulative revenue total exceeded $1.5 million annually.

Step 8: Reap the benefits It was time to implement the changes and deploy the most effective options. We used the next round of testing to fine-tune the design based on the two best-performing pages.

Understanding Post-Test Analysis

Throughout the testing process, there are three main points for data connection and analysis. First, you should establish a baseline for any change you attempt. In other words, you should know exactly how the page is performing before you tinker with it. Then, when the test has been executed, you should analyze the results. Finally, after you've run a test, determined the outcome, and made the recommended change, you should analyze the site to determine what happened once the changes were put into production. Interestingly, test results often aren't replicated when changes are placed into the live environment (although the direction of the change is almost always the same). For example, if a test shows that the design A performs 10 percent better than the control group, in the fully live environment you'll probably see results that are anywhere from 5 percent to 15 percent better than before.

This may be the result of a number of factors. However, it most often reflects sample-size discrepancies and customers' unfamiliarity with the new environment. If a customer comes to your site every day, a sudden change may initially make it more difficult for them to find a specific page. This will have a negative effect on performance. Once your visitors are used to the site, you may find that results improve.

Optimizing Segment Performance

One way to get the most out of site optimization is to test how different versions of pages perform for different audiences. As we touched on earlier in the segmentation portion of Chapter 10, the idea of the perfect page is a fallacy. Every visitor is different, and one size doesn't fit all. If you can, it's best to create pages for different segments.

The key to optimizing for segments isn't to test your user base as a whole, but to determine how each visitor segment responds to changes. In some cases, you'll test different designs and find that all your users prefer the same one; but in other cases, two similar designs will perform differently for different audiences. The key is to understand your segments and then test them. If there is a significant enough difference in performance, you may decide to create two versions of that page.

Let's see how this works.

Example One: Behavior-Based Testing

One way to segment traffic is to look at the behaviors users have performed on your site. For example, you may have multiple versions of a call to action about an automobile. The primary call to action, which involves requesting a quote for a certain vehicle, appears side by side with promotions for safety, reliability, fuel efficiency, and a few other key features. You may test the wording on the calls to action and find that reliability drives the highest conversion rate: 2.5 percent.

At that point, you may think that reliability should be your main call to action. But if you segment site visitors based on where they've spent the most time, you may find another story. Perhaps people who viewed at least three safety-related feature pages turn out to convert at a level of closer to 4 percent on a call to action that features reliability. You may then look deeper and find that people who viewed at least four fuel-efficiency-related pages convert at only a 1 percent rate on reliability, but at 5 percent on fuel efficiency. It may make sense to segment your calls to action according to what kinds of pages your users have viewed. In this example, if the value of the difference in conversion is significant enough, you may want to produce a dynamic promotion to take advantage of the opportunity.

Example Two: Day-of-the-Week Testing

Many sites see different types of user behavior on different days of the week. On a recent test for a consumer-focused service, for example, we tested copy, text length, and calls to action on a site segmented into Monday-through-Friday users and Saturday-and-Sunday users. We found out that longer, more descriptive copy performed significantly better on the weekends, and shorter, more bulleted copy led to greater conversion rates during the week. Eventually, the company decided to have two different versions of the page we were testing. Every Friday night, the page with the longer, more descriptive copy appeared. Then, on Sunday night, the site reverted to the other version. This didn't mean someone had to go in and work Friday night and Sunday night to throw a switch—the change was easily handled in an automated fashion.

Although understanding the different segments on your site is important, testing what gets each to convert is even more important.

Planning for Optimization

By now, it should be clear that optimization can benefit your company and allow you to better meet your customers' needs. The next challenge you face is allocating resources to take advantage of optimization.

Budgeting for Optimization

Because optimization is still rather new, most organizations don't budget for it. How do you decide how much to dedicate to this effort? One way is to total up your web budget and create a new line item for site optimization. Although numbers can vary, we typically recommend dedicating approximately 5 percent of the overall web budget to this effort. When you calculate this number, make sure you include all Web-related costs (internal and external), such as the following:

- Web design, development, information architecture, and project management
- Hosting
- Onsite advertising
- Search engine optimization (SEO) and search engine marketing (SEM)
- Web analytics and other business intelligence tools
- Competitive intelligence
- Attitudinal studies (surveys, expert reviews, and so on)
- Server costs and maintenance

As you add up these items, you may realize that 5 percent can be a large number, especially for organizations that buy a lot of media to drive traffic to their sites. Then again, if you spend a lot on media, you may also have a much higher potential to improve the returns on your media campaigns.

Allocating even a small percentage of the overall budget to a new line item can raise questions, especially if you ask for more money than last year. But once you explain how this 5 percent will be used, it may prove to be the easiest budget justification you make. Optimization can pay off quickly and will likely improve the overall website return and thus help to justify every other Web-related budget item.

If you need to justify the expenditure on optimization, it's relatively easy to do. First, pick two or three of your KPIs and look at their performance over the past 12 months. Next, model the financial impact if you improved their performance by even a small amount. For example, let's suppose a site has lead generation as the KPI. In one year, the company converts 2.38 percent of all site visits to leads, for a total of 2,800 leads per month. With its average lead closing rate and the average value of the close, the site's managers can determine that the lead's value is, for example, $213. The current monthly value of the leads will generate $596,400 (2,800 leads multiplied by the $213 lead value).

Through optimization, you can forecast an improvement of different levels to understand the potential benefit:

- A 5 percent improvement in conversion rate will yield a new conversion rate of 2.50 percent. That will add 140 additional monthly leads and result in a monthly benefit of $29,820, or $357,840 annually.

- A 10 percent improvement in conversion rate will yield a new conversion rate of 2.62 percent. That will add 280 additional monthly leads and result in a monthly benefit of $59,640, or $715,680 annually.

- A 15 percent improvement in conversion rate will yield a new conversion rate of 2.74 percent. That will add 420 additional monthly leads and result in a monthly benefit of $89,460, or $1,073,520 annually.

- A 20 percent improvement in conversion rate will yield a new conversion rate of 2.86 percent. That will add 560 additional monthly leads and result in a monthly benefit of $119,280, or $1,431,360 annually.

- A 25 percent improvement in conversion rate will yield a new conversion rate of 2.98 percent. That will add 700 additional monthly leads and result in a monthly benefit of $149,100, or $1,789,200 annually.

Although this model assumes that lead quality remains the same, it's easy to see how improving just one KPI by a small amount can lead to large improvements in the bottom line. If you model this for a number of your KPIs, you can make a case fairly quickly.

Skills Needed for a Successful Optimization Team

As we said before, testing and optimization require you to deploy nearly all areas and disciplines in overall site design. But management is probably the most crucial part. It's hard to find qualified people who can run this type of program, but it's not impossible. The skills can be learned, and many analytics, marketing, and user-experience professionals can step up to fill the void. A number of consulting companies are also springing up to take advantage of the opportunity.

For the rest of this section, we'll outline the specific tasks in a testing program and the underlying skill sets needed to develop to complete them. There are four main categories:

Test identification Knowing what to test requires a variety of skills. An understanding of analytics and data-based decision making is critical. Some knowledge of what typically works on a site is also vital. Finally, your candidate should have a solid understanding of the business goals. An experienced business manager with an analytical marketing background should be able to perform these tasks. Another possibility is a usability expert with a marketing or business administration background.

Test prioritization To prioritize tests, your candidate needs to understand both the financial impact of changes and their cost in human resources and technical requirements. In addition, this person may be confronted with the fact that the ideas of the online VP or director may not be so great. As a result, the candidate should be a good communicator. You may find that test prioritization is an iterative process that is determined by a number of individuals, so political skills are essential in this position as well.

Test design Skill in designing tests is probably the most difficult thing to find. Your test designer should have the ability to understand what can and should be measured in order to derive a meaningful result. As a result, this person should have a strong technical background as well as online analytics experience.

Data analysis and recommendations This the final piece of the puzzle. Once the test has been executed, the results must be analyzed and recommendations made. You need someone skilled at data extrapolation and statistical analysis. A strong web analyst should be able to perform these tasks.

You need a series of skill sets to execute a successful test program. Some of these are difficult to find in today's market, others not so much. But there is some good news. Most of these skill sets can be learned from existing roles. And with more companies turning to optimization, as time goes on there will be more individuals able to perform these tasks.

Challenges and Benefits of Testing: Interview with Nigel Morgan

Nigel Morgan has a number of years' experience managing online testing and analytics programs, most recently at Dell.com. He shared some of his optimization experience with us.

Authors: Nigel, what is the benefit to the company of testing?

Nigel: At its most base level, testing drives tremendous financial upside to a company. Because most companies are in business to make money, it's well aligned with the corporate goals! At a deeper level, it allows companies to understand what resonates most with their customers and ultimately allows them to deliver the right content in the right format at the right time. With the prevalence of high-speed Internet access and your competitors only a click away (my apologies for the cliché), you have to get it right straight away. Testing allows you to statistically prove that one design or price or click-though process is preferred over another, and therefore it can make a direct impact on the profitability of your business.

Authors: What is the most surprising change one of your tests made?

Nigel: There have been many surprises. Rather than give one instance, I would like to say that you shouldn't write off the smallest changes. They can often have a much larger impact than the big changes. The biggest surprise to me was how much upside there is in testing. You think you've got it right because you've done focus groups and brought in the best agencies. But that is just the start. I like to use a cooking analogy to illustrate this point. A chef doesn't put together a random set of ingredients that they think will taste good and then serve them to a customer. No. They will taste, refine, remake, and so on until they get it right. Site design is the same. You always need to be refining. And just when you think you've got the perfect recipe, the customers' preference

Challenges and Benefits of Testing: Interview with Nigel Morgan *(Continued)*

changes, and you need to start again. That's the beauty of the online world and the thing that keeps me interested in it. The world is always changing, and the only way to stay on top is to constantly improve and never be satisfied that you've nailed your site and that you have no more work to do.

Authors: Have you ever witnessed any political roadblocks with any testing program?

Nigel: Is this a trick question? Of course! Although there is often executive support for the concept of testing, the management team that needs to be proactive in support of a testing program can often be in conflict. Marketing managers may not want to admit that their expertise isn't perfect and think that the analysts are taking over their patch. IT managers usually have a million other priorities and don't have the resources for your program. Financial managers may not want the risk of change. All these people must be on board for a testing program to work.

What I can say is that once you start getting the small wins under your belt, there is a sudden insatiable appetite for testing across the whole organization. That is the moment of clarity in an organization and one which I am particularly fond of. All of the management team now gets it, and along the way, unnoticeably, the organization has now become one that is data driven.

Authors: Can you summarize testing in a sentence for us?

Nigel: How about two? Testing and optimizing your site can lead to tremendous financial upside to your company's bottom line; the return on investment can literally be in the thousands of percent. My advice is to start a testing program now and stick with it, because the rewards will be dramatic.

Overcoming IT Doubts

When it's time to act on data and use either A/B or multivariate testing, be prepared for roadblocks. And know you can overcome them. We've already discussed some of these roadblocks, including a lack of focus on KPIs, incorrect interpretation of visitor behavior, resource limitations, and lack of skills to identify potential problems. Even if you overcome those issues, there's one that you'll always see.

Every time we recommend a client do A/B or multivariate testing—not sometimes but every time—we're told it's not possible "in our environment." Although this is clearly not true, this statement can result from a number of reasons:

- IT doesn't understand the process and how it will affect the website.
- IT doesn't know testing's prioritization in its queue.
- There's no executive support to help push this paradigm shift in the organization.

Let's look at these in detail.

IT Doesn't Understand the Process

It's natural for the IT team to say "no" immediately. They're frequently buried in other work and think testing is one headache they don't need.

There are a number of ways to mitigate this resistance. You can work with a company such as Offermatica or Optimost to conduct multivariate tests. You can also have a developer create a basic script that points people to the different versions of an A/B test, something that should take only a day. Such a script will only allow for the most basic testing, but it isn't a bad place to start.

Testing Prioritization

The IT group probably isn't waiting around to help you institute the test. When you invite them, they're usually pulled away from other work. We've seen this problem most prominently in IT, where months of initiatives are lined up to be worked on. To increase testing and site optimization priority at a company, we monetize the recommendations and determine the range of return we expect to see from the test. Then, we monetize the opportunities. That tends to help testing climb up the list of company priorities.

Lack of Executive Support

Without executive support, getting people to move as fast as you'd like may be tough. You need to share the plan, monetization, and potential outcome with a senior person. Get their buy-in. Once you do, you'll be amazed how fast barriers come down.

A few months ago, we worked with a large organization that had invested a significant amount in their analytics tool. But they hadn't been able to identify opportunities and act on findings to improve site performance. After working with them to define overall site goals, proper metrics, and KPIs, we helped get the tool configured to report on those elements. We also rolled out our methodology of how to use the data.

We identified a series of priorities and started talking to the IT group about different testing opportunities. Of course, we were told it wasn't possible on their platform, they didn't have any resources, and they weren't cleared to get any more.

We worked with IT to help them understand the effect and requirements for the different testing opportunities. It turned out the only real issues were resource constraints. We'd already gained conceptual support on the process from the executive group, so we went back and showed the monetized impact making changes would have on the bottom line. We also estimated the costs of conducting the first two tests working with an outside partner, as well as internal costs for the company.

Based on the changes' estimated outcome, it was easy to get the company to free up the budget and resources to accomplish these goals. The initial test was rolled out and was within the estimated range for the monthly impact in terms of lift in the mon-etized metric.

Don't take no for an answer. Make sure you're clear about the potential finan-cial outcome, be sure everyone understands the process, and get executive support.

Learning from Your Successes and Mistakes

There's a great saying about testing that goes something like this: Experience is what you get when you don't get what you want. With testing, you won't always get the result you desire, but whether you're successful or you fail, you should learn some-thing. And that should inform your efforts. Most tests have three possible paths:

- The test yields statistically relevant changes to site metrics.
- The test yields no meaningful results.
- The test appears not to have been executed properly.

If you're starting out with a testing program, you'll probably see many more tests fall in the last two categories than in the first. Don't be discouraged. This is pri-marily due to both a lack of experience and a formal process not being followed. As your organization gains experience in testing and as managers reap the benefits of the often-substantial upside, the process will become more formalized and the number of mistakes will drop.

Let's look at each of these outcomes and see what happens. There are three rea-sons a test may not be executed properly, and they're largely technical in nature:

Reporting The metrics were not properly identified, defined, or captured.

Technical issues The test filter didn't work properly. Pages weren't tagged.

Lack of strategic focus The test was cancelled midway through. Executive support was lost. Sudden changes were made on the page being tested, which made the test redundant.

If a test yields no meaningful results, the cause could be any of the following:

- The wrong thing may have been tested.
- The prioritization exercise didn't work properly.
- The test design solution wasn't optimal.

If the test yielded statistically relevant changes to site metrics, congratulations: The test group performed as you hoped it would.

Learning from the Good and the Bad

Because all the previous scenarios happen, it's important to know how to learn from each one. All testing managers must understand and preach that there is no such thing as a bad test. You can always learn something, even if it's only how not to do something. Testing requires that a wide range of disparate disciplines, some of which are highly technical, come together and work in harmony.

Executives should know ahead of time that tests are complicated, that they often don't yield positive results, and that any program requires a learning curve. If an organization isn't aware of this, its leaders may feel that in the early days of the program they have laid out a significant financial commitment to a program that has yielded no results. This can be disastrous for the longevity of an optimization process. It's important to both control expectations and explain that even a failure represents a learning opportunity.

A Quick Way Up the Learning Curve

A good way to get up the learning curve faster is to bring in outside consultants to start any program. If you lack experienced staff, you should bring in people who have done this before. Although relatively expensive in dollar terms, an outside agency can deploy fully functioning test programs in a matter of weeks rather than months. Typically, this approach pays for itself in spades.

One of the most tragic outcomes we've seen is a company with no experience in testing that made bad decisions about what should be tested, had the technical design fail, captured the wrong metrics, and ultimately made its senior management believe that testing doesn't work. Some failures at the start are almost inevitable for any company trying to build out a program from scratch on their own. These failures can be reduced dramatically by bringing in outside experts.

Spreading the Word

Once a testing program is in place and positive results are flowing in, it's important to publicize that information throughout your organization. This can be done a number of ways. Some companies have company-wide online conferences; other prefer more informal online councils, where best practices are included among other knowledge-sharing sessions. In either case, whether your company is large or small, spreading the word about testing can help maximize the ROI of a program and yield a significant level of executive support and recognition.

Test Examples

Earlier in this chapter, we outlined six areas into which testing normally falls. Here, we'll give some specific examples of each so you can see how they work in the real world. The six functional areas are as follows:

- Price
- Promotional
- Message (content/images/headlines/promotional messaging, and so on)

- Page layout (what goes where on the page)
- New site launches or new functionality
- Site navigation and taxonomy

These six also are given in order of increasing difficulty, where ease of testing and implementation are concerned. Price testing is often the easiest to perform (when you have a site with multiple products), whereas navigation and site hierarchy testing can be costly and difficult.

Price

Price tests are perhaps the simplest to execute, and yet they can return high ROI. These tests can vary from changing a price point to having a series of tests to determine price elasticity. E-commerce sites are particularly well suited to this type of testing.

Figure 11.2 is a screen shot from landsend.com. The price is set at $59.50. But how do you know whether this is the ideal price that will drive the most profit? You could easily perform an A/B/n test that set the price at $54.50 and $64.50. From there, you could determine which drives the most sales, and whether the price changes increase or decrease your total revenue and profit margin. The math is relatively simple: If you drop the price 10 percent, you need to increase sales by a little more than 10 percent to make the same revenue. You may have to increase sales by considerably more to make the same amount of profit margin.

Figure 11.2 Price testing

Promotional

Another fairly easy test opportunity is in promotions. Some typical questions you may want to ask are, does a free giveaway resonate more than free shipping as a promotional offering? Does a percentage off a price point sell more products than a lowered starting price point? Again, this type of testing is great for e-commerce sites. and often the results are highly scalable across product lines.

Figure 11.3 presents a screen shot from *drugstore.com* as an example. Here you can see several promotions: a free shipping promo in the upper banner, a 30-day free trial of generic drugs on the left side, a 40 percent off seasonal promotion callout in the main image, and another 40 percent off promotion in the banner below the main image. In this example, you could easily test the main 40 percent off promotion by switching an alternative message with dollar savings, such as "Save up to $100." You could also change it to a different amount, such as "Take a third off!!!." Multivariate testing or A/B/n testing may be appropriate here.

Figure 11.3 Promotional testing

Message

Messaging is another fairly easy area to test, even though it can have a significant impact. Typically, these tests are done higher up in the funnel, while consumers are still doing research into a product or service. Message testing is also critical on landing pages, where visitors must make fast decisions about whether to continue to browse or navigate the site.

Figure 11.4 is a landing page from Honda.com, which we found by entering convertible into a major search engine. The page shows a sporty car, some body copy, and three clear calls to action: "Build your Honda," "Locate a Dealer," and "Request a Quote." In this instance, you could test the image by changing to a beach setting to focus on the lifestyle appeal of the car rather than its performance. You could also enlarge the three buttons and place them higher on the page. In each test, you would want to track click-through rates and possibly overall conversion.

Figure 11.4 General message testing

Page Layout

Page-layout tests can help establish what locations on a page have the highest value. In doing such tests, you ideally have only one desired action you want your customers to do (this isn't always applicable). Typically, the calls to action for that behavior are in the most conspicuous location on the page. For example, if you want visitors to click through to some additional content, you need two things:

- A conspicuous Next button
- A compelling message or call to action in a prime location

This is where testing can get more complicated. What is the compelling message that drives the desired behavior? Once you establish that, where do you locate that item on the page?

Let's look at a page from theknot.com (Figure 11.5), which has many different elements and modules. A robust testing plan would help you understand how to best lay out a page of this kind. For example, you might consider moving the banners and modules around the page to see what happens to the Next clicks and the leakage rates.

Figure 11.5 Page-layout testing

New Site Launches or New Functionality

Looking at new launches or functionality can be complicated. You may be testing a new microsite developed by a cutting-edge agency, or trying to assess the effectiveness to a sign-in/log-in process that appears on every page of your site. In both cases, you don't have a baseline of customer behavior. So, you should probably test every addition prior to a full launch. If your designers and developers have done a great job, chances are the test will be superfluous. However, if the project tests poorly, you'll want to know that as soon as you can. With a partial launch seen by only a small number of visitors, you can mitigate the risk.

The example in Figure 11.6 is the One-Click functionality introduced by Amazon.com. Because you'd typically be looking only at overall performance, this would be an A/B test.

Figure 11.6 Testing new functionality

Site Navigation and Taxonomy

Testing site navigation can be extremely complicated and is recommended only if you have a lot of experience. Even so, it's a powerful method for finding out if your architecture is working. A typical test takes many months to arrange and weeks—if not more—to conduct.

Let's look at the Dell.com homepage (Figure 11.7) to outline the issues involved in this kind of test. This page receives millions of visits per day. If you look closely, you can see that the company is working off the hypothesis that its customers primarily shop based on computer type (desktop or laptop) and that they should be segmented based on product. Later, they can choose their business segment. This is a simple concept, but testing it can be complicated. To ensure statistical confidence, the test must take all of the following into account:

- Where consumers go next
- The total revenue for each business segment
- The revenue for each product

Figure 11.7 Site-navigation testing

- The revenue for each product by segment
- The leakage from Dell.com
- How many additional leaked visits are created by adding a new customer segment page
- The opportunity lost by placing the consumer directly into a product purchase path and missing the cross-sell opportunity of directing them through the business segment homepage

A significant amount of analysis is required to define success metrics. Once those KPIs are identified, you also need to establish a baseline. Then, when the test is complete, you have a large amount of data to sift through. Finally, if you make changes, you should collect data on their performance as well.

Unfortunately, this is a simple example of testing site hierarchy. Imagine the complexities of changing purchase paths or global navigation elements. It's not surprising that these elements rarely change on large sites.

Recap

In this chapter, we looked at one of the most important aspects of the analytics process: testing and optimization. First, we examined the kinds of tests you can conduct on your site: A/B, A/B/n, and multivariate. The first two allow you to change one element on a page and measure the performance with great statistical accuracy. Multivariate testing, on the other hand, lets you look at a greater number of options, although the numbers you need for statistical significance are often large.

From there, we examined the kinds of things you can test, including pricing, promotion, page layout, messaging, new functionality, and navigation. We looked at how to create a test and emphasized that it's a holistic process that involves collecting data before, during, and after the test.

We also discussed the role of the tester. Not many people today have much experience in the field. So, we outlined the types of managerial, technical, political, and analytical skills you have to build on your team in order to get the most out of testing.

Next, we looked at budgeting for testing. Five percent of your total web budget is a good number to aim at for your program. At the same time, we emphasized that it's not easy to implement the process in many companies. In particular, we stressed that not all tests are a success, and any testing program takes time to become efficient. Even so, every test can teach you something about how to design tests and read results. If your company doesn't have the experience to create a testing program, consider bringing in outside consultants to build one. Finally, once a testing program is yielding results, it's important that these results are documented, shared with a company-wide audience, and kept as a record for future managers.

In the rest of the chapter, we looked at six examples of standard tests that companies can conduct on their websites. Looking at them should have given you a good idea of the kinds of things you may want to start testing soon.

Agencies

Much of our discussion so far has focused on how to define an analytics strategy and use it to drive business success. Implicit in this has been the presence of an agency to bring your strategy to life through implementation, analysis, and recommendation. Although some businesses choose to manage their web-analytics plan internally, most turn to an agency for help.

12

Chapter Contents

Why Use an Agency at All?

In previous chapters, we've discussed the skills and breadth of understanding you need in order to be successful at delivering high ROI through the effective use of web analytics. It's unlikely you'll be able to hire all the people you need to do a complete job (see Chapter 15 for an in-depth discussion of how to hire the right people). Eventually, you'll need to turn to outside resources. That typically means finding an *agency*. Let's provide a simple definition of an agency to make this discussion easier:

An agency, sometimes called a *web agency* or an *interactive agency*, is a company or firm dedicated to providing a range of services to clients that may include strategy, design, web analytics, web optimization, search-engine optimization, and other ROI-enhancing processes. Agencies service multiple clients, have specialized resources and experience, and usually have either a project or agency of record relationship with their clients.

Some companies see agencies as a necessary evil: a part of the marketing ecosystem that can't be avoided but should never be trusted. Others view agencies as a fast and easy solution to all their marketing problems. As usual, the truth lies somewhere in the middle. Agencies can succeed when they have clear direction, clear goals, and adequate resources and support to achieve those goals. In other words, agencies are usually no different than any internal specialist or team.

Many agencies become part of your extended team, often working with you across multiple projects. Knowing and trusting them is one of the keys to getting great work. If you can find a solid agency to do your web analytics now (and perhaps your web design and implementation as well), it will help make your company successful—and contribute to your professional success in the long term.

Some agencies are as small as two or three people, but most have anywhere from 20 to 100 employees. Often, agencies are part of larger full-service marketing and advertising firm such as WPP, Interpublic Group, or Publicis Groupe. Agencies may specialize in certain aspects of the interactive lifecycle such as analytics, or they can offer a full spectrum of services. Likewise, agencies may have geographic and/or industry-specific expertise. The authors of this book help lead the agency ZAAZ, which consists of more than 70 people who span the entire array of services. It's part of the WPP family of companies.

There's one last point we should make clear: Agencies charge money for their services, often lots of it. The more they do and the more time they spend doing it, the more money they stand to make. The goals of the agencies may be in direct conflict with the goals of the company that hires them. Avoiding this conflict, or at least understanding it, will make everyone happier.

Finding an Agency

Once you've decided to hire an agency, you have to find one. This usually isn't difficult. Agencies often find you first: They usually have business-development people out looking for companies just like yours. If you have a significant web presence, you're on the target list for one or more agencies. They know who you are and how your site is doing.

If they haven't found you already, you may to have to search for them. Sometimes this is as easy as talking with the direct-marketing or advertising agency you already have. Many of them have teams or divisions dedicated to online work. But be careful: Many large marketing agencies try to be all things to all clients. Although they may have good capabilities in the interactive space, they may not have a strong analytics practice (or may not have read this book!). Agencies don't want their clients to go elsewhere if they can avoid it. The rule here is to evaluate an existing agency against the same criteria you would use for a new agency. Keep everyone honest by making them demonstrate their competency.

It may seem easy to call up some associates and ask them to recommend their favorite agency (or the last one that did some work for them). Again, even the best of recommendations may not be appropriate for your needs. Great agencies are able to succeed because they work closely with their clients to identify the real business objectives, establish a high degree of trust, and create mutually compatible work styles. Just because an agency succeeded in doing this for your associate doesn't necessarily mean they can do the same for you.

Because none of these options can guarantee success, the best thing to do is to compile a list of agencies and invite them all to submit a proposal to your company. Where can you find them? Try some of the following:

- **Internal references:** Ask your co-workers for their experiences at your company and at other places they may have worked.
- **Internal vendor listings:** Many larger companies have a set of preapproved vendors across a variety of categories.
- **Industry associations:** You may find references for agencies with experience in your specific industry.
- **Sites you admire:** It never hurts to send an e-mail to a company that has a site you admire (try webmaster@*<sitename>* or marketing@*<sitename>*). They may be happy to recommend their agency (or reluctant, if they want to preserve their advantage).
- **Search engines** like Google, Live, and Yahoo!: To find agencies, try terms such as *web analytics* and *interactive agency*.

- **Web Analytics Association:** www.webanalyticsassociation.org

- **Web and advertising industry publications:** These include AdWeek, MediaWeek, and AdAge.

- **Design publications,** such as Communication Arts: Particularly useful are awards issues, like CA's Interactive Annual, which usually comes out in September.

- **Industry events and tradeshows:.** Such as Emetrics, eTail, and some of the other common web conferences or tool provider conferences such as Omniture's Summit.

We hope these methods allow you to identify a handful of agencies. From there, the best approach to selecting one of them is a Request for Proposal (RFP). It's a comprehensive model for identifying the type of services you want across several criteria. To get the most out of your RFP, however, you have to do some groundwork first.

First, you need to identify the type of agency you want. Many of these choices are driven by your own business and experience, but they should all be considered part of the equation. We can't tell you the answers to these questions, but we can help you ask the right questions. A list of some of the most important ones follows:

Agency size Do you need a boutique or a multinational? The former are good at consumer advertising; the latter are essential if you're delivering an internationally localized site.

Agency focus Is it an analytics-only group, a full-service online agency, or one that offers both online and offline services?

Agency specialty Does it cover all industries, or is it expert in specific verticals? Most healthcare companies, for example, rely on agencies with experience in their field.

Agency portfolio Can you find agencies that do work similar to your own; work for your partners, suppliers or customers; or work for other parts of your larger company?

Agency pricing model Does it bill by project or by time and expense? Depending on how you allocate resources in your company, this may be an important consideration.

Creating an RFP

After you narrow your choices based on the criteria we just described, you'll probably spend some time meeting with agencies and getting to know them. If you feel that they may be suitable for your work, invite them to respond to your RFP.

An RFP is a little like an employment ad, a little like an online personal ad, and a little like a project functional specification. It represents both the qualities you want in your agency and the outcomes you want from your project. The best RFPs can be informative ("here is the simple statement of the problem to be solved") and represent the ideal to which you aspire ("here is the pinnacle of success we hope to achieve in our business"). They also have to convey enough information to allow the agencies responding to craft a good response. At the same time, they should not be so specific that the agency declines to respond because they fear all the decisions have been made for them or that you might micromanage the project.

The RFP is both art and science, much like the analytics work the winning agency will eventually do for you. If the agency gets excited about your business and about the analytics challenge you present, they will go out of their way to give you the best response possible. They will want to win your business.

RFPs have a lot of components, and no two ever look alike (much to the dismay of the agencies that have to respond). Some RFPs cover the full range of services from design all the way through ongoing analytics and optimization. Others focus on a component, such as analytics, and make it clear that other site work is neither included nor open to review. When you create your RFP, remember that you want the agency to be able to respond in full, and you want your intentions to be clear. However, you also want to leave some room for the agency to suggest solutions to problems you may not have seen.

Although the contents of RFPs may vary, they all contain a few standard sections. Here is a general outline of what you should always include in yours:

1. Introduction
2. Company/brand background
3. Scope of work/business goals
4. Specific project requirements and deliverables
5. Timelines and financials
6. Technology assumptions/requirements (often including a requirements table or matrix)
7. List of questions the agency must address
8. Expected format of the response

We'll go through some of the sections briefly, using excerpts from fictional RFPs, and discuss the key points for you to include.

Introduction and Company Background

We recommend that you spend considerable time and effort on these sections, because it may be your only opportunity to explain your business to the agency. You want them as informed as possible so they can make the best proposal and suggest the most robust solutions. Often, clients assume that the agency knows a lot about them because they have a well-known brand or product. This assumption can sometimes leave the agency struggling to craft their response correctly.

In order to make sure you provide a good overview, follow these guidelines:

- Be explicit. Assume the agency knows nothing about your business.
- Reference any brand research or branding exercise you've previously completed.

- Paint a picture of the market and competition (the agency will want to look at competitive sites).

- Make it clear that you have high expectations for your brand, and the agency will need to help deliver on those expectations.

Example 1: RobotWear

RobotWear is a fictional clothing company. In the following RFP, they take a clear approach to explaining their company's brand and market position. This part consists of three sections: an overview, a market assessment, and a brand assessment. The company does a great job of following all four of our guidelines:

Overview RobotWear Products is the originator of the Automatic Cleaning Clothing system. Since 1989, RobotWear's state-of-the-art shirts and cleaning systems have benefited businessmen, outdoor enthusiasts, and law-enforcement personnel around the world. RobotWear continues to deliver innovative cleaning products to the market with the belief in the performance advantage that proper cleaning can deliver in any situation. The company is privately held and is headquartered in Rochester, New York.

Market assessment In recent years, the world of cleaning has become a crowded marketplace. And although the RobotWear brand has been around for more than 15 years and is deeply rooted in the spirit of innovative freshening and cleaning activities, today RobotWear's leadership position is challenged on many fronts by competition.

Brand assessment A brand study was recently (February 2005) completed with consumers across all our markets (business users, sports teams, and law enforcement). Key findings of the brand assessment are listed here, as well as the brand audit chart:

- RobotWear is viewed as highly valuable and innovative.
- Productive innovation is a fundamental brand equity for RobotWear, and our history is rooted in innovation.
- RobotWear isn't linked to one specific type of clothing or activity.
- RobotWear is perceived as in a class of its own (no competition).
- Clean clothing is essential; thus RobotWear is considered essential.

Example 2: Snappy Scissors

Our second fictional company, Snappy Scissors, keeps their request to the agency simple—too simple, in fact. They keep the focus on what they expect from their agency, and they don't provide much guidance about their own business. They don't explain themselves sufficiently to elicit a good response:

Overview Please prepare an executive summary of your proposal to include a summary of your firm's type of ownership and parent company and subsidiaries, if any capabilities, years in business, number of full-time employees, similar projects, transition methodology, and the proposed resources you would dedicate toward fulfillment of a contract with Snappy Scissors. *The proposal should also include an explanation of why Snappy Scissors would realize a competitive advantage by doing business with your company and what differentiates your firm from your competitors.*

Recap: Company/Brand Background

In the two examples, RobotWear gets all the details right and Snappy Scissors falls short. The former company manages to explain its business clearly, reference branding exercises, describe its market and competition, and explain its high expectations for the engagement. The latter, unfortunately, seems much more interested in the performance of their agency than in giving the kinds of information that would allow them to make an informed decision during the selection process.

Scope of Work and Business Goals

When you're designing a scope of work and outlining business goals, you have a lot of ground to cover. You need to make sure the agencies understand exactly what you want, while leaving some room for discussion. For example, even though you may want a 200 percent increase in site traffic, the agency should be able to use available analytics data to demonstrate that such a goal isn't reasonably attainable.

In constructing these sections, you should follow these guidelines:

- Drill into the details. Conduct your research before you write the RFP, so you know the facts about your existing site.

- Involve your team. There will be a lot of opinions about this section, and it's better to get them on the table now instead of in the middle of implementation.

- Ask big. If you don't set ambitious goals now, you may find yourself scrambling to make and meet them later.

Example 1: RobotWear

Having made a good case for their business and brand, RobotWear now goes on to state the goals for their project. Let's look at this section of their RFP:

Overall goals and objectives
- Establish robotwear.com as the core marketing vehicle to deepen the relationship that cleaners have with our brand
- Develop and deploy a scalable core applications platform that will support current and future development of rich content delivery; e-commerce and fulfillment; content, customer, and campaign management; communities; online cleaning tips; reporting; and web analytics
- Gain knowledge about our customers (who are they, what they like, and so on) via a centralized repository with comprehensive analytics and reporting

- Rank as a top-10 site for our consumer segment over the next three years
- Increase site traffic 200 percent to 80,000 monthly unique visitors by June 2008, and to 120,000 monthly unique visitors by June 2009
- Increase the repeat visitor rate to four visits/month
- Increase the average visit duration to six minutes/visit
- Increase online sales revenue in FY 2006 by 30 percent

Specific project requirements and deliverables—ongoing projects

- Website management: Database maintenance, network monitoring, daily backups, domain renewals
- Website design and development
- E-mail newsletter design, development, and reporting (for both U.S. and international)
- Product updates for all channels/markets
- Search-engine optimization and monthly reporting
- Monthly, robust reporting of user traffic across entire site and within each individual silo

Specific project requirements and deliverables—short-term projects

- Navigation/architecture upgrades (enhance user-friendliness by better font treatments and more intuitive and consistent ways to get to the information they want; enable use of the Back button throughout the site; and so on)
- Ability to enable RobotWear to self-edit/update key sections of the website
- Deep analytics implementation with an opportunity for optimization through A/B testing and product-feature testing

Long-term project (site redesign)

- Enhanced design and architecture to enable website as an easy to use/ navigate, user-friendly brand marketing and merchandising tool, including:
  - Strengthen online experience in a way that leverages RobotWear brand essence and equities
  - Create cleaning resource/information microsite/portal
  - Create product selector tool
- Enable areas for increased merchandising of products
- Display only the products available in each markets (on the U.S. site, only U.S. products; for international sections, display only international products)
- Multilanguage translation of the site that gives international users a robust experience, specifically:
  - French, Italian, and German translations for the entire site
  - Links to approved distributor RobotWear sites

- Products specific to international markets (don't show U.S. products if not available in that market)
- Global Dealer Site that is a restricted access/password protected, multilevel site to enable sharing of information with key customers and distributors, both U.S. and international, including:
  - Account-specific pages containing viewable/downloadable account reports, programs, and so on
  - Regional and global-distributor pages containing viewable/downloadable offerings/content for regional/global distributors (sales and marketing tools such as logos, ads, and so on)
  - Media-level pages containing viewable/downloadable PR information
- Ability to enable RobotWear to self maintain/update key sections of website
- E-commerce capability

Example 2: Snappy Scissors

Unfortunately, our friends at Snappy Scissors aren't so comprehensive or detailed. For this section of the RFP, they stay far too holistic. It's hard to know what they would or would not consider a success. Here are their goals and objectives:

Search engine optimized It's highly important to us to have a site that can be read by search engines and to increase our traffic received from the engines.

Cacheable pages Because of the amount of traffic we receive on a daily basis, and most especially a peak basis, we require that the majority of the pages be cacheable.

Checkout experience The checkout experience is just as important as the purchasing experience. We want a rich full-page experience for a customer when they're seeing their shopping cart.

Ease of use We're trying to accomplish a lot with this redesign; but many users initially come to the site for a utilitarian purpose, so the navigation changes can't be overwhelming but must be viewed as helpful. The site redesign needs to make sure these users can find the right product quickly and easily. Most buyers choose from a narrow range of scissor choices. Getting them to the right product line is important, and they're looking to narrow their searches with more options and more quickly.

Timelines

Each RFP response should clearly define a phased approach to implementation. The extent and detail of that timeline is often a reflection of a company's internal project-management system. If you rely on such a system, it's important to remember that your proposed timeline may be impossible to achieve given your business goals and the agency's capabilities. Rather than setting everyone up for failure by imposing unreasonable constraints, you should work with your agency to determine what is possible.

Following is a sample timeline. It may seem vague, but it relies on its respondents to best determine what is achievable in each phase based on the priorities of each requirement.

RobotWear Example

RobotWear constructed the following timeline for its RFP:

Milestone	Deadline
Phase I—Site Launch	07/25/2008
Phase II—RFP Respondents' Recommendations	10/01/2008
Phase III—RFP Respondents' Recommendations	3/5/2009
Phase IV—RFP Respondents' Recommendations	6/4/2009

As part of this timeline, they also request that their agency submit a detailed schedule for elements in each phase of the project.

Financials

The financial section of the RFP can be tricky. It needs to achieve two distinct things: (1) make your budget constraints clear to the agency, and (2) explain your expectations for how the agency should be compensated. Both of them touch on delicate subjects (how much you have to spend and how you want to spend it) and, if you aren't careful, may leave you more exposed than you should be.

Here are the simple steps to getting this section right:

- Know your budget before you send out an RFP! We can't emphasize this enough. Too often, clients expect the agency to come back and tell them what the work will cost, and then a lot of negotiation ensues.

- Know how you want to spend your money. If you have an RFP for analytics work only, then expect to spend your money on analytics. Selecting an agency for analytics and then telling them the budget has to cover site redesign as well will make everyone unhappy.

- Know how you want to pay the agency. Are you comfortable with a retainer, or do you want to work on a project basis? Will you accept billing by the hour, or do you want a fixed price/fixed time relationship? Are you willing to "pay for performance"?

The *pay for performance* model is gaining a lot of momentum in some parts of the industry, particularly for analytics and optimization engagements. If you have specific KPIs, and you expect your agency to help you achieve them, you should be prepared to provide a financial incentive. An agency may be willing to provide a fixed price for an engagement with built-in *accelerators* or incentives for meeting and beating your targeted KPIs. For example, you might build a model that gives them 10 percent incentive if they achieve 150 percent of a goal KPI in the first 6 months. Pay for performance tightly couples the agency's success with your success, and that means everyone has a great incentive to win.

The Rest of the RFP: Asking the Right Questions

Most of other sections in the RFP depend on the unique requirements of your business. The kind of technology you can deploy, the kind of response you'd like, and most of the rest are elements that will be specific to you. However, you should spend some time thinking about the specific questions you'll ask your agency. Let's look at how to do this.

One of the first things you'll get from an agency is a list of past and present clients and the work done for those clients. This is a good opportunity for you to look at their portfolio and for them to show off their expertise. By asking the right questions when you look at past work, you can find out some interesting facts about an agency.

Any agency that only does web analytics will likely point you to a site and then show you various scorecards and the KPIs they track for that site. If they also designed the site, they will demonstrate the various features and innovations they created. In some cases, the agency may even show you how they improved KPIs over time. This is all critical information as you begin to evaluate the work presented.

Your evaluation, however, needs to start with simple questions for the agency. Answering these will quickly change the nature of the discussion from "show and tell" to "prove and show."

Here are some key questions (and guidance on answers) for past client work:

- For client X, please specify the business problem you were hired to solve. (The agency should be able to articulate the client business problem as clearly as the client. If they say "to increase sales," that isn't a sufficient explanation of a business problem.)

- Having specified the business problem, please describe the methodology you used to craft a solution to the problem. (Most agencies have their own specific methodology. When they present it to you, you should try to envision working with it. Does it align or conflict with your own methodologies?)

- What were the KPIs the client was interested in tracking? (If the client didn't have any specific KPIs, then the agency should have helped them create some.)

- What were the KPIs that the agency was evaluated against during the project? (This is the heart of the discussion; the agency must be measured the same way your business will be measured.)

- If the project involved design, describe the process from concept to wireframe to implementation, including user experience and behavioral research. (Can the agency show that they have capabilities in both art and science, design and testing? Many great design firms in the marketplace position themselves as full service, but their work is closer to art than it is to the reality of online commerce.)

- How big was the analytics team assigned to the project, and what roles did they fill? (If it's just one person, or even just a part-time or multitasking person, you may want to consider whether the agency can deliver what you need.)

- How was analytics used across every aspect of the engagement? (Analytics can't be something tagged on to the end of an engagement. It needs to be integrated from strategy through design and implementation and then on to optimization.)

- What were the next steps for the project, and how has that progressed? (Great sites stay great by constant improvement. Is the agency signed on to help deliver that continuous improvement?)

- What were the criteria for overall success of the agency on the project?

- What was the compensation model for the agency? Project based? Pay for performance? Time and resources?

These are some of the questions that will allow you to quickly get to the core of the projects you're shown. Agencies do a variety of work, and not all of it is appropriate to your specific needs. The agency will often want to show off their sexy, big-brand projects, but you want them to show the work that delivered real results in situations similar to yours.

Ideally, you'll have a chance to get references from the agency and to follow up on them. If you do, you should ask the same questions as you did of the agency. You can also probe deeper to determine what type of relationship existed between client and agency. If the client loved the work, but it didn't drive the performance of the business, then the agency might not be for you. Likewise, if the client gives a lukewarm vote of approval on an agency because they were focused too much on measurement and not enough on building a great-looking site, then the agency might be exactly what you're seeking.

Mutual Objective: Success

A number of years ago, our CMO, then working for a different company, held a bake-off between two agencies to see which one would be his overall brand agency of record. Their brief explained clearly that his goal was to find an agency that could not only think creatively and strategically, but also deliver results that would meet his business goals. Both agencies were eager to participate and put together senior teams to address the opportunity. Over the course of several weeks, they did interviews with the company's team, held brainstorming exercises, interviewed his customers, and generally found out as much about the business as they could.

When the time came for them to each present their pitch, our CMO had a team of about six senior leaders sit through both presentations. In typical agency fashion, they both came to the table with color printouts, flashy PowerPoint presentations, posters, and sample collateral. Each agency presented for about two hours and then left. The

CMO's internal team half-heartedly had a discussion about the relative merits of each vendor, but they all knew who had won the business. The difference wasn't the specific substance of that vendor's pitch; both pitches were equally creative and substantive. The difference was the fact that one vendor began their pitch with a simple statement: "The business goal we are trying to achieve is...." The other agency began their pitch with "We are the best agency for you because...."

You and your agency need to have a mutual objective: success. That success has to be measured by specific KPIs, and those same KPIs should drive your measurement of the success of the agency as well. The alignment between your business goals and their project goals must be 100 percent. You should be clear up front that you expect measurable performance from the work provided, and your preference is to pay for that performance. That pay can include accelerators as well as penalties. In either case, the agency must be measured on the same things that drive your success.

This principal applies regardless of the scope of the work being done for you. Building agency relationships based on agreed-upon KPIs applies as much in the offline agency world as in the online agency world. Here is an example that illustrates this point.

Suppose a large consumer products' company has hired a direct-marketing agency to create and run a coupon campaign for a new product. Traditional models for this type of engagement have the agency charge for strategy and design on an hourly rate and execution (printing, mailing) on a quantity rate. If the campaign is a success (assuming a measure for success is agreed on up front), then the agency will likely get the business for the next campaign.

The problem is that the agency has no opportunity to demonstrate the real business value of their efforts to the client. The best they can demonstrate is that the campaign achieved certain results (assuming they can measure them) at a certain cost. This is classic direct marketing: The cost per lead was $X. The benchmark for the client was likely that a previous campaign generated Y number of leads or cost $Z per lead.

In a KPI-driven engagement, the client and the agency should work together to determine the specific results necessary to meet business goals up front. These results might include a certain percentage increase in coupon redemption in a specific geographic region. That way, the client can put the agency in a pay for performance agreement. If the goals are achieved, the agency gets paid, and they also have the potential for accelerators based on goals being exceeded. If the goals aren't achieved, the agency has to go back to the drawing board and do it again until the targets are hit.

Offline or online, agencies need incentives to do the right thing. They can only do that if their client knows and can articulate that specific "right thing." Your role as the client is to be informed sufficiently to find an agency and then be able to communicate your business goals clearly to the agency. If you can't tell the agency what you want, you can't expect them to deliver it.

We've always believed that the reason many agencies fail with clients is as much the fault of the client as anyone else. Clients are like chefs in a restaurant: They need to lead by example, demonstrate what a great finished product looks like, and ensure that everyone on the team has clear and specific instructions and goals. If the client is targeting everyone being served cheap food quickly, and the agency is building a system to serve quality food slowly, then everyone will walk away hungry.

Doing the Work

After all the practical and diligent efforts you've taken to find an agency and formalize a relationship, it comes time to do the work. For many companies, this can be a time of confusion and disappointment, particularly because many of the people you've been talking to at the agency up to now are replaced by a new set of people that will be working on your account going forward. Knowing how to manage this change is critical.

Many agencies operate with a model that divides the team into people who bring in new business, those who manage existing business, and those who oversee specific projects. Likewise, agencies have creative directors, designers, analytics directors, analytics managers, planners, strategists, user-experience experts, and about 10 other roles. The larger the agency, the more people you may have to deal with in the relationship. Sometimes the value these individuals bring to your business will be clear, and other times it will be fuzzy. The burden of clarity rests on both the agency and the client. If you don't understand the role of an individual on your account, you have to ask questions. There are often good reasons to have experts across different specialties involved, but you need to make sure you know why they're there.

The agency also has expectations of you and your team. They want to know who their points of contact are and who will make the decisions for the business. If an agency is hired to do a large analytics project and then finds there is no one to take the results and act on them, the agency can become disappointed. Your company owes it to the agency you hire to provide guidance and make decisions when they need to be made.

During the span of a project, there will be many opportunities to expand the scope of the work you're doing together. Often, with analytics projects, a few months of effort identify many areas where specific KPIs can be improved. If you've aligned your agency's success with your KPIs, the agency will want to do the next phase of the work. Creating a shared success model up front continues to pay back through the evolution of the working relationship.

Expect to have regular meetings with the agency and ask them to demonstrate progress on the work through their own scorecards. Over the course of long projects, you should also set specific milestones and deliverables associated with those milestones. No business likes paying invoices each month without a clear picture of the value they're getting. With long-term analytics projects, it's easy to lose sight of the ongoing work as everyone is marching toward a bigger goal. To avoid getting discouraged, you should build checkpoints into the plan from the beginning.

From time to time, it may also become necessary to terminate your relationship with an agency (depending on the situation, you may just want to fire them). There are many reasons for termination, and they aren't all negative. Sometimes an agency does a great job solving your business problem, and you're ready to have them hand off ongoing work to your internal team. If this is the case, you should be sure you have a full and robust knowledge transfer between your team and theirs. It's difficult to go back to an agency after the fact and ask for help. Other times, the agency has truly and spectacularly failed. Nobody likes it when this happens, and it's highly likely the result of poor communication somewhere in the process. Nonetheless, failure happens. The best approach is to make a careful examination of what went wrong, have a frank discussion with the agency about the situation, and then terminate the relationship. The agency should provide you with all the material they have created and any special training your team might require to make it work. By the time you're ready to let the agency go, you'll likely have started the selection process all over again.

The Secret Agency Sauce

If there is one thing—the *secret sauce*—that often separates great agency work from mediocre agency work, it's passion. Passion isn't easy to quantify, but it's easy to recognize. You want an agency that is thoroughly excited about web analytics and the value of using data to drive decisions. An agency that gives a nod to analytics but wants to focus on rebuilding your website is probably not the right fit for a KPI-driven analytics partnership. The agency should show its passion through dedicated staff, deep expertise, innovative approaches, and 100 percent alignment with your business goals. The best agencies realize that having an analytics engagement with you will give them the deepest possible understanding of how your business operates. That understanding will help them become a strategic partner instead of just another vendor.

In summary, a great agency can be one of your biggest assets in driving business value and business growth. From large full-service agencies to small boutique shops, the opportunity exists to build a strong working relationship and become strategic partners. The only way to find the right agency is through a lot of hard questions, clear discussions about expectations, and relentless pursuit of the data that drives your online business.

Agencies are out there, and they want your business. Most of them will go the extra mile to give you the solutions you're seeking. However, you still need to staff your business with a team that knows how to do and interpret analytics. The next chapter gives you the information necessary to find and build that internal staff.

Recap

In this chapter, we've looked at how to hire agencies that will help drive your business. We began by discussing the different types of agencies and explaining why you need to find one that fits your specific needs. Some companies work well with one agency, others with another. The perfect one for you may not be great for everyone.

You've put a lot of time and care into selecting the right agency. The first step is to finding a list of agencies and narrowing them down. Then, you should write an RFP that tells them a considerable amount about your company and its needs. However, it should also give them a chance to assess your problems and begin to construct solutions.

From there, you'll have presentations from the agencies. Above all, you should make sure you ask the right questions that will determine if the agency is committed to improving your KPIs and not merely focused on building a new website.

Finally, we moved on to the work and how you can get the most out of your agency. We stressed that the overall goal of any engagement is to drive success in your company. The key to this, occasionally, is finding a special passion, or special sauce, that ensures you that the agency will be focused on every goal of every project and work seamlessly to achieve them.

The Creative Brief

13

A lot of our discussion in the book so far has been factual and focused on analytics and how to use them. There is another side to all this, however: the design of the sites themselves. For many marketers and analysts this can cause fear and apprehension because it means venturing into the realm of the "creative" department. Fortunately, they're eager to help and ready to learn and just waiting for your creative brief. This chapter shows you how to write one.

Chapter Contents
What Is a Creative Brief?
Analytics and Creativity
A Sample Creative Brief

What Is a Creative Brief?

We envy creative directors in many ways. They're designers, artists, and strategists all in one stylish package. The *director* part of their title is appropriate for the way in which they orchestrate all the players on the online stage and the sense of theater and drama they must bring to their creations. As the Web moves ever closer to the sensory richness of movies and TV and the rich interactivity of a day at the mall, the creative director is poised to control the entire online experience. When the awards for interactive sites are announced every year, the creative director gets to justifiably stand and cheer; the awards are specifically for creative innovation and aesthetic excellence. There are few awards for highest conversion rates and most effective A/B testing methodology.

We're also a bit afraid of creative directors. They often arrive at meetings fashionably late and fashionably dressed, their expensive watches set to a time zone halfway around the world. Through the frames of their stylish and retro eyeglasses, they peer out from behind the glow of their Macintosh laptops. They seem to know something we don't, and they aren't likely to share it with us anytime soon. They certainly don't seem aligned with the pragmatic and analysis-driven marketing culture this book encourages you to create.

If we turn the tables, however, the creative director may be concerned about the hard-core marketing department down the hall. Those folks have been driving a new way of thinking when it comes to the Web, and it appears to be paying off. A focus on timely updates and data-based decisions seems to be capturing the mindshare of senior management, and changes in the site are driven by the need for efficiency and improved user experience. Even pocket protectors seem to be coming back into vogue.

There you have it: a rich catalog of stereotypes and old-fashioned notions about one of the most important individuals driving success online. In reality, the creative director and the entire creative team are often your biggest allies in the quest for ROI. They want the user experience online to be as rich and stimulating a process as possible, but they also want to drive the business forward and see the ROI in everything they create. The creative team wants their customers—whether their own internal departments or the clients of an agency—to be happy. Happy clients usually mean more work for everyone and more rewards.

The Brief

Whether you're working with an agency or with your own creative department, the brief is where the work of bringing a site to life begins. Once you've selected an agency via the RFP process (see Chapter 12) or assigned the task to an internal team, the brief becomes the focus of your attention. It's the blueprint for everything you're about to build and run.

The way in which a creative brief starts establishes the tone for the entire project. Some briefs begin with a grand vision of how a site will look, how the colors of the brand will be brought to life, and what kind of multimedia experience every visitor should have on arrival. Other briefs begin with an eye toward analytics: describing the business goals, enumerating the KPIs, and cataloging how site performance should be measured day in and day out. This isn't just a creative brief; it's a *data-driven* creative brief.

How's a data-driven brief different? In many ways, it isn't. Core messaging, campaign concepts, and company and brand descriptions are similar to those found in every company's creative requirements. But a number of extra sections set a data-driven brief apart.

Components of a Data-Driven Brief

A data-driven brief ensures that a campaign focuses on achieving clearly defined brand or business goals. It's not a straitjacket for online creative, but it should act as a guideline to keep everyone aware of the campaign objectives.

The creative brief usually includes the following important questions:

Who are we targeting? Data-driven organizations tend to know exactly who they want to reach and how to measure the effectiveness of their communications.

What do we want to accomplish? This may seem like an obvious point, but you should set reasonable benchmarks for the success of any initiative.

How does the campaign strategy map to the larger digital strategy? That's right, you should be clear about the overall strategy for your digital channel, and how this particular initiative supports it.

What are the campaign offers? If you're offering something (and most campaigns do), be aware of what those offers are, and be prepared to measure their effectiveness.

Creative Brief Metrics

In addition to being clear on these particular points, you should add an extra section to your brief that outlines the metrics you hope to achieve with the initiative. You should try to include at least the following:

Baseline measurements of key metrics The creative brief should state how the company or site is doing before the campaign starts, as well as average industry metrics.

Goals and success metrics You should also include a metrical description of what success looks like. These goals should be reasonably aggressive.

ROI estimate If possible, the creative brief should try to estimate the overall financial impact of the initiative. This may not always be easy if the objective of the campaign doesn't directly include revenue, but you should eventually work to understand how every user behavior affects your bottom line.

Customer satisfaction and attitudinal study insights In addition to purely financial considerations, you may want to measure the emotional or other impact of an initiative. If a shoe company specializing in sports is trying to move into high-end fashion, for example, it will want to conduct surveys before and after a campaign to see if customer perception has changed.

Motivation for the creative team to achieve goals Some data-driven organizations build team motivation into the brief. This can include financial or other incentives to make sure goals are met.

There are other ways you can ensure a brief is informed by analytics, but by following these guidelines, you should be well on your way to building a data-driven organization.

Unfortunately, most briefs are missing the following information:

Initiative success metrics This is essential and requires a strategic approach to the work being described in the brief. Success has to be quantifiable and discrete; you must be able to explicitly say whether your initiative has been successful. There isn't a lot of room for being a "little bit pregnant" when it comes to the six- and seven-figure investments made in online initiatives.

Monetized ROI estimate of the initiative(s) If you haven't been thinking about monetization by now, it's time to start. You should begin the ROI process as soon as you begin any initiative, not after it has already been built and pushed out the door.

Examples of different types of monetization Monetization can be calculated in many ways, and it isn't necessarily true that sites dedicated to brand awareness or other intangibles can't be measured in cold hard currency. Focus on where the value lives in your business, and connect your strategy to that. Some of them are easy (e-commerce and some lead generation sites) and some are a lot tougher (branding and customer service). Here are the easy ones:

- e-Commerce
- Lead generation
- Permission marketing: e-mail opt-in, alerts, direct mail, and so on

And these are the tougher ones:

- Indirect retail channel influence
- Brand impact
- Community
- Multichannel integration

The creative brief shouldn't be an arduous task. It should be an opportunity to capture your thoughts and aspirations about your project. Everyone has a certain sense of ownership and pride in their work, and the creative brief is a great way to express and share that.

Analytics and Creativity

Later in this chapter, we'll look at a sample creative brief. First, you need a better understanding of how the creative director and creative staff benefit from an analytics-driven strategy.

Using the model we've been discussing throughout this book, it might seem that everything becomes quantitative and that decisions about websites can be made by anyone who has learned to read the data and follow the progress of KPIs. Although a lot can be driven from this analytical approach, the expertise of the creative staff is essential to the finished product. Design isn't something that can emerge from data or a set of optimization tests. Many rules, such as the grid and color theory, drive great design, but learning the rules doesn't make a designer. Good designers are also inspired.

The big win that can come from an analytical approach is the rapid impact and iteration that data can have on design. As a marketer, this may be the most powerful technique you'll find to get the creative aligned with the larger goals of an analysis mentality. The data that comes from usability testing and website behavior mapping can give the designer a test bed for rapid iteration and improvement.

Traditionally, the marketer first interacts with the creative director through the review meeting. This is when the results of the creative brief are shown. Usually, a big group of marketers and business owners for a site gather for a couple of hours, and the agency or internal design team presents a series of comps. This is the opportunity for the creative director to share their vision of what the site could look like. Usually there are three comps, but you may see as many as five or six.

In lots of these comp reviews, we see the Big Dog Syndrome come into play. As we've mentioned before, the big dog in the room is the most senior person, usually a VP or CMO. As the designs are presented, the team shares their thoughts about the strength and weaknesses of each. The big dog may chime in a lot or sit quietly. In either case, after all the comps are shown and everyone has had a chance to express their opinions, the room gets a little silent and heads turn to the big dog. They then issue their vote and tell what they like best. Often there is quick agreement among everyone that the big dog's choice is the right one for this project. Meeting over.

We're being dramatic here for a purpose. Most organizations aren't filled with sycophantic behavior, but Big Dog Syndrome does take place regularly. It's natural for teams to defer to the most senior member. It's how organizational decisions are made.

Here is the secret. As an agency, we've found that when we present comps to a client, the big dog almost always picks the one that we think is the weakest of the lot. Something about the way the big dog thinks seems to drive them toward designs that are at the opposite end of the spectrum from what designers think is best. This sets up a tension between the creative director and the client early in the process. The good news is that this tension can be avoided.

The Iterative Design Cycle

The comps shown at the review are usually the result of lots of creative brainstorming and rough sketches that have been shaped into a sharp design. This process can be loose and flexible and is often a reflection of the creative director's personal style.

In the interactive design cycle, designs are brought as quickly as possible to a stage ready for testing. These designs end up in the usability lab and have target users working with them in controlled situations. The designers watch the process carefully, and any issues with the design almost always immediately surface.

This makes the designers smile. They're smiling because they want their design to *work* as much as they want it to be aesthetically pleasing. If the lab shows that users are having trouble differentiating the fonts used to express one concept versus another on the screen, the designers can change it immediately.

Immediate observation and change make iterative design work. In a few days, the team can work through a set of designs and have them tuned by the reactions of real users. Things that are tested in the morning can be changed and retested in the afternoon!

After this cycle, when the comp review happens, it isn't just design that is presented. The research itself can be presented along with a highly tuned design. Instead of a time for everyone to express their own opinion, it becomes a time for the voice of the customer to be heard and the design to reflect that voice. Now the design works, and the creative designer is the proudest person in the room.

One of the authors once sat through a comp review with a group of marketing managers from a large technology company. After the designs had been shown and the big dog had made his choice, the real fun began. Instead of letting the design team go back and revise the design chosen (this was a situation where the agency didn't use the iterative design process), the meeting became a discussion about the color of lines used to demarcate areas of the screen and the suggestions from the marketing team that using a serif font made more sense. You could see the pain on the creative director's face. This was unnecessary pain, and you should work hard to avoid it.

A Sample Creative Brief

The best way to understand what a creative brief looks like is to see one. We've seen a lot of them over the years, and they range across the spectrum in terms of quality as well as in terms of detail. Being able to understand and respond to a good brief is a key part of the creative director's job, but they should also be prepared to work with a less than perfect brief and find a way to understand its intent.

Creative Brief: Robotwear.Com

- Brief Date: 8/31/06
- Project: Holiday Campaign
- Client Lead: Robin Johanson

Purpose of the brief

The purpose of this brief is to provide the strategic foundation that informs the online creative strategy for the RobotWear holiday online campaign. The brief will ensure that the campaign concept is focused on achieving the business and brand goals for the campaign. The brief should answer the following questions:

- What do we want to accomplish?
- How does the campaign strategy map back to and support the larger digital strategy?

What is the overarching strategy?

The strategy for the holiday is to continue to support the platform of originality, while aggressively driving demand for holiday product and awareness for RobotWear 2.0. The campaign must also gracefully support the continuation of the RobotWear Fall campaign, which will run concurrently with the holiday campaign through December.

Many brands stake a claim to the theme of originality, but only RobotWear has the brand heritage and pedigree to own it. RobotWear is where originality lives. The Web is the ideal destination to demonstrate originality and bring it to life in a unique way for each consumer through brand and product democracy, inspiration, and consumer expression and participation.

On November 15, RobotWear is launching several new products for Fall. We'll promote product to drive incremental revenue between two larger campaigns: Back to School and Holiday. We'll continue to drive awareness and interest in RobotWear 2.0, which was officially launched in July.

Who are we targeting?

The fall campaign targets RobotWear innovators 28–44.

What makes them innovators?

RobotWear innovators search and question, seeking to find the thing that captures their imagination and fuels their passion. Limited only by what their imaginations allow them to become. Poets. Pioneers. Revolutionaries. Rebels. Inventors. World-record holders. Leaders. Scientists. They're true to themselves and what they're compelled to become.

Secondarily, we'll target The Organizer, who is a fashion enthusiast, with the initiation of the Martha Signature Program. The influencer within this group is the suburban, adult female who sees home organization as one of her primary lifestyle influences, whether she does it for relaxation or as her job.

What do we want to accomplish?

We'll measure the performance of the campaign against the following goals during the period that the campaign runs: 08/23/08 to 11/13/08.

BRAND GOALS

- Continue to build RobotWear's innovation position
- Extend and strength offline brand themes
- Demonstrate originality and bring it to life

BUSINESS GOALS

Purpose	Goal
Increase revenue	$231,432
Increase visitor-to-purchase conversion	1.65%
Increase orders	3,500
Increase registrations	11,644
Improve visit-to-registration conversion	2.14%
Drive visits	570,000

We'll closely monitor consumer behavior and interaction following the launch of the campaign in order to identify opportunities for experience optimization, and also to inform future initiatives.

What is the core message that we want to communicate with this campaign?

Practice the science of The Organizer. Whether you choose from our new Fall products or define a style all your own, RobotWear has something as innovative as you.

What is the campaign strategy? How does it support the larger strategy for the RobotWear web channel?

The brand message of innovation will be tightly woven into the overall concept in a way that actively demonstrates innovation through providing the choice to select a Fall product or begin with a blank canvas, design your ideal product, and share your creation with the world.

Equal weight will be given to the Fall product icons in order to support freedom of choice. Stylized photography, merchandising, and selection will encourage purchase, as will supporting offers (see campaign offers section that follows). Demand for the new products will also be driven by the campaign e-mail and the launch of the HGTV.com boutique.

We'll employ a balanced strategy that will also allow us to build interest and intrigue around Martha Wilson and the upcoming season with a teaser for signature items (see Martha Signature Program creative brief for additional detail).

What is the campaign concept?

The concept for the Fall homepage will be product-focused, offering consumers the choice to select from Fall products or to design one of their own. The page will be equally balanced between lifestyle and performance, giving emphasis to both the Fall message and the initiation of the Martha Signature Program.

On the home page, about 60% will be dedicated to design-your-own and hot new Fall product and 40% to the Martha teaser campaign. This balance will give a dominant presence to the Signature release while supporting the remainder of the core audience. In addition, a notification for international shipping and a 15%-off offer will also be present.

The Robot2 and Junior Robot pages will be updated to include a more integrated Martha promotion/link. The Lifestyle and Julio pages will remain the same.

What are the campaign offers?

Supporting offers to drive sales and registration:

- Primary offers:
  - Register and receive 15% off your order. (Doesn't apply to Julio orders.)
  - Preorder the Martha line.
- Secondary offer: Sign up to be notified when subsequent Martha "stories" are available and ultimately when the Martha signature line is available for retail sale.
- Proposed tertiary offer: Submit your RobotWear success story.

What are the main campaign components?

ROBOTWEAR.COM

- Brand site background image will be updated.
- Brand site homepage will be redesigned per strategy above with associated registration page for the offer.
- Martha Wilson teaser campaign on the home and entertainment site with an associated registration page for the offer (see Martha Signature Program Creative Brief).
- The following brand pages will be updated with new product:
  - Outdoor Lifestyle page will add a Martha teaser.
  - Nighttime Lifestyle page will get a "Coming Soon" Martha banner for the Evening Robots line.
- Store banners will be updated to feature new products (see merch. calendar for details).

MARKETING

- E-mail to registered base (updates list, Martha list: de-duped).

What are the key milestones for the project?

Date	Milestone
Tuesday 8/2	Present draft creative brief
Friday 8/5	Final feedback provided by Converse
Friday 8/12	Present revised creative brief, feedback provided in meeting
Tuesday 8/16	Present sketches
Wednesday 8/17	RobotWear approves creative brief, sketches
Wednesday 8/23	Present brand site design comps (includes legal and MarthaCo review)
Tuesday 8/29	Present all design comps (revised brand, remaining comps) (includes legal and MarthaCo review)
Thursday 8/31	RobotWear approves all design comps (includes legal and MarthaCo)
Tuesday 9/13–Monday 9/26	Final site review and acceptance (includes legal and MarthaCo)
Monday 9/26	Launch Fall campaign with Martha teaser

Recap

In this chapter, we looked at how to write a data-driven creative brief. We began by looking at the role of the person most likely to receive the brief: the creative director. You saw that in a lot of ways, the kind of brief you'd ideally like to deliver to this person isn't much different from what they're used to seeing.

However, a few aspects are unique. In particular, the brief is much more specific when it comes to target audiences and campaign goals. It also should define success metrics carefully. These briefs should never be straitjackets and should always allow the creative director some leeway in how to achieve the goals. Ultimately, analytics and creativity aren't diametrically opposed. The use of benchmarks and goals can eliminate one of the biggest impediments to creative freedom: the big dog who makes uninformed decisions based on their gut instincts.

From there, we looked at an example of a well-written, data-driven creative brief. If you're able to create similar guidelines for your in-house team or outside agency, you should be well on your way to getting the most of out your data-driven design initiatives.

Staffing and Tuning Your Web Team

We've talked throughout the book about web analysts. But who are they, and what do they do? In this chapter, we'll focus on the essentials of finding or training a good web analyst, as well as other role types in a data-driven organization. We'll also look at what an analyst does from day to day. Hiring the right people with the right skillsets is an import step toward getting the most out of web analytics.

Chapter Contents

Skills That Make a Great Web Analyst

The preceding chapters have emphasized the importance of making decisions based on solid data *and* real-world experience rather than mere gut feelings. We hope that from now on, you won't select designs and headlines for a page in a meeting room. Instead, you'll roll out multiple versions of every change you make on your website and let your visitors tell you which one performs best.

At the same time, your company will ideally build different versions of the same page and serve them to different visitor segments. You may even have plans in the works to leverage behavioral, attitudinal, and competitive data, not in silos but all together to help identify the best opportunities. Key behaviors on your site will be monetized and projects prioritized based on them. There will even be a time down the road where all projects you undertake will be prioritized not by managerial preference, but by real forecasted business impact.

In the beginning of this book, we discussed something called a *culture of analysis*, and you saw how it's a long process to build one. Along the way, you'll probably want to make some important staffing changes, the most obvious of which is adding a good web analyst (or several).

Hiring a web analyst isn't like hiring a designer or writer. Those employees have traditional roles, along with formal training and experience. If you need a designer who can review overall goals and desired behaviors for a page and then create a few different design components for different aspects of the page, you can easily find one. Even if some of the work is new to that person, they're a designer, and they can leverage things they learned in school, training sessions, and on the job. Being a data-driven designer doesn't require a new skill set; it involves a shift in the way those skills are leveraged.

A web analyst is a different story. They fill a new role in corporate America, one that is essential in transforming your company into a successful data-driven organization. As of today, you won't find many web analysts with any formal education in the field. And judging their experience can be tricky. As you'll see, a lot of people have "web-analytics experience" that won't be much use to you.

Technical vs. Interpretive Expertise

When we talk to new or prospective web-analytics clients, we often hear stories of how disappointed they are with the performance of the people they've chosen to lead their analytics initiatives. There seems to be a major disconnect between the analytics roles companies need to fill and the skill sets available in the current workforce. At ZAAZ, we face this problem every day as we try to grow our team. Who are these people, and what types of backgrounds do they have?

If you search job-board sites for people with web-analytics experience, you'll find a large number of résumés. Nowadays, it's considered a valuable skill set, but people who list it on their CVs don't necessarily have the experience you're looking for. Often, they've had contact with web-analytics tools, but at a higher, more technical level. Companies need technical leads, but these aren't the kind of people who can spearhead the transition a data-driven organization.

To narrow your search, you may want to add the company names of several common analytics tools, such as WebTrends, Omniture, and WebSideStory. If you do that, you'll find a number of qualified people to help you run the servers and web-analytics tools. This is again a valuable skill set. But there's a significant difference between someone who can manage the tool and someone who understands visitor behavior, testing, and strategies that can help you act on data.

One particular thing to watch for is people who say they have WebTrends experience. It turns out that WebTrends is the company that put web analytics on the map, and it built a broad client base early on. Unfortunately, because of the way the software works, you can find many people who can say they have "web analytics experience with WebTrends" and don't know much about analytics in the sense that we're talking about. Having said that, you also can find people who have solid experience in analysis using WebTrends data.

You need technical skills that can keep servers and analytics tools running perfectly. But to take the next step in web analytics, you need something more.

Key Web Analyst Skills

When we hire a new web analyst, we look carefully at their resume. Often, you can find people who are qualified or will quickly master the skills they need. And it's not merely knowledge of tools that we're talking about—that can be learned fairly easily. Usually, we try to find someone who has the right background. That includes the following:

- Experience in web strategy. Have they run or been a part of a team running an enterprise-level website?
- An understanding of different data types. They should have the ability to analyze and interpret data types—everything from financial systems to behavioral, attitudinal, and competitive data.
- Experience in identifying opportunities to improve online businesses.
- Direct marketing experience.
- An MBA or MBA-type experience.

We also look for people with an understanding of statistics, a business intelligence background, or experience in analyzing data from specific tools. Over time, we've found we have the most success with people who can blend a strong web-strategy and business background with a solid understanding of data.

Most important, when you're choosing a web analyst, remember that the job is not only about analytics; it's also about improving web businesses. Web analytics investments and initiatives are supposed to drive your company's bottom line success. Analytics are only a means to an end. Make sure they understand the big picture.

The Roles of the Web Analyst

A web analyst's job shares many characteristics with a number of more traditional jobs in corporate America. A successful, business-focused web analyst should have many of the same skills and qualities of the following professions:

Accountant Good web analysts can track the financial performance and ROI of the web channel, including campaigns, affiliates, and other online initiatives.

Actuary They should also be able to assess and reduce the risk of undesirable things happening, such as rolling out a new site page or section that doesn't meet needs and reduces conversion and revenue significantly.

Scientific investigator Just as a scientist studies difficult and often unknown things, a good web analyst may work with a company to help crack the conversion nut. A site that has had low visibility in the past needs to break new ground to find answers.

Computer systems analyst Web analysts aren't normally systems analysts, unless you classify the web channel as a system. That said, a reasonable level of technical experience is required to understand site performance. Things you see with web-analytics tools may lead you to identify system problems, such as slow download speeds.

Financial planner The ability to forecast the financial outcome of potential site changes is what separates great from merely good web analysts. They must identify opportunities and make recommendations and then prioritize those opportunities based on the potential outcome of the site changes. And they have to be able to monetize opportunities and forecast results.

Parole officer A web analyst is often required to hold people or initiatives accountable. Before people understood individual campaign performance, for example, they were free to spend money in the wrong place. In their role as parole officer, the analyst helps the web team make better decisions and understand the effects of their actions.

Marketer This is an easy one. Web analysts should know how to generate interest in and help people understand the value of opportunities.

Software engineer Web analysts must know how sites are built and function. To work effectively with tool providers and make good use of customization capabilities, a web analyst requires a solid technical understanding of the site.

Statistician To interpret and derive meaning from data, the analyst needs a strong statistics background.

Motivational speaker They also must have the ability to get people excited and motivated about opportunities, particularly about the ability to improve web performance and the overall business.

Website manager Although the people in charge of analytics don't usually manage the entire site, often it's their responsibility to manage its metrics and KPIs.

That's a tall order. It helps explain why so few truly qualified web-analytics professionals are available on today's market. Even so, we've managed to find some excellent analysts among the stacks of resumes we see. With a little luck, you should be able to as well.

Building Your Web-Analytics Team: Internal and External Teams

One of the first steps you need to take in building a team is to budget properly for the effort. Unfortunately, most companies typically only think about the technology costs and fail to estimate the full cost of professional implementation and business consulting services. Not surprisingly, the biggest complaint we hear about web analysis is that a company purchases an expensive solution but gets little more than meaningless statistics out of it. Without an experienced analytics team, that's exactly what happens.

There's more than anecdotal evidence to support this. In a recent report, Jupiter-Research noted that "Staffing is strongly correlated with the likelihood that analytics applications will be used well…. Companies assigning at least one dedicated resource are at least twice as likely as those assigning none to measure conversion rates, integrate external search marketing data, measure marketing spending, as well as use A/B testing strategies and funnel analysis tools to incrementally improve Web sites."

The first step to building a web team is make an accurate assessment of what the entire effort will cost. This depends largely on the route you decide to take. When it comes to building a team, you have three options:

In-house team You can hire dedicated staff to oversee and implement your analysis internally.

Outsourced agency You can hire an experienced, outside consultancy.

Combination You can hire both your own people and others. Optimally, what we've seen to be most successful is to pair an experienced outside team with an internal dedicated team.

Estimating Your Cost

You also need to know exactly what it will cost to get you up and running. These expenses vary, but they include obvious things such as your tools, if you don't already have them. Some other items you should consider include the following:

Full-time employee (FTE) costs By far your biggest potential cost is FTE expenditure. To get the most from your web-analytics software, you must have a team of people dedicated to internal communication, data integration, internal meetings, tool maintenance and configuration, and so on.

If you have one FTE dedicated to web analysis, calculating the expense is easy. If you disperse duties across several individuals in different departments, such as IT and marketing, you must estimate the time associated with common analysis tasks on a weekly and monthly basis. Once you've figured out the total time needed, calculate it as a percentage of the FTE's salary for gross cost. A dedicated FTE can cost you anywhere from $50,000 to $100,000 in annual salary, plus overhead expenses.

Implementation services You'll encounter additional expenses in customizing an analytics tools to conform to your business requirements. Be sure to ask your analytics software vendor about pricing for these types of services.

Training and skill development Technical and business-user training costs can be high, particularly because they often involve on-the-job training. Don't underestimate the training needed to get maximum utilization of the technology.

External analysis services External web-analytic companies can provide success metric definitions, financial modeling (including TCO analysis), analytic tool recommendations, implementation, accuracy audits, and ongoing analysis. Even though such services add to the initial cost, they're invaluable in helping you save money and get better information in the long run.

Key Analytics Positions

At ZAAZ, we've worked with smart, nimble boutique firms and Fortune 100 juggernauts alike. When an enterprise analytics team clicks, it clicks for similar reasons, no matter what the scale. Looking at successful teams, we see recurring models, assignments, and action plans. At its base, a good team has a strong foundation, typically anchored by two starring roles: a technical lead who serves as the manager of the tool and tagging details, and a strategic analytics lead who can turn data into solid business recommendations and be the champion for changing the ways business decisions are made and opportunities prioritized:

Technical lead Companies that are successful with analytics invariably have an analytics technical lead. This individual isn't typically a real web analyst as we discussed earlier. Instead, they deal with the nuts-and-bolts issues of web pages and tracking tools. The position's responsibilities include the following:

- Managing software and servers.
- Managing the tagging strategy. They determine the best way to place visitor-tracking tags on website pages and then ensure that those pages show up

correctly and consistently in the analytics tool. Where applicable, they also work with third-party content providers and partners to tag pages.

- Ensuring that new pages or site changes carry proper tracking tags.
- Managing tracking-tool changes and upgrades.

Analytics lead The person leading your analytics effort should be much like the web analyst we discussed earlier. Analytics leads are the champions, evangelists, and advocates of all web-analytics efforts. Their responsibilities include the following:

- Helping key stakeholders define site or section goals and the data readouts needed to drive improvements
- Developing a data-distribution strategy that features weekly, monthly, and quarterly reports, as well as ways to bring them to the attention of stakeholders
- Helping interpret data as a basis for site architecture or design changes
- Driving A/B testing to solve specific site problems identified through analytics

Expanding the Circle of Influence

Technical and analytics leads typically come from different places and have different skill sets, so it's unlikely you'll find one person who does both jobs. We've found that organizations that can dedicate two full-time people to these positions typically do much better with them.

Beyond these two, you should try to build an influential circle of advocates who can provide vital support to your fledgling analytics team. They should include the following:

- Executive management who often prioritize initiatives and help define website success metrics at the highest level
- Web designers, information architects, and developers who implement data-driven improvements
- Business group leads

Internal vs. External Teams

As we've said, our most successful clients have leveraged both internal team members as well as outside expertise. Even though we run a web-analytics practice and a data-driven design team, we still don't advocate outsourcing 100 percent of your web analytics on a long-term basis. For stability and some oversight, you should always have someone in house. On the other hand, it doesn't make a lot of sense to launch web-analytics efforts without outside help. The ideal mix will change over time depending on your organization, growth, and potential upside in optimizing your site.

When looking at the pros and cons of each approach, you should consider the following:

Going it alone

Pros

- **Avoid outside costs.** Although it may seem tempting, this advantage should be taken with a grain of salt. The loss of opportunity in only a few months often far exceeds what you could pay to get started with an outside agency.

- **Build internal expertise.** On the other hand, this is a valuable asset and needs to happen either way you go. Long term, you want analytics fully integrated into the overall organization.

Cons

- **Long learning curve.** Building up your own expertise will take considerable time.

- **Opportunity cost.** Most likely, you'll spend 12 to 18 months before you start getting the kinds of actionable insight you need. You won't be able to take advantage of opportunities to improve your business right away. Most likely, you'll leave a lot of money on the table.

- **Myopic view of analytics.** You won't have the benefit of an outside perspective from someone who has seen how other companies implement analytics. In other words, you won't be sure that what you're seeing is normal.

Leveraging external expertise

Pros

- **Greatly reduced learning curve.** You'll begin reaping benefits right away.
Learn from the agency's past experiences. This will help you avoid common problems and allow you to leverage the agency to overcome stumbling points.

- **Build credibility internally.** Instead of starting, stopping, and changing processes internally, you can begin with a clear roadmap and executive support. That way, you can roll out an overall plan to get everyone excited.

- **Training.** The agency can train and teach your staff members how to use the data.

- **Maximize the opportunities that you identify.** A solid, experienced agency should be able to share solutions to the opportunities that data unveils through testing.

Cons

- **Exterior cost.** As we noted earlier, when you work with the right experienced partner agency, the agency fees are dwarfed by the return you should realize. If they aren't, you should find a new partner.

- **Lack of control.** This can be a real problem, and you should explore it with whatever partner you're thinking of employing. Make sure they help you build internal expertise and that they're helping other groups in your organization understand how they can leverage the insight analytics can provide.

Ideally, you'll find a way to leverage internal resources as well as work with outside experts. Make sure you find someone with proven experience not only with analytics but also with transforming an organization. If you're talking to someone and all they're talking about is analytics and not the other parts of your organization that will be impacted, you probably aren't talking to the right agency.

Education and Training for Web Analysts

As we discussed earlier, it isn't easy to find experienced web-analytics experts who can help you leverage data to improve site performance. Often, "experienced" people are experienced only in using or managing a specific tool. More often than not, they don't understand business strategy or how to transform data into insight and drive changes on the site.

Where do you find people experienced in turning data into insight and recommendations, and how do they get the training and education they need? The following sections describe a few of the different types of training and education that are available to web analysts today as well as other ways they gain experience.

Web Analytics Association

The Web Analytics Association (WAA; www.webanalyticsassociation.org) was created in 2004 and is a diverse industry group mainly composed of analytics professionals and tool providers. Its goal is to promote a better understanding of web analytics in business.

The WAA can be a great resource for learning the ropes of analytics and benefiting from the experiences of others. The membership is diverse and is a great educational resource in an industry where most people are self-taught by one-of-a-kind experiences.

Conferences

Industry conferences are another good way to learn. Although most conferences are starting to include at least a few sessions on web analytics, they're still fairly sparse. A few focus exclusively on analytics, such as Jim Sterne's outstanding Emetrics Summit (www.emetrics.org).

The Emetrics Summits are currently held a few times a year around the world. The content presented at these conferences is usually excellent, and the events are always sold out. It's a great way to learn and network with others in the space.

The good news is that the Emetrics Summit content and focus is branching out from standard web analytics into questions of how to improve your website through the use of both analytics and other data.

You should make sure that at minimum your lead web analysts attend this annually (if not the extended team) if you want to take full advantage of web analytics and other data types.

University of British Columbia Courses

A few years ago, the University of British Columbia (www.tech.ubc.ca/webanalytics) began offering a remote-learning course in conjunction with the WAA, making it the first formal university course focusing on web analytics. This is another great way to learn the basics of web analytics.

Message Boards

A few message boards offer a good volume of participation and insight. The most popular one today was started by Eric Peterson two years ago on Yahoo!. You can find it at:

http://tech.groups.yahoo.com/group/webanalytics

Whenever you're on a board anywhere, remember that just because someone gave an opinion, it may not be accurate. But message boards can be a great way to find out what people are thinking about and what kind of work they're doing.

ClickZ and Other Online Media

Another way to learn from others is through online marketing sites such as ClickZ (www.clickz.com). On this site, you can find a lot of great columns (including two from the authors of this book) focusing not just on web analytics but also on online marketing in general.

Blogs

As of the writing of this book, new web-analytics bloggers are popping up daily. As with all blogs, some are insightful and others not so much. Among the best is Avinash Kaushik's "Occam's Razor" (www.kaushik.net/avinash). Avinash continuously explores great topics and provides insight that often leverages other web-analytics experts' options.

If you're going to read only one web-analytics blog this is the one, but there are other good ones out there to explore. And surely many more will be launched in the future.

Web Analytics Wednesdays

Analytics advocate Eric Peterson started the idea of Web Analytics Wednesday (www.webanalyticsdemystified.com/wednesday) in 2006 in Portland, Oregon, and then encouraged people in other cities around the U.S. to do the same. The event is a casual get-together for like-minded web analysts. On one Wednesday per month, participants can network, share war stories, and have a good time. It's an especially good idea because most organizations have only one or two analysts, and it's great to find like minds who can help you explore new ideas.

Vendor Training

Training from analytics tool vendors such as Omniture, WebSideStory, Google Analytics, Coremetrics, and WebTrends can give you a great education about how the tool works. Most of the top analytics software providers offer both in-person training and some form of remote Web-based training.

Most of the training unfortunately revolves around configuring and using the tool. It doesn't usually focus on how to *use* the data. Because you've read the book, you probably understand that unless you put the data to work, you're wasting your time.

You should leverage your tool-provider's training to ensure that you're using the tool correctly and understand what is available to you; that knowledge is imperative. But it's more important to focus on the training you need to act on the data as well. Again, you shouldn't expect to get this type of training from the tool providers. It isn't in their DNA—they're all about their product.

Agency Partners

Experienced agency partners are another great way for your organization to learn best practices. Because the top-tier agencies that focus on leveraging web analytics and building data-driven organizations have most likely worked with many different clients, you may find working with them to be a fast and efficient way to get your team up to speed.

Hands-on Experience

Of course, the best way to learn how to analyze and make recommendations based on data is to jump into the trenches. Many of the ideas we've mentioned will help you, but there's no substitute for real-world experience. Pick the most important conversion on your site, and start by trying to understand one step in the process. Remember, you're looking for opportunities and formulating recommendations, not just seeing how the site is doing!

Recap

In this chapter, we've looked at how to build a proper web-analytics organization. You first saw that web analytics is a new field, and it can be difficult to find a person with the experience and temperament needed to succeed in the profession. Because web analytics is a hot topic, it's showing up on more people's résumés. However, that doesn't mean they can take data and use it to drive positive change and better ROI on your site.

Instead of focusing on skill with a particular tool, we recommend looking for a person with different kinds of real-world business, marketing, and statistics experience. Good web analysts exist, but you should be careful in making a hiring decision.

We also looked at the role web-analytics agencies can play in helping to build up your capabilities. Should you hire an outside company or go it alone? We hope you agree with us that to achieve rapid and enduring success, you should probably do a combination.

From there, we discussed staffing your organization with two key people: a technical lead and an analytical lead. The first manages your online analytics efforts, and the second serves as an evangelist and change agent for your company. Having both is a great step on the road to success.

In the final section, we examined opportunities for training in web analytics—either for you or for your staff. Unfortunately, you won't find many ways to do that, but as the field grows, so will the educational base supporting it.

Partners

This closing chapter brings together everything we've discussed so far in the book and focuses on choosing an analytics tool and tool vendor. We've intentionally left this topic for last because it's often easy to focus on the tools first—software is tangible—and forget the basics of why we use the tools. We hope this discussion will help you make sense of a complex landscape.

Chapter Contents

When to Choose an Analytics Tool Vendor

Many people may find it strange that we've left the discussion of analytics tools to the end of the book. Why did we do this? Because whenever we enter an engagement with a new client, we typically start by asking them a series of questions:

- What are the goals for your e-business channel?
- What are your key performance indicators?
- Are you confident in the accuracy of your data?
- Do you have dedicated staff (internal or external) responsible for online behavioral analysis?
- Are you acting on these insights?
- Are you happy with your web-analytics vendor?

By reading the rest of this book, you know that we're interested in the first five of these questions. Goals, KPIs, accuracy, staffing, and action are of paramount importance if you're going to have success with web analytics. Tools? Unfortunately, the vast majority of our clients focus on them: They typically see their analytics vendor as the root of all evil. As you learned in Chapter 4, this is typically a false assumption. Tools—no matter how sophisticated—can't ensure success without a plan.

Unfortunately, most organizations kick off their analytics efforts by purchasing a software package. They implement it, look at the standard reports, and try to gain insights. We once attended a vendor sales demonstration where a slick-looking salesman confidently stated that his software could deliver more than 2 million out-of-the-box reports. Our eyes got big—not because we were impressed with the volume of reports available at our fingertips, but because we were wondering what in the world they expected people to do with 2 million reports. Most organizations need fewer than 10. Determining which 10 reports you need out of 2 million options is the task, and it requires both the art and science of analytics.

When we looked around the room, many of the people looked impressed. What they felt they would do with 2 million reports, we're not sure, but they certainly felt those reports had some value. That's why we've purposely put this chapter last in the book. We want to counter most organizations' intuition that they can buy software, and everything will be better. Of course, we're sometimes guilty of the same kind of thinking. When we started writing this book, we had an old version of Microsoft Word. We thought if we bought the latest upgrade, we'd be in a better position to finish. We already had a decent tool to do word processing; what we lacked was a comprehensive strategy to get the book done.

More than half a dozen tools in the industry can solve 97 percent of the e-business questions and problems out there. Recently, there has been much debate and activity around companies like Google that are offering an analytics tool for free. Free software? This must be heresy? How can it work?

The truth is that Google's tools may not be the best. But it's also true that the gaps in web analytics have little to do with the software available. Therefore, we recommend that you strongly consider a free tool as a start for your organization. They're becoming more sophisticated every day.

Methodology for Selecting a Tool

Most companies want something more than a free tool, however. How do you go about purchasing one? As with most sophisticated business decisions, if you're planning to select an analytics vendor, following a proper methodology is important to ensure success. We suggest the following steps:

1. Appoint a review committee.
2. Set up a timeline.
3. Determine investment and ROI expectations.
4. Write an RFP.
5. Meet each vendor in person (if possible), and ask specific questions.
6. Select the tool, and implement.

In the following pages we will outline some of the important aspects to lead you through the selection process. This information will get you started with the six steps above.

Selecting a Review Committee

Your first step should be to set up a review committee to evaluate all the vendor options. This should be a cross-functional team led by your e-business marketing group (or similar corporate structure). It should include a strong partnership with your IT and site-development teams.

The committee's first task should be to determine the kinds of metrics to collect. By this point in reading this book, you should have a pretty clear idea of how to determine those metrics. What kinds of things will your organization be looking at with web analytics? Although we've said that the top-tier tools deliver mostly the same kind of data, there are differences, and you should make sure you can easily get the kind of data you want.

Another important early task for the review committee is to secure executive sponsorship. Throughout this book, we've demonstrated the need to have high-level backing for your analytics initiatives, and selecting a tool is no different.

It is imperative that this committee not get caught up in all the features of the tool and make an emotional discussion on a cool feature within a given tool. We have seen far too many companies get into the selection process and get wooed by something that "would be great down the road" and miss the boat on what is going to help them solve their business problems. While making sure that it's a solution that can work for your site and team from a technical standpoint, the most important factor must be how it is going to help you understand your visitors to directly improve your business. Don't take your eyes off of this point during this process.

Establishing a Timeline

How long should you take to determine what tool you'll buy? This depends on the nature of your organization and the number of tools you have to select. Typically, we recommend that you spend at least a month determining your success metrics. After that, we recommend writing an RFP that outlines your needs to your vendor. From there, the following timeline should apply:

- Three weeks for vendors to prepare a presentation
- One week for presentations
- Two weeks for your company to select the provider
- One to four weeks for contract negotiation and final tool selection

Criteria to Review and Select Vendors

When you're selecting vendors, you need to consider a variety of factors. Mainly, they fall into three categories: technical and implementation, reporting and analysis, and customer service. Each vendor's presentation should span all three of these issues (a lot of times, they'll want to talk about reporting but gloss over customer service). You should be sure that they cover a wide range of questions, which are both general and specific to your organization. In the following sections, we'll list the most important of these. There's no need to read them exhaustively, but you should look at them closely enough to understand the kinds of issues you should raise. They will also give you a handy checklist as you prepare for your selection process.

Technical and Implementation Questions

These questions cover the nuts-and-bolts aspects of the implementation. Because tools often provide the same kind of data, the answers to these questions may be more important to your organization than any others. The most important technical questions include the following:

- Provide an overview of the analytics tool, and discuss the underlying technology. Describe how information is collected, processed, and made available to the end user.
- Describe the process for the initial placement of site-tracking code on the website. How is this process affected by different technology platforms?
- How do you validate the implementation? How are the final sign-off and acceptance documented and handled? What are the responsibilities of each organization?
- Can you implement a proof of concept on a microsite?

- What is required to capture visitor behavior when interacting with Flash sites or embedded Flash content?

- What security measures are in place to ensure that data isn't lost, stolen, or compromised?

- What technical support is provided during the implementation phase?

- What kind of documentation is available on the tool, and how is this information maintained and distributed?

- Is there a single point of contact for implementation? How do you handle post-implementation support requests? What about future customization requests?

- What types of external data can be imported into the analytics tool? How is this done?

- Discuss the infrastructure, architecture, and system monitoring that ensures reliability and data backup.

- Do you provide a web service or some other server-side interface that we can use to supply and retrieve data for tracking?

- How do you monitor performance (in terms of speed) to ensure that there is no slowdown in transactions? Is there redundancy? Are disaster-recovery procedures in place?

Reporting and Analysis

So much for getting the tool up and running. You should also be interested in what kinds of data you can get from it. As we've said before, most high-end tools can probably deliver all the data you need. But one tool may group and deliver that data in ways that work better for your organization. Some of the questions you'll want to ask include these:

- What are the key features and benefits of the tool? Which features differentiate your tool from the competition?

- How are audience segments created, and what types of reports can be developed against these segments?

- How does your tool define a unique visitor? How does the tool define a returning visitor?

- How does the tool track onsite search functionality?

- How does your solution handle onsite advertising—ads or promotional placements that may drive users to other sites or deeper within the site?

- Demonstrate and describe the functionality used to manage campaigns of the following types:
  - Search marketing
  - E-mail marketing

- - Onsite promotion/merchandising
  - Integration of third-party campaign information (publishers, agencies)
- What integration do you provide for pulling in data from third parties?
- What kind of integration from offline data sources can you provide?
- Is there a means for a power user to do self-directed exploration through the data? How can a user expose the full scope of the data and mine it for personal discovery?
- What kinds of ad hoc reporting can be done with the tool?
- What are the most frequent causes of data-accuracy issues? What tools and processes are available to detect and correct accuracy issues?
- How does your tool create scorecards and dashboards and send them to business users?
- Can the system support the push of reports to users on a recurring basis?

Account Service and Support

Equally important is how the vendor will support your implementation and ongoing use of the tool. Some of the important questions here include the following:

- How is pricing determined for the tool?
- What features come standard, and which ones require an additional charge?
- What is your standard service level agreement?
- What ongoing training is available?
- What other sorts of services are available, including consulting, analysis, and optimization services?
- What other tools are available, such as campaign tools, search tools, and scalable professional and junior versions of the tool?
- What other clients do/have you worked with in the financial services vertical?
- How do you handle contract renewals?
- Please provide two referrals that we may contact.

10 Questions to Ask Web Analytics Vendors

Our friend Avinash Kaushik has offered his own take on 10 questions you should ask any web analytics vendor. We've included them here:

1. What is the difference between your tool/solution and Google Analytics (or any other free solution that may emerge from Microsoft, Yahoo!, or another large software vendor)? Please share your top five—just five—reports that are different from the free reports available.

2. Are you 100 percent application service provider (ASP), or do you offer a software version we can buy and install in-house? Are you planning to do a software version?

3. What data-capture mechanisms do you use? JavaScript only? JavaScript and weblogs? Weblogs only? Others?

4. Please help us calculate the total cost of ownership (TCO) for your tool.

5. What kind of support do you offer? What is included for free, and what would cost more? Is free 24/7? What are the limits? How far will you go to help me solve my technical problems and answer silly questions from my business users?

6. What features in your tool allow me to segment the data?

7. What options do I have to export data from your system into our company system? Can I get all the raw data? Can I export processed data? How easy is it for me to export 100,000 rows of processed (not raw) data out of your tool into my other company systems? What happens if I terminate my contract with you?

8. What kinds of features do you provide for me to integrate data from other sources into your tool?

9. What are two new features/tools/analytical advancements/acquisitions that your company is cooking up that will keep you ahead of your competition for the next three years?

10. Why did the last two clients you lost cancel their contracts with you? Who are they using now? Would you permit us to call one of them?

Comparing to Free Tools

1. What is the difference between your tool/solution and Google Analytics (or any other free solution that may emerge from Microsoft, Yahoo!, or another large software vendor)? Please share your top five—just five—reports that are different from the free reports available.

The first question ("how do you differ from a free tool") is not as simple as it might seem. For many businesses, there are free tools available that can more than satisfy their basic analytics needs. However, tools vendors so often push all the features they offer that buyers can feel a bit intimidated into spending money unnecessarily. If free works, then free might be good enough for you (and your vendor might be charging too much if they can't convince you they offer more value).

Now to dig into some of the details of the key questions you will want to understand:

ASP or Software Version

2. Are you 100 percent application service provider, or do you offer a software version we can buy and install in-house? Are you planning to do a software version?

We're on the record saying that one of the challenges vendors will face is that clients will want to have solutions that are software based and in-house rather than ASP based. Currently, most vendors are ASP based with no software-based offerings (except WebTrends and ClickTracks). That's OK for now, but it may not be so in a year or two.

With this question, you're trying to probe for how ready the vendor is for the future in terms of differentiating offerings for you, should you want them (and you will, if not tomorrow, then in the near future). You're also looking for the intangible: how they react to this question, as much as the content of their answer.

You can also ask them about first-party and third-party cookies, which ones they use, and how much pain and cost first-party would require. You should almost always use first-party cookies, and most vendors enable this. You're looking for their reaction. Do they proactively advise you to have first-party cookies? Do they insist on it? It shows the mindset of the vendor.

Data Capture

3. What data-capture mechanisms do you use? JavaScript only? JavaScript and weblogs? Weblogs only? Others?

There are many different ways to capture data: JavaScript tags, packet sniffers, sensors, and so on. JavaScript tags and weblogs are the most common, and each has its merits.

In the answer to this question, you're looking for the kind of flexibility a vendor has natively in dealing with different data-capture formats. You want a vendor that may evolve beyond JavaScript tags (or logs or sniffers) as the Web evolves and becomes much harder to track (as in Flash, Flex, RIAs, RSS, mash-ups, and things we don't even know about yet). No current methodology will survive for a long time. Is the vendor you're considering ready for the near future's data-capture challenges?

You aren't looking for them to brainwash you that JavaScript tags are the answer to all your prayers (or weblogs or packet sniffers or sensors). If they try that, chalk it up in the suboptimal sales choice column.

Total Cost of Ownership

4. Please help us calculate the total cost of ownership (TCO) for your tool.

Most vendors will tell you that that the cost of their tool will be $30 per month for any site of any size, and it's an all-you-can-eat buffet. OK, we're stretching that a bit, but not by much.

The TCO of a web-analytics tool can be massively different depending on who you are as a company, what you already have in place, and, mostly, who your vendor is and what their pricing strategies are. We encourage you to poke and dig for data to get a clear understanding of the TCO for each vendor you're considering.

Here are the elements of TCO that you should consider:

TCO = Cost per page view (because most ASP-based vendors charge per page view)

+ Incremental costs beyond initial lump sum (charge if you go over your allocated page views; if there any advanced features such as RIA tracking, RSS, extra modules that cost more, or anything else you might buy from the vendor that you may need later—for example, pay-per-click integration with Google/YSM or a keyword-bidding feature—it's better to know now)

+ Annual support costs after year one

+ Cost of professional services (initial install and then post-launch troubleshooting or customizations)

+ Any additional hardware you need at your end (PCs, laptops, web servers, data-storage drives, and so on; these can vary by vendor)

+ Cost of administration (managing the vendor relationship; this may be a partial head count, or someone to create all the reports and publish them, or someone to coordinate between vendor and IT and marketers, or these could be one person; it's better to know now)

+ Cost of analysts needed to draw insights (you can lump this with the previous cost if you want, but it's important to be aware of the 10/90 rule and realize that you can't just buy the tool—you also have to hire a relatively intelligent brain to interpret the data; some vendors have stated that their tools are so smart that you don't need analysts, which would work in your favor, but make sure you buy that)

+ Additional head count (partial or full) to maintain the tags, liaise with IT, update pages on the site, and so on

Total that up across vendors, and make an informed choice. The only item that isn't in the "unique to each vendor" camp is the analysts you'll need. Stress-test whether it's OK to break the 10/90 rule because the tool inherently is so smart.

Also notice that although some of these factors are eliminated with a free tool, others apply even in the case of a free vendor.

Support

5. What kind of support do you offer? What is included for free, and what costs more? Is free 24/7? What are the limits? How far will you go to help me solve my technical problems and answer silly questions from my business users?

During vendor pitches, you'll hear that everything is free (and some web-analytics vendors do offer loads of absolutely free support, as long as you stay with them). But often there are limits and caveats that aren't explicit, and you have to dig them out.

Signing a contract and implementing the solution signifies the start of your problems—not the end. It's critical that you understand exactly what you'll get and exactly how much it will cost to get what you need. For example, if a vendor only provides business-hour support during weekdays, what would 24/7 support cost? Or if they only answer questions about the tool and not about why the tool isn't working with your site, what would those additional answers cost? These are just suggestions to get your juices flowing; you'll have to make up your own unique questions.

You'll need support and professional services. Understand what the vendor will provide or what the vendor's authorized consultants will provide.

Data Segmentation

6. What features in your tool allow me to segment the data?

Without segmentation, data isn't insightful. That sounds extreme, but segmentation is the fastest path to insights. You should stress your vendor about exactly what options you have to segment data and how easy it is to do. Try it yourself, and see if you can segment data in the tool.

Also ask for one important point: Do you have to precode everything in custom JavaScript tags on each page on your site to be able to segment the data post capture? Or can you capture data with a standard tag and do segmentation later (even though you didn't implement all the segmentation possibilities before launch in custom JavaScript tags)?

Most vendors are in the *former* camp—custom JavaScript tags on pages to enable any segmentation—and that makes segmentation much harder (how can you think of all the questions you'll ask of the data up front before you install the tool?). Again, understand where the vendor is, and make an informed choice.

Data Export and Options

7. What options do I have to export data from your system into our company system? Can I get all the raw data? Can I export processed data? How easy is it for me to export 100,000 rows of processed (not raw) data out of your tool into my other company systems? What happens if I terminate my contract with you?

That's a lot of questions, but it's really one important question: Who owns the data? And if the vendor stores it and you want to export it, do you get the raw logs (huge data files with no intelligence in terms of computed metrics, so you have to figure out how to do that) or processed data (computed data that is much easier to integrate into wherever you're taking it)?

This question is a process of you discovering what you need and realizing that you aren't going to get it and then being OK with that (or not). Typically, most vendors will say that you can export everything. Ask them these specific questions, understand exactly what you can export (remember that "you can get an Excel dump" isn't the answer, which is why we mentioned 100,000 rows earlier), and then form an opinion about whether that is sufficient for your company.

We aren't recommending that you insist on getting all the data or getting it in a particular way; we recommend that you ask the hard questions so you aren't disappointed later about what you'll get, if you need it.

Data Integration

8. What kinds of features do you provide for me to integrate data from other sources into your tool?

Bottom line: No matter what vendor you use, your clickstream data will feel limiting after a while when you want real insights, and you'll be forced to integrate it with other sources of data. Because the export route (question 7) is so hard, you'll have to bring that data in. This question goes to the heart of figuring out how easy it is to do that for each vendor you're considering.

Examples of data you may want to bring into your tool are meta-data from other sources in your company, your CRM data, data from your ad/search agency, data from surveys that includes the primary key (such as cookie values), A/B or multivariate testing integration so you can measure conversion from the MVT tool but also analyze site overlay (click density) for each recipe, and so on. You must be able to import data efficiently (without needing humans, if possible) and then use it for segmentation or reporting.

Some vendors can automatically pick up data from Google AdWords and do direct integration without your having to do anything. Others require you to do a daily download yourself and upload a text or CSV file into your tool. Others can't do anything. Figure out the line in the sand for the vendor you're considering for the kinds of data you want to integrate.

The Future

9. What are two new features/tools/analytical advancements/acquisitions that your company is cooking up that will keep you ahead of your competition for the next three years?

At the core of this question, you're trying to see if your vendor is good at dealing with today or if they're worried about tomorrow and have plans to deal with it.

It also gives you a sense of how much they know about their own position and that of their competitors (you don't ask for two things they're doing that are good; the framing is in the context of competition). As our conference experience at Emetrics 2006 Washington DC event experiment proved, some vendors are much better at forming a good reality check about themselves.

You want one of the two things to be a complete surprise to you (which means they're ahead of you, which is always a good thing), and you want to get the feeling that your vendor has a good sense for themselves and their competitors.

If you ask this same question across a few vendors, they will talk about each other. The differing perspectives are a source of valuable insights for you.

References

10. Why did the last two clients you lost cancel their contracts with you? Who are they using now? Would you permit us to call one of them?

A vendor taught us this question, and it's fantastic. You want to be confident that you're making the right choice, and there is no better way than to learn why each vendor recently lost someone's business.

You'll probably hear marketing/sales speak and not reality, but even hearing the marketing/sales speak can be of value. Of a whole bunch of vendors we've asked, only two have answered this question honestly (in both cases, VPs of sales were answering the question). The interesting thing is that we're doing business with both today, even though in both cases they aren't the most awesome vendor technologically.

Remember with any vendor that you're buying a relationship and not just the tool. In the long run (and even the near short term), using a tool whose people you can do business with far outstrips the value of using the most advanced tool on earth whose people you can't have a relationships with.

Recap

In this chapter, we've outlined a strategy for selecting an analytics tool. We began with an observation that tools are rarely the cause for success or failure in web analytics-initiatives. You need a tool to do analytics, and the important thing is to choose one that's right for your organization.

To do this, we first recommended that you set up a review committee to assess the various options. The committee begins by defining success metrics for the organization and then sending out an RFP to tool vendors. From there, the committee's task is to evaluate the presentations that vendors make. We gave you a long series of questions for doing this. They focused on three different topics: technology and implementation, analytics data and delivery, and customer service. By considering each of these carefully, you should end up with a tool that serves your organization well.

We ended by offering you the thoughts of our friend Avinash Kaushik about tool selection. In addition to offering advice about data integration and other topics, he also made the excellent point that buying a tool means establishing a long-term relationship with a vendor. In addition to everything else, you should make sure you like the people you'll be working with. Given that most tools can deliver the data you need, that may be the most important consideration in your decision.

Conclusion

Somehow, the end of a book always becomes the beginning of something more. In this case, as we bring *Actionable Web Analytics* to a close, it opens the door to new business opportunities and new success for our readers.

Throughout this book, we've tried to balance the realities of a dynamic business environment with the opportunities for creating the culture of analysis needed for success. Sometimes the balance isn't easy to maintain; quarterly profits and budgets can become overwhelming, and the demands of your customers are never-ending. But we've tried to take a systematic approach to giving you the tools necessary to get your hands around the massive amount of valuable data being generated by your websites every day and then using that data to take action. By building a culture that values action as much as it values analysis, you'll be able to make fast headway in the quest for more ROI.

In the introduction, we said that this book is first about marketing. We hope you've seen that our definition of marketing is broad and that this book touches on disciplines that range from marketing to analytics and from design to data. In all these areas, our message of accountability and responsibility remain the same. No matter what your profession, you should be able to look at the Web with new eyes and new questions.

If there is a single message we want you to take from this book—and this is the same message we want our clients to take away when we engage with them—it's that without action, there is no ROI. This book should inspire you to go do something now, because your customers are busy clicking while you're reading. We wish you the best of luck and hope to visit your website soon.

Web Analytics "Big Three" Definitions

 *Let's be up front about this: There are a lot of specific terms relevant to web analytics and lots of different calculations and data-collection and aggregation techniques. We've touched on many of them throughout this book, but with our continued focus on the big picture and the things a marketer needs to know, we decided to give you the definitive take on the most important. In the culture of analysis you should be creating in your organization, these three metrics should be a core part of every discussion and the touchstones that everyone from the CEO down to the new interns should be able to reference and explain. Cut out this appendix, and put it up on your office wall. Your website success depends on your mastering the Big Three.*

How We Define Terms

During the second half of 2006, the Web Analytics Association (WAA) Standards committee, co-chaired by one of the authors (Jason Burby) and Angie Brown, embarked on an effort to define what was agreed on as the three most important metrics: unique visitors, visits/sessions, and page views (see Figure A.1).

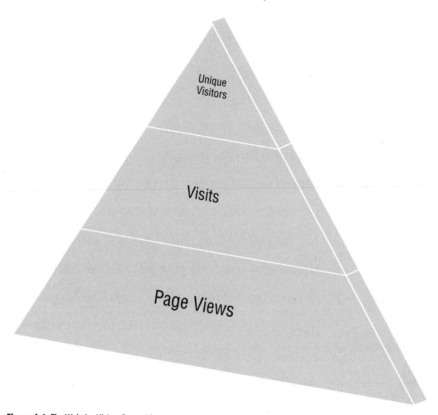

Figure A.1 The Website Visitor Pyramid

The Standards committee determined that these three metrics make up the foundation for most web-analytics definitions. In addition, because many other metrics rely on an understanding of these three, the decision was made to focus on these metrics first.

After multiple rounds within the committee, a request was sent for feedback to the entire WAA membership base. Comments and feedback were reviewed and the definitions tuned.

Definition Framework Overview

There are three types of web analytics metrics:

Count The most basic unit of measure; a single number, not a ratio. Often a whole number (Visits = 12,398), but not necessarily (Total Sales = $52,126.37).

All of the Big Three definitions are counts and are the foundation for many more ratios, such as page views per visit or revenue per visitor.

Ratio Typically, a count divided by a count, although a ratio can use either a count or a ratio in the numerator or denominator. (An example of a ratio fabricated from ratios is *stickiness*.) Usually, it isn't a whole number. Because it's a ratio, *per* is typically in the name, such as "page views per visit." A ratio's definition defines the ratio itself as well as any underlying metrics.

Key performance indicator (KPI) Although a KPI can be either a count or a ratio, it's frequently a ratio. Although all website types can use basic counts and ratios, a KPI is infused with business strategy—hence the term *key*—and therefore the set of appropriate KPIs typically differs between site and process types.

A metric can apply to three different universes:

Aggregate Total site traffic for a defined period of time.

Segmented A subset of the site traffic for a defined period of time, filtered in some way to gain greater analytical insight: for example, by campaign (email, banner, PPC, affiliate), by visitor type (new vs. returning, repeat buyers, high value), or by referrer.

Individual The activity of a single web visitor for a defined period of time.

Term: Unique Visitors

- Type: Count
- Universe: Aggregate, segmented
- Definition/calculation: The number of inferred individual people (filtered for spiders and robots) within a designated reporting timeframe, with activity consisting of one or more visits to a site. Each individual is counted only once in the unique visitor measure for the reporting period.

Authentication, either active or passive, is the most accurate way to track unique visitors. However, because most sites don't require a user login, the most predominant method of identifying unique visitors is via a persistent cookie that stores and returns a unique ID value. Because different methods are used to track unique visitors, you should ask your tool provider how they calculate this metric.

A unique visitor count is always associated with a time period (most often day, week, or month), and it's a *non-additive* metric. This means unique visitors can't be added together over time, over page views, or over groups of content, because one visitor can view multiple pages or make multiple visits in the time frame studied. Their activity will be over-represented unless they're de-duplicated.

The deletion of cookies, whether first-party or third-party, will cause unique visitors to be inflated over the actual number of people visiting the site. Users that block cookies may or may not be counted as unique visitors, and this metric is handled in different ways depending on the analytics tool used. Ask your tool provider how blocked cookies are managed in their tool: It's important to understand how this impacts other metrics with regard to these visitors.

Term: Visits/Sessions

- Type: Count
- Universe: Aggregate, segmented
- Definition/calculation: A *visit* is an interaction by an individual with a website, consisting of one or more requests for an analyst-definable unit of content (page view). If an individual hasn't taken another action (typically, additional page views) on the site in a specified time period, the visit session terminates.

Different tool providers use different methodologies to track sessions. Ask your tool provider how this metric is computed. A typical time-out period for a visit is 30 minutes, but this time period is configurable in many web-analytics applications.

A visit typically consists of one or more page views (see the definition of *page view*). However, in the case of sites where interaction consists solely of file downloads, streaming media, Flash, or other non-HTML content, a request for this content may or may not be defined as a *page* in a specific web-analytics program but could still be viewed as a valid request as part of a visit. The key is that a visitor interaction with the site is represented.

Visits can be added together over time, but not over page views or over groups of content, because one visit can include multiple pages.

Term: Page Views

- Type: Count
- Universe: Aggregate, segmented
- Definition/calculation: The number of times a page (an analyst-definable unit of content) is viewed.

Most web-analytics tools allow the client to specify what types of files or requests qualify as a *page*. Certain technologies including (but not limited to) Flash, Ajax, media files, downloads, documents, and PDFs don't follow the typical page paradigm but may be definable as pages in specific tools.

Content such as XML feeds (RSS or Atom) and emails that can be delivered to both web browsers and nonbrowser clients aren't typically counted as page views because the request or receipt of the content doesn't always correspond to the content being displayed. As an alternative, image-based page tags can be placed inside such content to track the views of all or portions of the content.

Web server responses that return status codes indicating the requested content was missing (400 to 499) or there was a server error (500 to 599) should not be counted as page views unless the web server has been configured to return a real page in the same response with the status code. Returning a page such as a site map, search page, or support-request form instead of the default missing or error messages is configurable in the most widely used web-serving applications (Apache and IIS).

Web server responses that return status codes indicating redirection to another page (300 to 399) also aren't typically counted as page views but can be used to track events such as click-throughs with systems specifically designed to use the redirect as a counting mechanism. Most redirect counting is done with a status code of 302.

A few status codes that indicate a successful response (200 to 299) also may or may not be counted as a page view: The 202 status code (Accepted) is returned in cases where the request has been accepted by the server and the server may or may not return content to the request at a later time. It isn't possible from this response to determine if the content was ever sent, so it would typically be excluded from page-view counts. The 204 status code (No Response) tells the web browser there is no content to return but no error has occurred, so the browser should stay on the page prior to the request. It's essentially a non-event. The 206 status code (Partial Download) usually occurs with the delivery of larger file downloads such as PDFs. This code indicates that only part of the file was delivered, so it typically should not be counted as a page view.

Filtering by status codes to remove requests that should not be counted is generally needed only when you're processing raw web server log files; it isn't usually necessary in page-tag-based implementations. Vendors make different distinctions in deciding what should be counted. Consult your tool provider for more information about your implementation.

Index

Note to the Reader: Throughout this index **boldfaced** page numbers indicate primary discussions of a topic. *Italicized* page numbers indicate illustrations.

A

A/B testing
    in data-driven organizations, 48
    overview, **162**
    using, 163
A/B/n testing
    overview, **162**, *163*
    using, 163
abandonment issues, 133–135
accelerating release cycles, 33
acceleration analysis, **133–134**
accelerators in RFPs, 194, 197
account service questions for vendors, **228**
accountant role of web analysts, 214
accuracy
    in data-driven organizations, 48
    issues, **50–52**, 132
    mandate for, 35
action
    importance of, **67–68**
    plans for, 58, *58*
active subscriber base metric, 86
actuary role of web analysts, 214
ad-supported content site monetization models, **106–108**, *107*
ads served monthly metric, 107
advertisers in culture of analysis, 39
advertising-based site metrics, **85–86**
advertising click ratio, 86
advertising publications as agency source, 188
advertising strategy shifts, 8
agencies, **185**
    benefits, **186**

for education and training, 221
finding, **187–188**
mutual objectives, **196–198**
passion in, **199**
RFPs for. *See* RFPs for agencies
steering committee mandates for, 35
for web teams, 215
work by, **198–199**
agenda blending, **81**
aggregate data
    behavioral data for, 111
    definition, 239
aggregate search terms, 137
always-on consumers, 8
analysis, **67**, **129**
    branding content, **138–140**
    campaign landing pages, **140–142**
    case study, **137–138**
    commitment and acceleration, **133–134**
    for decision-making, **134**
    delayed conversion, **146–147**
    drivers to offline conversion, **144–145**
    fine-tuning for audience, **134–135**
    home page effectiveness, **138**
    lead processes, **135**
    onsite search data, **136–137**
    optimization tests, 172
    purchasing processes, **132–133**
    vs. reporting, **130–132**
    search terms, 137
    segmenting traffic, **142–143**
    user steps, **133**
analysis mandate, **13–14**
    innovation, **15–16**
    ROI marketing, **14–15**
analysis questions for vendors, **227–228**
analytics intervention
    recovery. *See* gaps, analytic intervention for
    steps, **44–48**, *47*

Web Analytics Wednesdays, 220
web award fallacy, **19**
web cast sign ups, 103, *103*
web-only offer codes and coupons, 97
web publications as agency source, 188
web team manager/leaders, 38
web teams, **211**
    analyst skills, **212–215**
    building, **215**
    circle of influence, **216–217**
    cost estimates, **215–216**, 218
    goals and incentives, 48
    internal vs. external, **217–219**

    key analytics positions, **216–217**
    training, **219–221**
website manager role, 215
website visitor pyramid, 238, *238*
whatamigonnadonext.com site, **20–21**, *21*
winning sites, **9–10**
wireless phone company case study, **126–128**
word of mouth marketing, 13
Wunderman, Lester, 8

Z

ZAAZ Exit Ratio, 138

INDEX

Praise for *Actionable Web Analytics: Using Data To Make Smart Business Decisions*

"Relationship marketing continues to evolve in new and exciting ways, and Actionable Web Analytics provides a clear and concise guidebook for the marketing executive. Shane and Jason have captured the essence of creating relationships online, which lead to meaningful customer dialogues, and then measuring the success of those efforts."

—LESTER WUNDERMAN, Founder and Chairman Emeritus, Wunderman

"Some people build web analytics tools. Some work tirelessly, deep in the hearts of their organizations drawing the rich value out of those tools. And then, there are those like Shane and Jason who have spent close to a decade helping a wide variety of companies optimize their advertising spend, supersize their website value, and maximize their online marketing ROI. These guys are in an amazing position to help you figure out all of the above. But that's just the half of it. While their position is nice, their scary IQ, their awesome curiosity, and their uncanny ability to drill down to bona fide business value make this book a must read."

—JIM STERNE, President, Web Analytics Association and Producer, Emetrics Summit

"The real money is made when the initial click leads to a customer journey filled with meaningful, relevant dialogues that motivate action. Actionable Web Analytics helps marketers take customers on that journey and generate a good ROI doing it."

—DANIEL MOREL, Chairman & CEO, Wunderman

"We have been fortunate enough during the past decade to see our business grow in parallel with, and in partnership with, the team at ZAAZ. As true thought leaders in the web analytics and marketing space, Jason and Shane have captured the important issues facing marketers and business people every day and explained them eloquently in Actionable Web Analytics."

—JOSH JAMES, CEO & Co-Founder, Omniture

"These guys have forgotten more about analytics than we mortals will likely ever understand. Most analytics folks revel in the complexity of their work. Jason and Shane know how to simplify and communicate how analytics can really change marketing, and it is incredibly effective."

—MATTHEW ROCHE, CEO, Offermatica

"If you're one of the many people who view web analytics as a necessary evil, this book will spin your perception 180 degrees. That Jason and Shane know web analytics backward and forward (not to mention upside-down and inside-out) is a well-known fact. But these two possess another singular talent: the ability to make analytics palatable, understandable, even digestible for even the most data- and math-averse right-brain thinker you know (perhaps you're that person?). These two go way beyond the numbers. They can explain with crystal clarity how to use data to improve processes, businesses, and their bottom lines."

—REBECCA LIEB, Editor-in-Chief, The ClickZ Network

"*Digital Marketing excellence is paramount for today's marketers. In this book, Jason and Shane provide straightforward web analytics insight and instruction to help marketers achieve greater performance and profit from their communications activities.*"
> —SCOTT LENNARD, Advertising Director—Central Marketing Group, Microsoft Corporation

"*Jason and Shane have been sharing their extensive experience and insight with clients and through conferences for a while, so it's about time they committed it to print.*"
> —LAURENT BURMAN, VP Web, Helio

"*Jason Burby and Shane Atchison are two guys in the web analytics world that truly understand what success looks like. They wisely took much of what I wrote about in* The Big Book of Key Performance Indicators *and attached a dollar sign to it, dramatically improving their client's desire to understand and deploy KPIs. I have little doubt that* Actionable Web Analytics *will long be considered a critical work in the web analytics body of knowledge.*"
> —ERIC T. PETERSON, author, *Web Analytics Demystified, Web Site Measurement Hacks* and *The Big Book of Key Performance Indicators.*

"*I have been waiting for a book like this. They've helped me understand some of the finer points in web analytics and taught me how I can put those concepts into action with my team. What I like best about working with them is that their knowledge goes beyond finding the data and pulling the numbers—they know how important it is to tell the story behind that data.*"
> —KRISTEN FINDLEY, Manager, Website Analytics Interactive Marketing, Ameriprise Financial

"*Shane, Jason, and the rest of ZAAZ are the preeminent leaders in outsourced professional services and analysis in the web analytics space. They have helped propel the industry forward in both the high end and the mainstream through client engagements, thought-leading articles, and presentations for the past 10 years. Their presence is only growing, so watch closely as they impact the industry over the next 10-plus years.*"
> —BRETT CROSBY, Senior Manager, Google Analytics

"*Jason and Shane have been at the forefront of helping organizations drive actions based on data; it is indeed a privilege to have all their wisdom gelled into a book for the rest of us to benefit from!*"
> —AVINASH KAUSHIK

"*Burby and Atchison bring to web analytics the kind of practical expertise every online marketing manager should have access to. Finally, a book on web analytics that cuts through the clutter and delivers the kind of actionable insights online marketing managers need.*"
> —TOM TAYLOR, Expedia